CHALLENGE AND REJECTION

AMERICAN DIPLOMATIC HISTORY SERIES

GENERAL EDITOR: *Armin Rappaport*

Prelude to World Power: 1860–1900
Foster Rhea Dulles

The Uncertain Giant: 1921–1941
Selig Adler

Challenge and Rejection: 1900–1921
Julius W. Pratt

CHALLENGE
AND REJECTION

*The United States
and World Leadership, 1900–1921*

Julius W. Pratt

THE MACMILLAN COMPANY, NEW YORK

COLLIER-MACMILLAN LIMITED, LONDON

For Bill and Helen, Walden and Janice

First Printing

The Macmillan Company, New York
Collier-Macmillan Canada Ltd., Toronto, Ontario
Library of Congress Catalog Card Number: 67-15051

Printed in the United States of America

Contents

Preface   vii

I   THE FIRST AGE OF ROOSEVELT   1

II   THE PANAMA EPISODE   7

III   POLICEMAN OF THE CARIBBEAN   22

IV   FURTHERING THE CAUSE OF PEACE   37

V   FRIENDS AND RIVALS IN EASTERN ASIA   54

VI   THE EPIGONI   70

VII   THE POLICEMAN TURNED DEMOCRAT   84

VIII   MEXICO—THE INTRACTABLE REVOLUTION   102

IX   WAR AND NEUTRAL RIGHTS   118

X   "THE RIGHT IS MORE PRECIOUS THAN PEACE"   133

XI   WARTIME DIPLOMACY   152

XII   THE PEACE CONFERENCE IN PARIS   174

XIII   THE RENUNCIATION OF WORLD LEADERSHIP   195

Appendix   The Fourteen Points   220

Further Reading   225

Index   243

Preface

This volume covers the period from the death of President McKinley and the accession of Theodore Roosevelt, to the inauguration of President Harding and his final rejection of all thought of American participation in the League of Nations, or even the shadowy "association of nations" of which he had talked during his campaign. The United States had emerged from the war with Spain with new responsibilities stretching from the Caribbean to the Philippines on the fringe of Asia, and had found itself, as never before, under the necessity of taking a hand in world politics. The rivalry of the great powers of Europe over their ambitions in Asia and Africa, and their frictions at home, presented a challenge to a United States that stood apart from those rivalries—a challenge to lead the way in resolving them by peaceful means. A conflict among these powers could not leave the United States unscathed, since the nation was a part of what had become, in Wendell Willkie's later phrase, "one world." Roosevelt sought to meet the challenge piecemeal, crisis by crisis. Wilson, after years of hesitation, proposed what he thought to be an over-all solution, the League of Nations, in which he had cast the United States in a star role. But Wilson, through illness and obstinacy, played into the hands of the isolationists, who believed that America could still be insulated from the lethal currents that racked Europe and Asia. Thus came America's rejection of the League, and with it rejection of the challenge of world leadership. This challenge and this rejection constitute the main theme of the book, though other phases of American policy are not neglected.

The writer of such a volume as this, which offers a condensed narrative of a complicated story, must necessarily depend very heavily upon the research of his predecessors in the field, as embodied in articles, monographs, and biographies. The more significant of such works for this period, together with the more accessible types of source material, are listed under "Further Reading." Lack of space forbids more specific acknowledgment of indebtedness to individual authors. My former colleague, Selig Adler, performed the generous service of reading the entire manuscript and giving it the benefit of his accomplished scholarship. Armin Rappaport, the editor of the series, and Peter V. Ritner, Executive Editor of The Macmillan Company, also read the manuscript and made valuable suggestions. While gratefully acknowledging the assistance of these authorities, I assume full responsibilities for any errors that may remain in the book despite their efforts. My wife, Louise W. Pratt, has not only devoted countless hours to the mechanical tasks of typing, proofreading, and indexing, but has also given invaluable aid as a perspicacious and constructive critic.

JULIUS W. PRATT

University of Notre Dame
January 1967

CHAPTER I

The First Age of Roosevelt

William McKinley, victim of a bullet fired by the anarchist Leon Czolgosz, died in Buffalo in the early hours of Saturday, September 14, 1901. Theodore Roosevelt, hastily summoned from a vacation in the Adirondacks, took the oath of office at three o'clock that afternoon in the Buffalo home of Ansley Wilcox. Despite his assurance that he would continue McKinley's policy "absolutely unbroken," the new President was a man of too much dynamism and initiative to walk for long in the footsteps of the placid McKinley.

In the seven and a half years from September 1901 to March 1909 Theodore Roosevelt shaped the foreign policy of the United States as well as much of its domestic history. Those years might in fact be called the first Age of Roosevelt. The young and dynamic ex-police commissioner, ex-Rough Rider, and ex-governor of New York, whom the politicians had consigned to the limbo of the vice-presidency, was by a stroke of fate elevated to the highest office in the land. From the White House, which he described as "such a bully pulpit," he was free to preach his version of international as well as national morality. He was, however, averse to words without action. Perhaps his best-known aphorism was the counsel, "Speak softly and carry a big stick," and he seldom took a position in international affairs which he had not the will and the power to support.

Fundamental to Roosevelt's thinking, writes John Blum in *The Republican Roosevelt*, were two "related constants: his quest for order, his faith in power." Every nation, he believed, had a duty to maintain internal order and meet its international obligations. For peoples whose governments failed in this duty—certain of the Latin Americans, the Koreans, the Chinese—he showed a pitying condescension, not to say contempt. Such incompetents must expect that the work they could not do would be done for them. It was increasingly "incumbent on all civilized and orderly powers," he told Congress in 1902, "to insist on the proper policing of the world." Thus the United States was soon to take a hand in policing several disorderly states in the Caribbean area— for the general good, Roosevelt believed. Similarly, with Roosevelt's approval, Japan would take over the policing of a disorderly Korea, and Roosevelt soon thereafter found himself wishing that "all of uncivilized Asia and Africa [were] held by England or France or Russia or Germany."

Roosevelt, it is safe to say, was the first American President to think of United States foreign policy as a factor in world politics. As early as 1897 he had remarked that old-fashioned isolation was no longer possible; that on east and west, in Europe and Asia, new responsibilities faced the American nation. Aside from its own material interests in the other hemisphere, the United States had, Roosevelt realized, a serious stake in the maintenance of world peace. He worked to promote the resort to international arbitration, with important reservations, and he professed a belief in the eventual limitation of armaments; but believing that for the present the preservation of peace and the prospering of American interests depended on the balance of power in Europe and Asia, he was ready on occasion to throw American weight into the scale. The weight that counted was measured in armies and navies—navies in the case of the sea powers, England and America. A convinced disciple of the naval historian A. T. Mahan, Roosevelt worked untiringly for the upbuilding and improvement of the United States Navy. On its efficiency and his own readiness to use it, he believed, depended America's influence for peace in Europe and Asia and its success in discouraging violations of the Monroe Doctrine in Latin America. This "big stick" he revealed (accompanied by soft words) in salutary gestures to the German Kaiser in 1902 and to Japan six years later. No longer holding, as in his younger days, that occasional war was essential to a nation's health, Roosevelt believed, nevertheless, that every self-respecting nation must be ready and willing to fight in defense of its interests and honor.

Power alone guaranteed a nation's security. Roosevelt had little faith in the written word. Treaties could be unilaterally abrogated; in fact, should be when incompatible with a nation's vital interests. He would not have hesitated to proceed with a canal at Panama in violation of the Clayton-Bulwer Treaty had England not agreed to abrogate it. International law and the amenities of normal international relations gave way to force in time of crisis. Roosevelt gloried in his own disregard of Colombia's sovereign rights in Panama. He and Elihu Root (former Secretary of War and future Secretary of State) exchanged felicitations upon the Japanese surprise attack (without declaration of war) on the Russian fleet at Port Arthur. In a "just" cause, all was fair, and when the chips were down, power alone counted.

Much of the work of a Foreign Office or State Department Roosevelt carried on himself. He corresponded with Kaiser Wilhelm II of Germany, engaged in personal diplomacy with favorites in foreign diplomatic corps—Speck von Sternburg [1]

[1] The German's name often appears as Sternberg. His signature in letters in the National Archives is indubitably Sternburg.

of Germany, Sir Cecil Spring Rice of England, J. J. Jusserand of France—and wrote confidential letters to a few intimates among his own envoys, such as Henry White and George von L. Meyer. In some important negotiations he bypassed the State Department almost completely, thus setting precedents for Woodrow Wilson and for his cousin Franklin. Cases in point were the Venezuela crisis of 1902, the Russo-Japanese peace negotiations of 1905, and the Algeciras Conference of 1906.

Roosevelt, nevertheless, was served by two very able Secretaries of State. John Hay (1898–1905) was an inheritance from President McKinley. A one-time private secretary and biographer of Abraham Lincoln, Hay had spent some years dabbling in literature before being named ambassador to England by McKinley in 1897. Called back to Washington to head the State Department in 1898, he handled the peace negotiations with Spain and in the next year penned the "open door" notes on China with which his name is associated. He handled the still more delicate Boxer crisis of 1900 and the negotiations resulting in the Hay-Pauncefote Treaty with England in 1901. Under Roosevelt his most important work concerned the canal negotiations with Colombia and Panama and the Alaska boundary controversy with Great Britain. The closing months of his tenure were a long struggle with illness, and he died on July 1, 1905.

Hay's successor, Elihu Root (1905–09), had also been inherited by Roosevelt from McKinley, but as Secretary of War. A brilliant and successful New York lawyer, he had been brought in by McKinley to straighten out a badly disorganized War Department. He had succeeded admirably and, continuing under Roosevelt till January 1904, had effected important reforms in the regular Army and National Guard. Returning to Washington as Secretary of State in July 1905, Root concerned himself especially with Latin American relations and the Far East. His success in improv-

ing relations with the lands to the south has led to his being
called "the first good neighbor." Root was strong in one de-
partmental function where Hay had been weak: relations
with Congress. Hay had been rather supercilious in his attitude to Congressmen and Senators, holding it beneath his
dignity to plead his cause before committees or to conciliate
Senators before submitting treaties. The result had too often
been bitter disappointment. Root, much more the politician,
was adept at getting on with the legislators and usually had
his way, in whole or by reasonable compromise.

Though Roosevelt, after Hay's death, spoke disparagingly
of the Secretary's ability, the President's relations with him
and with Root appear to have been excellent. There is little
if any evidence that either Hay or Root resented the President's assuming responsibilities and initiatives that normally
would have belonged to the State Department. Root, a man
of great independence, would hardly have remained in office three and a half years had he felt that his prerogatives
were infringed or that his dignity was compromised. Actually, he and "T.R." seem to have been on the most cordial
and intimate terms. On policy matters they usually agreed.
If not, Roosevelt recorded later, "He fought me every inch
of the way. And, together, we got somewhere." Seldom in
the American experience has there been so strong a foreign
policy team as that of "the two R's"—Roosevelt and Root.

One important feature of American foreign policy on
which Roosevelt, Hay, and Root were all agreed was the
necessity of cordial relations with England. Hay returned
from London an Anglophile. Roosevelt, though he could ex-
hibit bellicosity when interests clashed, soon found that he
needed British support in his world policy. Root seems never
to have questioned the thesis. Recent and contemporary
events contributed to Anglo-American understanding. British
opinion had warmly supported the United States against a
censorious Europe in the war with Spain. American govern-

mental policy was benevolently neutral in Britain's South
African war with the Boers (1899–1902). Neither nation
looked with friendly eye upon the rise of German sea power,
and both had a stake in preserving the open door in China.
It was easy, furthermore, for American and British statesmen of that day to understand each other. Roosevelt, Hay,
and Root, men of means and of broad culture, had much in
common with such Englishmen as Lord Lansdowne, Joseph
Chamberlain, and Arthur Balfour. Thus after Britain met the
United States rather more than halfway on the isthmian and
Alaskan controversies, there was unprecedented cordiality
between the Anglo-Saxon powers.

CHAPTER II

The Panama Episode

In the field of foreign policy Roosevelt was destined to act with characteristic vigor in three areas of the world—in the Caribbean, in the Far East, and in Europe. In two of these areas, when he took office, no immediate action was called for. Europe was quiet, and, in the Far East, the Boxer crisis in China was being liquidated. In the Caribbean, too, the problem of Cuba, freed from Spain but still under military government by the U.S. Army, had been partially solved through the initiative of Elihu Root as Secretary of War. At his suggestion Congress had attached to the Army Appropriation Act of March 3, 1901, an amendment introduced by Senator O. H. Platt of Connecticut. This required the Cuban Constitutional Convention then in session to agree, among other things, that the Cuban government would contract no excessive debt, would consent to intervention by the United States for the preservation of Cuban independence or of orderly government in the island, and would permit the United States to establish a naval base in Cuban territory and territorial waters—a privilege for which Guantanamo Bay was later chosen as a site. Informed that acceptance of the Platt Amendment was the price of the withdrawal of U.S.

troops, the Cuban Convention reluctantly agreed to attach
the amendment to the new constitution and to see that it
was embodied also in a treaty with the United States. Cuba
attained this somewhat limited degree of independence in
July 1902, and became—though never so called officially—
the first protectorate of the United States.

Still unsettled, however, was the long debated question of
an isthmian canal. That there was to be one, and that it was
to be built and controlled by the United States government,
was no longer in doubt in most American minds; but whether
it should be cut through Nicaragua or through the Isthmus
of Panama, and whether it should be undertaken with Great
Britain's good will or in the face of British protest, were
questions still to be determined.

A half-century earlier, at a time when the United States
was weak in the Caribbean area and Great Britain was
strong, the two governments had agreed that neither of them
would seek exclusive control over any canal that might be
constructed. Any such canal, they then promised, should be
neutralized under international guarantee. This Clayton-
Bulwer Treaty (1850) had seemed fair enough when it was
negotiated; but as the United States grew stronger and the
strategic importance of an isthmian canal more apparent,
the idea that such a canal must be neutralized grew more
and more objectionable. A canal owned and controlled by
the United States and forming a vital link in its defense
system came to be settled American policy. An American-
owned canal, however, was expressly forbidden by the
Clayton-Bulwer Treaty, and until the year 1900, England
persisted in refusing either to modify or to waive it. Meanwhile, early in 1899 an impatient Senate passed a bill calling
for the construction of a canal without awaiting British
permission.

The Senate bill, sponsored by the Alabama Senator John
T. Morgan, proposed a canal through Nicaragua, where a

combination of lake and river provided a natural waterway
for small vessels over all but a dozen miles of the distance
between Caribbean and Pacific. Nicaragua had long been
the site favored by American opinion, and an American
corporation had actually undertaken to dig a canal there
but had failed for lack of adequate funds. Primarily for the
same reason, a French company, originally headed by Ferdinand de Lesseps of Suez Canal fame, had failed at Panama,
where it had secured canal rights from the government of
Colombia at Bogotá. With an estimated two-fifths of the work
completed and with no more funds in sight, the company
had collapsed. Its rights and properties had been taken over
by a newly organized corporation, also French, calling itself the New Panama Canal Company. The new company,
with no prospect of completing the canal itself, hoped to sell
its rights and property on the isthmus to the United States.
Each of the two routes had its attractions and each had its
sponsors in the United States. Those desirous of giving the
Panama site a chance persuaded Congress to substitute for
Senator Morgan's bill a measure calling for a new investigation of all practicable canal routes, with emphasis on those
by way of Nicaragua and Panama. An Isthmian Canal Commission, appointed by the President of the United States,
was to conduct the investigation.

Secretary of State John Hay, a strong devotee of friendly
relations with England, naturally hoped to secure British
consent to the canal enterprise rather than proceeding in
disregard to the Clayton-Bulwer Treaty. In reality, Britain
was no longer averse to accepting the American desire for
a canal owned and controlled by the United States. Canada,
however, was opposed to concessions to the United States
on the canal question unless they could be coupled with
American concessions on certain controversies with Canada,
especially a boundary dispute between Alaska and British
Columbia. When a Joint High Commission, designed to settle

such disputes, adjourned early in 1899 without reaching
agreement, Canadian opposition prevented for a time any
agreement on the canal question. But the Boer War, beginning in October 1899, strengthened Britain's need for American friendship. A temporary *modus vivendi* was reached on
the Alaska boundary, and Canada dropped its objection to
a canal treaty.

More than a year before Roosevelt's accession to the presidency—while he was still governor of New York in fact—Hay
and Lord Pauncefote, the British ambassador, had reached
tentative agreement on terms, and on February 5, 1900, they
affixed their signatures to a treaty by which Great Britain
gave its consent that the government of the United States
should construct and manage a ship canal to connect the
Atlantic and Pacific Oceans. Thus the old ban of the Clayton-Bulwer Treaty was withdrawn, though that treaty was
not expressly abrogated. In fact, in accordance with the
principles of the earlier treaty, the new agreement stated
that the canal should be neutralized, specifically that it
should not be fortified, and that other powers should be invited to become parties to the agreement.

John Hay was so pleased with his work that he actually
hoped the Senate might approve the treaty unanimously.
Unfortunately, he had, as was too often his custom, neglected to consult Senate opinion during the negotiations.
Critics, both in the Senate and outside, objected particularly
to the ban on fortification of the canal and to the inclusion
of other powers in the guarantee of its neutrality. Among
the critics was Governor Roosevelt, who from Albany attacked the treaty in the press and explained his objections
in a letter to his friend, Secretary Hay. In agreement with
an earlier statement of Captain Mahan, Roosevelt contended
that the proposed canal, unless fortified by the United States,
"strengthens against us every nation whose fleet is larger
than ours." The invitation to other powers to join in the

guarantee he deplored as contrary to the Monroe Doctrine. He counseled Hay and the President to "drop the treaty and push through a bill to build *and fortify* our own canal." In other words, simply disregard the restrictions of the Clayton-Bulwer Treaty!

The Senate preferred to rewrite the treaty signed by Hay and Pauncefote. It postponed action until December 20, 1900, when it approved the treaty with three amendments. The first declared the Clayton-Bulwer Treaty superseded. The second reserved to the United States the right to take necessary measures for the defense of the canal. The third eliminated the provision for the adherence of other powers.

Lord Lansdowne, now British Foreign Secretary, objected to the unilateral rewriting of the treaty by the Senate and refused to accept the amendments. His objections, however, were to the manner rather than to the substance of the Senate's action. Hay and Pauncefote were encouraged to try again. On November 18, 1901, they signed a new treaty which met the wishes of the Senate and of Roosevelt, now President, and also satisfied the British government. It terminated the Clayton-Bulwer Treaty. It dropped the prohibition of fortifications and made application of the other rules of neutralization the responsibility of the United States alone. Reference to powers other than the two signatories was conspicuously omitted. Thus the United States would be answerable to Britain alone for its adherence to the terms of the treaty. Of primary importance for future users of the canal was Rule No. 1, which stated:

The canal shall be free and open to the vessels of commerce and of war of all nations observing these Rules, on terms of entire equality, so that there shall be no discrimination against any such nation, or its citizens or subjects, in respect of the conditions or charges of traffic, or otherwise. Such conditions and charges of traffic shall be just and equitable.

The treaty (usually referred to as the second Hay-Pauncefote Treaty) was promptly ratified by both parties—the Senate approving by a vote of 72 to 6—and ratifications were exchanged on February 21, 1902.

In the meantime the Isthmian Canal Commission, created by Congress in 1899, had taken a new look at both the Nicaragua and Panama routes and, during a session in Paris, had inquired as to the legal capability of the New Panama Canal Company to sell its rights at Panama to the United States. On this last point the commission was satisfied, assuming that the government of Colombia would consent to the transfer. The price asked by the company, however, seemed to the commission prohibitive. Although virtually all engineering data favored Panama, therefore, the commission in its supposedly final report (November 16, 1901) recommended the route through Nicaragua. Thereupon it appeared that the excessive price asked by the New Panama Canal Company had been a bluff, which the commission's report successfully called. The company's Paris office cabled that it would accept forty million dollars (the figure which the commission had suggested as fair) instead of the one hundred and nine million dollars originally asked. Reconvened by President Roosevelt, the commission presented a supplementary report (January 18, 1902) recommending the Panama route if satisfactory arrangements could be made with Colombia.

The Senate of the United States now became the battleground for the advocates of Panama and of Nicaragua. Before the Senate was the Hepburn Bill, passed by the House of Representatives, authorizing the President to initiate steps for a canal at Nicaragua. After the Canal Commission's supplementary report, Senator Spooner of Wisconsin proposed an amendment giving preference to the Panama route but empowering the President to proceed via Nicaragua if it should prove impossible to make satisfactory arrangements with the French company or the government of Colombia. Champions of the two routes lined up for and against the Spooner Amendment.

Leader of the forces favoring Nicaragua was Senator John T. Morgan of Alabama, chairman—though a Democrat in this Republican Senate—of the Committee on Interoceanic Canals. Long a proponent of the Nicaragua route, Morgan apparently saw it as more profitable than Panama to his state and section, but only a feeling that his own prestige was involved seems adequate to account for his emotional dedication to Nicaragua. Morgan's chief opponent on this issue in the Senate was Mark Hanna of Ohio, the body's leading Republican in terms of power and influence, and also a member of Morgan's committee. Hanna argued forcefully for Panama as the site most feasible on grounds of engineering and most practical for shipping, but it seems probable that many of his facts and some of his arguments were supplied by the legal representative of the New Panama Canal Company, New York attorney William Nelson Cromwell.

Cromwell, a member of the law firm of Sullivan and Cromwell, was one of two able and active propagandists who served the New Panama Canal Company in its time of crisis. Cromwell was skilled at pulling wires and guiding legislation. He claimed to have diverted the proposal for a Nicaragua canal in 1899 into the creation of the neutral Canal Commission. Whether an alleged gift by him of sixty thousand dollars to the Republican campaign fund in 1900 influenced Hanna or secured a noncommittal plank in that year's platform is a moot question. The company's other efficient agent was the Frenchman Philippe Bunau-Varilla. He had been chief engineer of the original French company and had become a stockholder in its successor. Skilled as a pamphleteer and propagandist, he was able to influence opinion in the press and in political circles. He had an uncanny faculty for divining American policy from chance remarks or circumstantial evidence; and he had a way of turning up at crucial moments with key information, wise counsel, or essential funds.

Morgan's committee divided, 7 to 4. The majority, led by Morgan, reported in favor of the original Hepburn Bill without the Spooner Amendment—in other words for the Nicaragua route. Hanna and his three colleagues of the minority submitted a report recommending the Panama route and hence the Spooner Amendment. The decision was up to the Senate. While the issue hung in the balance, nature dealt a telling blow for Panama. In the far-off Caribbean island of Martinique the volcano Mt. Pelée became suddenly active, burying the town of St. Pierre under a flood of lava and a storm of volcanic ash. Such activity in the vicinity of a canal might have blocked the waterway for months, perhaps years. And there were volcanoes in Nicaragua! In fact, Nicaraguan postage stamps advertised their presence, depicting a smoking volcano, Mt. Momotombo, rising from the waters of Lake Nicaragua. A day or two after the explosion of Mt. Pelée every Senator found such a stamp on his desk—a thoughtful gift from M. Bunau-Varilla! Timely press reports, whether genuine or inspired, brought news of an eruption from Mt. Momotombo and an accompanying earthquake.

These events, natural and human, coupled with the fact that Panama was without the expensive luxury of volcanoes, were thought by the press to have had a determining influence on the Senate's decision. Whatever the reason, the Senate on June 19, 1902, approved the Spooner Amendment by a vote of 42 to 34. A few days later it passed the amended bill, the House concurred, and on June 28 the Isthmian Canal Act received Roosevelt's signature. It directed the President to seek the necessary agreements for a canal through Panama and to fall back upon the Nicaragua route only if these were not obtainable on reasonable terms.

Secretary Hay, in the meantime, had been active in clearing the diplomatic roads to both Nicaragua and Panama. Nicaragua was ready to grant the necessary concessions if Congress should elect that route. For a treaty with Colombia for the Panama route, Hay had exchanged ideas not only with the Colombian minister, J. V. Concha, but also with interested Senators and with Cromwell, representing the Canal Company. Negotiations were apparently going well when in September 1902 the minister took offense at the landing of United States marines at Panama during disturbances there and refused to continue the discussions. Concha was recalled at Hay's request, and Dr. Tomás Herrán, secretary of the legation, took over as chargé d'affaires. Negotiations were resumed, but not until January 22, 1903, was the treaty with Colombia actually signed. Whether Herrán actually had authority to sign as he did is in some doubt. Three days after signing, at any rate, he received from Bogotá instructions not to do so. He let his signature stand, nevertheless, and on March 17 the United States Senate approved the treaty.

By the Hay-Herrán Treaty Colombia agreed that the United States might acquire all the rights and property of the New Panama Canal Company and might construct, operate, and control a canal across the isthmus. Its control would extend to a zone ten kilometers wide, half on either side of the canal. These rights were granted for a period of one hundred years and were renewable at one-hundred-year intervals at the discretion of the United States. The United States recognized the sovereignty of Colombia in the zone; justice, however, would be administered by a system of mixed courts, and the United States reserved the right to use its armed forces to protect the canal if Colombia should be unable to do so. For these privileges the United States would pay Colombia ten million dollars down and two hundred and fifty thousand dollars annually beginning after nine years, the estimated time required for completion of the canal.

In Colombia as in the United States, approval of the Senate was required—normally at least—for the ratification of treaties, and to the Colombian Senate the Hay-Herrán Treaty was sent with a buck-passing letter by President José Manuel Marroquín. Marroquín, an aging intellectual, was in a difficult position. He had just weathered one threat of revolution and was not anxious to court another by identifying himself too closely with a treaty that seemed sure to be unpopular. He preferred to let the Senate bear the odium, if odium there was to be, of accepting a treaty tinged with "Yankee imperialism" or of rejecting it and perhaps losing the canal.

The treaty was promptly attacked in the Colombian press. The compensation, it was charged, was too small, the grant of privileges was in effect unlimited in time, the mixed courts were an infringement on Colombian sovereignty. The second and third criticisms were not unreasonable, but apparently Colombian opinion might overlook these if it could be satisfied on the first—the demand for more money. The United States minister in Bogotá was told on good authority that the Senate was unlikely to approve the treaty unless it were modified to permit Colombia to exact ten million dollars from the New Panama Canal Company and an additional five million dollars from the United States—a total of twenty-five million dollars instead of the ten million dollars of the treaty.[1]

It is hard to see how the Senate of Colombia had a moral, to say nothing of a legal, obligation to approve the treaty without amendment. Yet Hay, who had witnessed, and Roosevelt, who had approved, the recent mutilation by the United States Senate of Hay's treaty with England, waxed

[1] Some Colombians hoped to do even better than this. A committee of the Colombian Senate contended that an executive decree that had extended the life of the grant to the French company from its original terminal date of 1904 to 1910 had been illegal. Hence if action were postponed until after 1904, the company's right would lapse and Colombia instead of the company would collect the forty million dollars.

indignant at the suggestion that the Colombian Senate might exercise a similar right. Hay warned Colombia that amendment or rejection of the treaty might lead the American Congress to take action "which every friend of Colombia would regret." Privately he denounced the Colombian politicians as "greedy little anthropoids" while to Roosevelt they were "jack rabbits," "contemptible little creatures," and "foolish and homicidal corruptionists." The Colombian Senators were not aware of the name-calling, but they resented the threats and the State Department's take-it-or-leave-it attitude. Hay, normally a reasonable diplomat, had in this case, thinks his biographer Tyler Dennett, fallen too much under the influence of Cromwell. In any event, the Colombian Senate voted overwhelmingly to reject the treaty and some weeks later, October 31, 1903, adjourned without further action.

Roosevelt's proper course now seemed clear. Having failed to secure Colombia's consent to the work at Panama, he was authorized by the Isthmian Canal Act to turn to Nicaragua. This possibility was kept before him but not urged upon him by Secretary Hay. Another alternative, of course, was to reopen negotiations with Colombia and pay a price that would win the assent of the Colombian Senate. But Roosevelt had been impressed by technical reports setting forth the superiority of the Panama route. He was unwilling to be diverted from that choice, and neither he nor Hay was willing to submit to what they considered highway robbery by the politicians of Bogotá. In the weeks between the rejection of the treaty and the adjournment of the Colombian Senate, Roosevelt's mobile mind played with several possible courses of action. One, brought to his attention by the distinguished international lawyer John Bassett Moore, was to seize the canal site and dig the canal in defiance of Colombia's refusal. Such a procedure, Moore argued, would be justified by an old treaty with New Granada (the earlier name for Colombia). By this treaty of 1846 New Granada had guaranteed to the United States the right of way across the Isthmus of Panama, while the United States in return had promised to ensure peaceful transit across the isthmus and New Granadan (Colombian) sovereignty over it. The United States, said Moore, having fulfilled its part of the bargain for over fifty years, had every right to avail itself of the use of the transit route as it saw fit, even for the purpose of constructing a canal in the face of Colombian objection.

Roosevelt thought well of this plan. He even drafted a message to Congress asking legislative approval and stating that if this were not given he would "proceed at once with the Nicaragua canal." But Roosevelt had also a different plan, which depended in the first instance on the initiative of others. Rejection of the treaty in Bogotá led to widespread rumors that the Department of Panama would declare its independence from Colombia and proceed to make its own treaty with the United States. This was what Roosevelt hoped for, but, as he wrote Senator Lodge, "for me to say so publicly would amount to an instigation of a revolt, and therefore I cannot say it." It was not necessary that he should. A small group of men at Panama, headed by a Dr. Manuel Amador Guerrero, to whom choice of the Nicaragua route would mean disaster, had for months been plotting to revolt if Colombia finally rejected the treaty. Their scheme was abetted by Bunau-Varilla, who provided funds and last-minute assurance, based on his own clever inference, that a revolt in Panama would be supported by the United States.

Bunau-Varilla's forecast was correct. How much advance knowledge Roosevelt had of the conspiracy has never been determined, but United States naval vessels were on hand at Panama and Colón when the revolt occurred on November 3, 1903; and their orders directed them to prevent landing of troops within fifty miles of the transit route. Nominally, these orders were a means of preserving peace on the transit route. Actually, they made it impossible for Colombia to suppress the insurrection. Four days after the revolt, the United States extended de facto recognition to the new government of Panama. On November 13 President Roosevelt received Bunau-Varilla as its accredited agent, and on the eighteenth Hay and Bunau-Varilla signed a new canal treaty between the United States and the Republic of Panama. It had all been done with unseemly haste.

The new treaty was largely the work of Bunau-Varilla. At his insistence and in recognition of his indispensable contribution to the revolution, the Panama government had reluctantly designated him as its first diplomatic representative to the United States. His powers were limited, however, and Dr. Amador and a colleague, Federico Boyd, sailed for New York, carrying a letter which instructed Bunau-Varilla to do nothing without their consent. They landed in New York on November 17 and lingered there for a day to consult with Cromwell, quite unaware that while they were at sea Bunau-Varilla had used the cables to exact full diplomatic powers from the acting head of their government. They learned with consternation upon their arrival in Washington that Bunau-Varilla had already negotiated and signed the treaty as envoy extraordinary and minister plenipotentiary of the Republic of Panama.

How a treaty negotiated by Amador and Boyd would have differed from that signed by Bunau-Varilla we can only conjecture. Undoubtedly they must have approved his action in dissuading Hay from following a senatorial proposal to divide the ten million dollar down payment between Panama and Colombia. They probably did not object to the first article which declared, "The United States guarantees and will maintain the independence of the Republic of Panama." Whether they approved of the expansion of the canal zone from a width of ten kilometers (about six miles) to ten miles, or the authority granted the United States to ensure public order and sanitation in the cities of Colón and Panama and to defend the canal with fortifications and the use of its armed forces, may be doubtful. They would hardly have accepted, in place of the mixed courts to which Colombia had objected, the provision that the United States should exercise in the zone "in perpetuity" all the rights and authority that it would possess if it were sovereign. Nominal sovereignty remained with Panama. All the rights that it implied were exercised by the United States. The compensation, the same as that offered Colombia—ten million dollars upon ratification and an annuity of two hundred and fifty thousand dollars beginning after nine years—would no doubt have been acceptable to Amador and Boyd.

Whatever chagrin the new arrivals from Panama may have felt, Bunau-Varilla had control of the situation. Having stolen a march on them in securing authority and making a treaty to his taste (and that of the United States), he now demanded and got from Panama assurance that the newly elected Congress would accept his handiwork. Consequently, when the United States Senate approved the treaty on February 23, 1904, the matter was settled, and President Roosevelt was free to proceed with plans for the construction of the canal. He maintained then and ever after that he had followed a perfectly correct and justifiable course.

Colombia, naturally, thought otherwise. Marroquín's government offered, too late, to ratify the original treaty by executive act alone, if the United States would enable it to recover sovereignty over Panama. When this offer was refused, Colombia proposed that the question of America's culpability for allegedly instigating and supporting revolution against Colombia be submitted to the Hague Court for arbitration. This proposal the United States refused. For the United States, no doubt, this question involved the national honor, and such questions were excluded from the obligation to arbitrate by the treaties then being proposed and later completed between the United States and other powers.[2] Various attempts to placate Colombia failed until 1921. Then, two years after Roosevelt's death, the United States paid Colombia twenty-five million dollars, the amount for which the latter presumably would have granted canal rights in 1903. Though the motive behind the settlement of 1921 was no doubt tinged with expediency, that settlement nonetheless was a belated confession of wrongdoing.

[2] See pp. 51–52. The United States maintained that its intervention in Panama had been for the purpose of maintaining peaceful transit under the treaty of 1846 with New Granada. The guarantee in the same treaty of New Granadan (Colombian) sovereignty in the isthmus was interpreted, as it had been by an earlier administration, as applicable to aggression from without, not revolution from within.

CHAPTER III

Policeman of the Caribbean

The treaty with Panama made that small state the second protectorate of the United States in the Caribbean area. Terms of the relationship were not spelled out as fully as they had been for Cuba in the Platt Amendment; but the United States had undertaken to protect Panama's independence on the one hand, and on the other had received the right to maintain order and sanitation in Panama's principal cities, as well as to use its armed forces for the defense of the Canal Zone.

Indirectly, too, the Panama treaty set the stage for the institution of other protectorates in the Caribbean region. The assurance that a canal would be built and would become a vital link in the defense system of the United States made any European encroachment in the area seem more than ever a threat to American security. The specter of such an encroachment had come to haunt American dreams while the canal negotiations were still in progress. Britain and Germany, later joined by Italy, had waged an undeclared war against Venezuela. The danger exemplified in this episode led Roosevelt to propound a new theory and to apply it in the establishment of a new protectorate.

The Venezuelan government, now headed by dictator Cipriano Castro, was delinquent on a variety of international obligations, and its creditors had lost patience. In July 1901 Castro refused a German proposal that the German claims against his government be submitted to the Hague Court for arbitration. Germany thereupon began considering the use of force. The German ambassador in Washington, Theodor von Holleben, informed Secretary Hay of these intentions in December 1901, but added the assurance that there would be no permanent occupation of Venezuelan territory. The communication caused no immediate excitement in Washington. Hay made no objection; he merely quoted from Roosevelt's first annual message, December 3, 1901, a passage in which the President had remarked, speaking of the Monroe Doctrine, that the United States did not guarantee any American state against punishment for misbehavior, provided only that the punishment did not involve acquisition of territory. Some months before, in fact, while still Vice-President, Roosevelt had written his German diplomat friend Speck von Sternburg: "If any South American country misbehaves toward any European country, let the European country spank it."

With the road thus apparently cleared, the Germans and British decided upon a combined naval demonstration against delinquent Venezuela. The British seem first to have suggested joint action, early in January 1902—rather surprisingly in view of popular resentment at Germany's unfriendly attitude toward England during the Boer War. Formal discussion began in July, and on November 11, 1902, Foreign Secretary Lord Lansdowne, in the so-called "ironclad bargain," promised the German ambassador that England would stick by Germany until their purpose was achieved. Two days later British ambassador Sir Michael Herbert informed Hay of their plans. The two powers presented their ultimatum to Castro on December 7 and on the eighth established a *de facto* blockade of Venezuelan ports. On the next day the allies captured a number of Venezuelan gunboats. Two of these the Germans sank in local waters, explaining to the State Department that they were too small and unseaworthy to be sent to Trinidad with other captive vessels. Troops from the allied squadrons landed at the port of La Guaira to rescue British subjects, who feared violence from the enraged local populace. Germany had proposed a "pacific blockade" of Venezuela (convenient as not requiring consent of the Bundesrat) but dropped the proposal in response to British and American objections. On December 20 the allies instituted a regular, or "warlike," blockade of the Venezuelan coastline. The two powers had in the meantime been joined by Italy, another hungry creditor.

Cipriano Castro was neither loved nor admired in the United States, but these drastic actions against an American state by a combination of European powers aroused excitement and antagonism in the American press and public. Such antagonism was, however, directed principally against Germany. The British had largely disarmed criticism through public disclaimers of aggressive purposes. Ambassador von Holleben's repeated assurances that Germany would respect the Monroe Doctrine failed to carry similar conviction. Roosevelt, very much alive to the tides of public opinion, had already, if we can trust circumstantial evidence, had second thoughts about the green light that he had given in his letter to Sternburg and in his annual message of 1901. We cannot be sure here of cause and effect, but for whatever reason the Navy Department, soon after the first warning of the use of force against Castro, began planning for an impressive naval demonstration in the Caribbean. A temporary base of operations was found at Culebra Island, off the eastern end of Puerto Rico, and in June 1902 naval maneuvers from that base were ordered for the following December. Every available battleship was ordered to the area, and Admiral George Dewey, the Navy's highest-ranking officer, was given command of the maneuvers. He took charge on December 8, the day on which the first Anglo-German blockade was imposed. In the meantime the Navy, under orders from Washington, had been investigating sites for landing operations on the Venezuelan coast. It seems evident that Roosevelt was taking precautionary measures against possible trouble with Germany.

Castro now contributed to an easing of the tension. With his ports blockaded by three determined major powers, he thought better of arbitration as a mode of settlement. On December 11 he offered through the United States to submit the claims against him to arbitration. The State Department at once transmitted his offer to the allies. On the sixteenth, at the prompting of Venezuela, it urged that the offer be accepted. As late as December 15, Germany was counseling Great Britain against arbitration, but on the next day the German ambassadors in both London and Washington advised the Foreign Office in Berlin to accept Castro's proposal. A day later (December 17) the British and German governments accepted the principle of arbitration, with certain reservations, proposing that President Roosevelt act as arbitrator. The United States was notified of their decision, by Britain on the eighteenth, by Germany on the nineteenth.

Just what occurred between the eleventh and the seventeenth of December to induce the German Kaiser to agree to arbitration remains something of a mystery, but it seems reasonably certain that Roosevelt exerted pressure on Wilhelm outside regular diplomatic channels and in a manner that left no official record in the archives of either country. In a letter to Whitelaw Reid less than four years later Roosevelt gave the following account of what happened:

. . . I finally told the German Ambassador that in my opinion the Kaiser ought to know that unless an agreement for arbitration was reached, American public opinion would soon be at the point where I would have to move Dewey's ships, which were then in the West Indies, south, to observe matters along Venezuela; and that I would have to let it be known publicly that under conditions as they then were I would have to object even to temporary possession of Venezuelan soil by Germany, unless such possession was strictly limited to say three or four days to a week. This brought him to terms at once.[1]

[1] Elting E. Morison, ed., *The Letters of Theodore Roosevelt* (8 vols., Cambridge: Harvard University Press, 1951–54), V, 319. The letter is dated June 27, 1906. Roosevelt gave a generally similar account in a letter to Henry White, August 14, 1906. In this he emphasized the secrecy with which the matter was handled—"I saw the German Ambassador privately myself"—and his care to enable the Kaiser to retreat without losing face. *Ibid.*, V, 357–359. The story remained a secret between Roosevelt and a few intimates until 1915, when a more dramatic account, telling of two warnings served on the German Ambassador several days apart, was supplied by Roosevelt to W. R. Thayer for inclusion in his *The Life and Letters of John Hay* (2 vols., Boston: Houghton Mifflin Company, 1915), II, 285–288, 411–417. Roosevelt's letter to Thayer is also printed in Morison, *op. cit.*, VIII, 1101–1105. There is no record of any such warnings in the State Department archives or in the records of the German Foreign Office, and a number of historians have regarded the entire story as a fabrication born of Roosevelt's later hatred of the Kaiser's Germany. It seems certain that he was at least exaggerating and overdramatizing his role in the later accounts to Thayer; on the other hand, despite the absence of official confirmation, there seems no good reason to doubt the essential truth of the story told confidentially to Reid and White in 1906, at a time when Roosevelt was still on very good terms with the Kaiser. For skepticism concerning the ultimatum story see, among others, Dexter Perkins, *The Monroe Doctrine, 1867–1907* (Baltimore: The Johns Hopkins Press, 1937), chap. 5; Tyler Dennett, *John Hay: From Poetry to Politics* (New York: Dodd, Mead and Company, 1933), chap. 31. For the contrary view see H. C. Beale, *Theodore Roosevelt and the Rise of America to World Power* (Baltimore: The Johns Hopkins Press, 1956), pp. 395–431; W. H. Harbaugh, *Power and Responsibility: The Life and Times of Theodore Roosevelt* (New York: Farrar, Straus & Cudahy, 1961), pp. 191–192; H. F. Pringle, *Theodore Roosevelt: A Biography* (New York: Harcourt, Brace and Company, 1931), pp. 282–289. The naval maneuvers and their apparent relation to the Venezuela episode are described in S. W. Livermore, "Theodore Roosevelt, the American Navy, and the Venezuelan Crisis of 1902–1903," *American Historical Review*, LI, 452–471 (April 1946). For the suggestion that Roosevelt's pressure on

A few days after the President's alleged warning to von Holleben, but apparently before the Kaiser's agreement to arbitrate was known, the battleships of the fleet were ordered south to Trinidad. This move was nominally a part of the dispersal of the fleet for the Christmas period. Whatever the purpose, it brought the big ships much nearer the Venezuelan coast, where they could be joined on short notice by other elements of the fleet; and it led to several anxious inquiries at the State Department by the German chargé d'affaires. Captain William S. Cowles, U.S.N., Roosevelt's brother-in-law and acting chief of the Bureau of Navigation in Washington, was reported as saying that the presence of the fleet "was probably a convenience to the administration in discussing the Venezuelan situation." A few months later Admiral Dewey told a newspaper reporter that the fleet maneuvers had been "an object lesson to the Kaiser, more than to any other person"—an indiscretion for which he was summoned to the White House and reprimanded.

The allies had agreed to arbitration in principle and had accepted Roosevelt's proposal that the Hague Court, not he, act as arbitrator. But many weeks were required for agreement on details, and until these were settled the allied blockade continued, accompanied by the needless bombardment of Venezuelan Fort San Carlos by the German cruiser *Panther*. A result of this incident was a new flare-up of anti-German feeling in the United States. The whole affair had been disturbing to Roosevelt. Public controversy with Germany had been avoided, but he clearly feared that some future episode of similar character might so inflame public opinion that a showdown with Germany would be inevitable. How could repetitions of the allied debt-collecting pro-

the Kaiser may have been applied at a later stage of the controversy, when there was disagreement over the terms of the proposed arbitration, see D. G. Munro, *Intervention and Dollar Diplomacy in the Caribbean, 1900–1921* (Princeton: Princeton University Press, 1964), pp. 72–74.

cedure be avoided? [2] British statesmen and newspapers were volunteering an answer. They endorsed the Monroe Doctrine, but with the suggestion that the United States should itself make some arrangement for preventing default by Latin American states on their obligations to Europe, already estimated at three hundred million dollars.

Whether Roosevelt was actually influenced by these thoughts from overseas is uncertain, but within a year and a half after the Anglo-German intervention in Venezuela he had reached two decisions: first, such European coercion of an American state could not be again permitted; second, the United States, which forbade coercion, must in justice see that there was no legitimate excuse for it. The United States must, in other words, prevent American states like Venezuela from giving provocation for European intervention.

This new concept, entailing preventive intervention by the United States, Roosevelt first expressed in May 1904 in a letter to Secretary Root, to be read by the Secretary at a dinner in New York. Seven months later he incorporated it in his annual message of December 6, 1904. In this official form it read as follows:

> Any country whose people conduct themselves well can count upon our hearty friendship. If a nation shows that it knows how to act with reasonable efficiency and decency in social and political matters, if it keeps order and pays its obligations, it need fear no interference from the United States. Chronic wrongdoing, or an impotence which results in a general loosening of the ties of civilized society, may in America, as elsewhere, ultimately require intervention by some civilized nation, and in the Western Hemisphere, the adherence of the

[2] The Hague Court, in arbitrating the claims against Venezuela, had given preference to the claims of the three powers that had resorted to armed force. This aspect of the decision seemed to put a premium on armed intervention and to make it more likely in the future.

United States to the Monroe Doctrine may force the United States, however reluctantly, in flagrant cases of such wrong-doing or impotence, to the exercise of an international police power.

First termed by Elihu Root a "corollary" of the Monroe Doctrine, the Roosevelt Corollary, as it came to be called, rested on a concept which would in sixty years no longer be tenable—the concept of the inequality of states: of first-class and second-class states, of which the latter, being incompetent to manage their affairs decently, must submit at least to supervision by the former. Roosevelt's thinking on this subject may have been influenced by a former teacher, the political scientist John W. Burgess, whose lectures he had attended while a law student at Columbia. In Burgess' philosophy, the "political nations" (to him synonymous with the "Teutonic nations") had a right and a duty to impose order upon populations "which manifest incapacity to solve the problem of political civilization with any degree of completeness."

This description, in Roosevelt's mind, would have fitted Castro's Venezuela. It also fitted the Dominican Republic, or Santo Domingo, to which he undoubtedly alluded in his "corollary" letter and message. A long series of revolutions, in which both government and opposition had borrowed abroad, had saddled the Dominican government with a debt which its corrupt and incompetent fiscal administration could not possibly service. Debts owed to American, British, German, Belgian, French, and Italian creditors had been guaranteed by liens on the customs revenue, both at large and at specified ports. Such liens conflicted with one another and with the needs of the government itself, and during 1904 the prospect grew that European governments might attempt to occupy ports and customhouses in behalf of their nationals. Such action Roosevelt now considered quite impermissible, and to prevent it he put his corollary theory into practice.

At a hint from Washington by way of the United States minister in Santo Domingo, President Carlos F. Morales invited the United States to take charge of the collection and disbursement of the customs revenues and to assist the republic in adjusting its debts and satisfying its creditors. An agreement to that effect was signed in Santo Domingo, the Dominican capital, on January 20, 1905. This was long before the day when executive agreements in foreign relations became common American practice, and the revelation that this document contained no provision for submission to the Senate but was to go into effect at once produced an angry reaction in the Congress and the press of the United States. The New York *Sun* warned that if the President should succeed in destroying the Senate's control of treaties, "the Republican form of government . . . would cease to exist; and irresponsible autocracy like that of Russia would be the hideous substitute." The President and the State Department bowed to the storm. The agreement, with a few changes, was put into treaty form and sent to the Senate on February 15, 1905. In the accompanying message Roosevelt observed that foreign creditors of the Dominican Republic had no means of ensuring collection of their debts other than by acquisition of territory or the seizure of the customhouses. Making it plain that either type of action by a European power would violate the Monroe Doctrine, the President drew the conclusion:

> The justification for the United States taking this burden and incurring this responsibility is to be found in the fact that it is incompatible with international equity for the United States to refuse to allow other powers to take the only means at their disposal of satisfying the claims of their creditors and yet to refuse, itself, to take any such steps.

When, despite Roosevelt's urging, Democratic opposition prevented Senate approval of the treaty, its essential features were temporarily put into effect by a new executive agreement, termed a *modus vivendi*, signed April 1, 1905. Unlike the earlier agreement, by which the United States would have guaranteed "the complete integrity of the territory of the Dominican Republic," the *modus vivendi* stipulated no obligation on the part of the United States. It provided, in the first place, that the Dominican government would appoint as receiver of customs a citizen of the United States nominated by the American President. This official would turn over forty-five percent of the receipts to the Dominican government. The remainder, less cost of collection, would be deposited in a New York bank, to be apportioned among the creditors of the republic if the Senate finally approved the treaty; otherwise it would be returned to the Dominican government for such apportionment.

This *modus vivendi* remained in effect for over two years, until a new treaty signed February 8, 1907, received the Senate's approval and was proclaimed in the following July. During those years, while the Dominican government that accepted the arrangement was sustained in power against its opponents by the presence of United States naval vessels, an American economist negotiated adjustments of the Dominican debt, which reduced its amount from over thirty million dollars to seventeen million dollars. At the same time a new twenty million dollar bond issue was floated in the United States and the proceeds were applied to paying off the adjusted debt and to the execution of neglected public works in the island. What had happened, obviously, was that the United States had assumed the role of debt collector in behalf of the creditors of the Dominican Republic, thus removing any excuse that European governments might have had for coercive action against the debtor state. By instituting honest and efficient collection and disbursement of the revenue, it was benefiting all concerned except those Dominican politicians who regarded public money as a source of private income.

The same arrangement, with some modifications, was continued under the treaty of 1907. Appointment of the general receiver of Dominican customs and his subordinates was now vested directly in the President of the United States. The general receiver was to have full control of the collection of customs duties until the twenty million dollar bond issue should have been liquidated, and until that time the Dominican government agreed not to increase its public debt without the prior consent of the United States. All revenues not required for expenses of collection (limited to five percent) and for interest, amortization, and cancellation of the bonded debt were to be turned over to the Dominican government. That government promised protection, "to the extent of its powers," to the general receiver and his assistants, and the United States promised to give them "such protection as it may find to be requisite." The United States assumed no obligation beyond the administration and protection of the receivership.

The Dominican Republic thus became the third Caribbean protectorate of the United States and the first to rest explicitly on the foundation of the Roosevelt Corollary to the Monroe Doctrine. Roosevelt had no further occasion to invoke the corollary during his occupancy of the White House, but his successors, Taft and Wilson, were to rely upon it, implicitly at least, in adding Nicaragua and Haiti to the circle of American protectorates.

The enunciation of the Roosevelt Corollary and the application of it in the Dominican Republic met with little criticism and with no official protests from foreign governments. The French and German press were critical, the British press approving. British bondholders regretted that application of the policy was not extended to other Caribbean republics. Even in Latin America there was little criticism and considerable outright approval. Roosevelt was careful to give assurance that the corollary would be applied only in extreme cases, and to flatter the more stable governments to the southward. Elihu Root, who became Secretary of State in July 1905, declared that the United States was "trying to perform the office of friendship and discharge the duty of good neighborhood towards Santo Domingo."

Root, indeed, made every effort to remove suspicion and cultivate good will in Latin America. The South Americans, he told a Senator, hated the United States, "largely because they think we despise them and try to bully them." He believed that their friendship was important to the United States "and that the best way to secure it is by treating them like gentlemen." In 1906 he attended the Third International Conference of American States at Rio de Janeiro and in the course of his journey there and back accepted invitations to visit nearly all the capitals of South America—something that no previous Secretary of State had done. He induced the Russian Czar to postpone the Second Hague Peace Conference from 1906 to the next year in order to avoid conflict with the conference at Rio; and he persuaded the Czar also to include the Latin American countries in the invitations to the Hague in 1907, whereas Mexico alone had been invited to the first conference in 1899. Through the United States delegation at the Hague he secured adoption by the conference of a modified version of the Drago Doctrine—proposed by the former Argentine Foreign Minister—declaring inadmissible the use of force by a European power for the collection of the debt of an American nation.[3] He promoted a Central American Peace Conference in 1907 and assisted, with the cooperation of Mexico, in the creation of a Central American Court of Justice and the adoption of a group of

[3] See pp. 49–50.

treaties designed to put an end to the frequent wars between the states of that area.

Not all relations with Latin America in Root's time were marked by sweetness and light. Colombia remained unreconciled to the loss of Panama and resentful at the United States despite Root's best efforts to settle the quarrel by treaty. Panama was angered by Roosevelt's warning, in Root's absence, that the United States would not permit a fraudulently elected president to take office—a seeming anticipation of Woodrow Wilson's policy of a few years later. But the worst problem for the United States in Latin America during Root's term as Secretary of State arose in Cuba, whose relationship with the United States Root himself had undertaken to define in the Platt Amendment.

Independent Cuba under its first President, Tomás Estrada Palma (1902–06), seemed at first on the road to order and progress. A beneficial reciprocal trade treaty was negotiated with the United States, and Guantanamo Bay was leased to the United States for use as a naval base. Estrada Palma, a popular figure who had served abroad during Cuba's civil war, had been chosen as the candidate of both leading political parties. As the time for new elections approached, however, he allowed himself to become a tool of the Conservative Republican (or Moderate) party. Cuban politicians, novices in democratic procedures, soon showed themselves adept in democracy's most vicious practices. An estimated one hundred and fifty thousand fictitious ballots were cast in the election of 1905. Estrada Palma was declared reelected, but the defeated Liberals, who had abstained from what they considered a rigged election, staged a revolt, in August 1906, in support of their candidate, José Miguel Gómez. The President had neglected to provide his government with an army. Unable to suppress the rebellion, he asked intervention by the United States. Roosevelt sent a high-level team to investigate: William H. Taft, Secretary of War, and, in Root's absence in South America, Assistant Secretary of State Robert Bacon. They found Estrada Palma determined to resign, leaving Cuba without a government, and reluctantly recommended that the United States intervene under the terms of the Platt Amendment. Taft became temporarily provisional governor. He was succeeded, October 13, 1906, by Charles E. Magoon, an American lawyer who had had experience in administering the new American acquisitions, in Washington and in the Panama Canal Zone.

Magoon administered Cuba in behalf of the United States from October 1906 to January 1909. His regime was not an unqualified success, but at least he restored order, promoted useful public works, sponsored a new election law, and paved the way for new elections in 1908. These were won by the Liberals, and Gómez took over the presidency in 1909. Roosevelt and Root had firmly resisted attempts by American and Spanish property owners in Cuba and by such American imperialists as Senator Albert J. Beveridge to convert the temporary occupation into annexation. "The machinations of the gentlemen who wish to turn this business into a reconquest of Cuba will not succeed," Root declared. The United States had intervened only when Cuba was on the verge of anarchy and had remained only so long as was necessary to restore order and revive normal processes of government. In conformity with the promise of the Teller Resolution of 1898, it had then returned "the government and control of the Island to its people." [4]

Under the authority of the Platt Amendment in Cuba and the Roosevelt Corollary in the Dominican Republic, the United States had indeed become the policeman of the Caribbean, enforcing order and responsibility upon small states that lacked them. These actions it had taken reluctantly and

[4] The Teller Resolution, an amendment to the war resolutions of April 20, 1898, had disclaimed any intention of acquiring Cuba for the United States.

with results that were beneficial to the people of the states concerned and in the interest of world order and stability in general. Thanks largely to Root's tactful approach, the interventions had called forth surprisingly little resentment in Latin America as a whole. Such "Yankeephobia" as existed at this stage was found largely in literary circles rather than among political leaders or the populace. One Argentine litterateur, indeed, Manuel Ugarte, took occasion to deplore the failure of the South Americans to resent the "wrongs" inflicted upon Colombia and Santo Domingo by the "Colossus of the North."

CHAPTER IV

Furthering the Cause of Peace

Writing to a friend from Albany while still governor of New York, Roosevelt had emphatically denied the charge that he was "an advocate of bloodshed." Asserting that he "very earnestly" desired peace, he remarked that "something was done for peace" at the Hague Conference of 1899, but that the American influence at the conference "was due to the fact that we came in as a strong man and not as a weakling."

The First Hague Conference, to which Roosevelt here referred (and to which the United States had come backed by a respectable and growing Navy), had failed to agree on any limitation of armaments—the ostensible purpose for which the Russian Czar had proposed it. It had adopted certain rules to make war more humane; and it had established the so-called Permanent Court of Arbitration with seat at The Hague. The court was actually merely a panel of judges— four named by each of the twenty-six participating governments—from among whom governments wishing to submit a case to arbitration could select members of a tribunal. The court, together with the Permanent International Bureau, which served as its secretariat, was eventually housed in a magnificent palace donated by Andrew Carnegie, the American steel king. The court was available for any contenders that cared to use it, but the nations that had set it up had made no promises to resort to it and for several years showed no inclination to do so. It fell to Roosevelt as President to break what looked like a boycott of the court.

It was suggested to Roosevelt by a French visitor, early in 1902, that he might reassure Europeans who suspected him of bellicosity "by giving life to the Hague Court." Roosevelt thereupon instructed Secretary Hay to find a controversy that could prudently be submitted to arbitration. The case that Hay selected was the long-standing Pious Fund controversy with Mexico. The Pious Fund had originated some two hundred years earlier from sums donated for the support of Jesuit plans to Christianize the natives of California. It grew to over a million dollars, and its proceeds were used in part, after the dissolution of the Jesuit Order, to support Franciscan missions in California. The independence of Mexico transferred control of the fund from the Spanish to the Mexican government, which first secularized the California missions and later, under Santa Anna in 1842, in effect confiscated the fund.

After California became part of the United States, the Catholic Church in that state laid claim to payment of interest on the fund. Its claim for interest from 1848 was filed with a claims commission agreed upon between the United States and Mexico in 1868. The commission directed Mexico to pay over nine hundred thousand dollars in back interest from 1848 to 1869 and to pay thereafter annuities of some forty-three thousand dollars. Mexico paid the arrears but failed to keep up the annuities, and it was the Church's claim for these that Mexico and the United States agreed to submit to arbitration at The Hague in 1902. The court sustained the American claim on behalf of the Catholic Church. Mexico was directed to pay $1,420,682.67 for sums due since

1869 and to continue the annuities as previously ordered.[1]

The Pious Fund arbitration was of minor importance in itself, but it set a precedent under which the Hague Court became moderately active. Within a year, nearly twenty controversies, including the Venezuelan controversy described in the last chapter, had been submitted to tribunals chosen from the Hague panel of judges. A much more serious controversy than that over the Pious Fund, Roosevelt was, however, unwilling to entrust to The Hague. This was the dispute with Canada and Britain over the Alaska boundary.

When the United States purchased Alaska from Russia in 1867, it inherited the boundary between Alaska and adjacent British Columbia which had been defined by the Russo-British treaty of 1825. This treaty had described the eastern boundary of the panhandle area as following a range of mountains from 56° north latitude to the 141st meridian of west longitude, which formed the boundary thence northward to the Arctic Ocean; but it also stipulated that this line from 56° to 141° should be nowhere more than ten leagues (thirty miles) from the sea. Since no mountain range corresponding to the description existed, it was assumed that the line should be drawn thirty miles from the sea.

This sounded simple enough. The United States assumed, and the Canadians for thirty years tacitly admitted, that the thirty miles were to be measured from the head of tidewater in the numerous fjords or "canals" that intersected the drowned coastline. This apparently was the intent of the 1825 treaty, for the records seemed to show a mutual understanding that the Russians were barring the British from

[1] Mexico kept up payments through 1912, when revolution had emptied the Mexican treasury. As of 1963, no further payments had been made. See F. J. Weber, "The Pious Fund of the Californias," *Hispanic American Historical Review*, XLIII, 78–94 (February 1963).

navigable water. Disagreement came after 1897, when thousands of prospectors, lured by the discovery of gold in the
Klondike, found that the best approach was by way of the
Lynn Canal and the Chilkoot Pass. At the head of the canal
(more accurately a deep inlet or fjord) two boomtowns,
Dyea and Skagway, blossomed almost overnight. Canada
now put forward the claim that the boundary should be
drawn not thirty miles from the head of tidewater, but thirty
miles from the outer fringe of the ragged coast. A line so
drawn would give Dyea and Skagway to Canada and would
leave to the United States little of the panhandle beyond a
few islands and a row of disconnected headlands. The
United States rejected the new Canadian claim as wholly
unwarranted.

The British, for their part, viewed the Canadian position
at best with skepticism but had to make an effort to satisfy
a loyal Dominion. During the sittings of the Joint High Commission (1898–99) they sought concessions from the United
States on the Alaska boundary in exchange for British consent to modify the Clayton-Bulwer Treaty. The United
States refused such a deal, but Hay and the British ambassador agreed on a *modus vivendi* which left Dyea and Skagway under United States jurisdiction until the boundary
could be definitively established.

This was the situation when Roosevelt entered the White
House. While willing for the time being to "let sleeping dogs
lie" by observing the *modus vivendi,* he believed that the
Canadian claim "had not a leg to stand on." When the British government, actually looking for a settlement through a
face-saving retreat, indicated a wish to reopen negotiations,
he permitted Hay to revive a proposal which the Secretary
had made and the British had refused three years before.
This called for submission of the boundary controversy to a
commission of six men, three chosen by each contestant. This
procedure could easily produce a deadlock, but Roosevelt,

who considered assertion of the Canadian claim "danger-
ously near blackmail," refused emphatically to submit it to
an arbitral body in which a neutral member or members
should have the deciding voice. Such bodies, as he knew,
were apt to look for compromise solutions, and on this question he considered the American case so strong that no compromise would be acceptable. The British must yield or
there would be no settlement. In that event, he let it be
known, he would order the United States Army to run the
line and hold it.

Friction over the Venezuela blockade (described in the
preceding chapter) made the British government now particularly anxious to remove other irritants in Anglo-American
relations, and on January 24, 1903, Hay and Ambassador
Sir Michael Herbert signed a treaty embodying Hay's proposal. The boundary question was to be submitted to a
tribunal [2] of "six impartial jurists of repute," three named by
the King of England and three by the President of the
United States. They were to "consider judicially" and determine within six months, "the geographical meaning of the
vague or disputed terms of the treaty of 1825."

Much would now depend upon the six "impartial jurists"
selected by the President and the King. Roosevelt was first
to reveal his choices, and they were greeted with astonish-
ment in the United States and with indignation in Canada,
if not in Britain. The least objectionable was Elihu Root,
Secretary of War, an eminent lawyer, but hardly in a position to view the issue impartially. The others were Senators
Henry Cabot Lodge of Massachusetts and George Turner of
Washington state, both notorious for emphatic champion-
ship of the American claim. On the surface these selections
were inexcusable, but the alternative to the naming of these

---

[2] Roosevelt insisted that the procedure was not arbitration; in fact he recalled the treaty from the Senate to delete the word "arbitral," which had
got in by error.

men or similar partisans would probably have been no treaty, no tribunal, and, if Roosevelt had carried out his intention, a possible clash of arms on the Alaska frontier. Even with the names of the appointees confidentially revealed to the Senators, Lodge, in charge of the treaty, had to resort to stratagem to secure its approval by a sparsely attended Senate. Had two Supreme Court justices, to whom Roosevelt later asserted he had offered appointments, agreed to serve, the treaty could well have been rejected.

The British government thought of naming equally partisan judges, but on the advice of Lord Minto, Governor General of Canada, resolved to live up to the spirit of the treaty. It had been understood that one of the King's appointees should be an Englishman, the other two, Canadians. The King named Lord Alverstone, Lord Chief Justice of Britain, and two distinguished Canadian lawyers, of whom one was a former justice of the Supreme Court of Quebec, while the other had declined appointment to the Supreme Court of Canada. In actual fact, however, the Canadian jurists proved to be as impervious to the other side's argument as were the American politicians.

The decision rested, as was no doubt foreseen, with Lord Alverstone, and the American exertions to influence him were at best unseemly. Roosevelt had already sent troops to southern Alaska, where they would be on hand in the event of border disturbances on either side of the line, but would also symbolize the President's determination to enforce the American claim if necessary. Through Henry White of the American embassy in London, through Lodge, and through Justice Holmes, who was also in England, Roosevelt and Hay warned Balfour, the Prime Minister, and Lord Lansdowne, the Foreign Secretary, of the danger inherent in a deadlock. Such an outcome, Roosevelt wrote White, while bad for the United States, "would be a very much worse thing for the Canadians and English," because it would leave the President no alternative but to take possession of the disputed territory "and to declare furthermore that no additional negotiations of any kind would be entered into." White spent a weekend with Balfour; Balfour conferred at least twice with Lord Alverstone. The Chief Justice, who had from the first leaned to the American side on the main issue, gave up his attempt to find a compromise and voted with the three Americans on every essential point. The tribunal, therefore, handed the United States a four-to-two victory. The Canadian members, outraged probably more at the methods than at the results of the proceedings, refused to sign the award.

Lord Alverstone maintained, then and later, that all his decisions had been based on judicial considerations, uninfluenced by the pressures and threats emanating from Washington. However that may be, his stand, though bitterly resented in Canada, was fortunate for all concerned. For him to have supported the Canadian view, a British historian has written,

> might well have spelled disaster for Canada, as well as Britain; that he took the American [view], caused pain and vexation for a time, but reinforced in the end the fundamental Anglo-American concord upon which Canada's life depends.[3]

The settlement, in fact, removed the last obstacle to cordial relations between Britain and the United States.

The Alaska decision was handed down on October 20, 1903. Early the next year Japan and Russia went to war over their rivalry in Manchuria and Korea. The story of America's relationship to that war and to other developments in the Far East is reserved for the next chapter. Soon after the Russo-Japanese War was ended—largely through Roosevelt's

[3] H. C. Allen, *Great Britain and the United States: A History of Anglo-American Relations (1783–1952)* (New York: St. Martin's Press, Inc., 1955), p. 613.

efforts—the President made a significant contribution to the preservation of the peace of Europe. The quarrel here was between France and Germany; the cause of strife was rivalry in Morocco; and the dispute was settled not by arbitration but by an international conference at Algeciras, Spain. Roosevelt played an important role in bringing about the conference and in ensuring its success.

The Morocco quarrel exhibited Germany's resentment at the progressive partitioning of Africa without her consent. France had already annexed Algeria and made Tunisia a protectorate. England controlled Egypt, and Tripoli had been earmarked for Italy. In North Africa there remained only Morocco, nominally independent under a Sultan, but ill governed and a tempting morsel to the colonial appetites of Europe. By a treaty of April 8, 1904, England conceded to France a free hand in Morocco in return for withdrawal of French claims in the Sudan. Later in the year France and Spain delimited their respective spheres of interest in Morocco—a narrow northern coastal strip for Spain, the hinterland and most of the Atlantic coast for France. At no point had Germany been consulted. German economic interests in Morocco appeared compromised, and the prestige of Germany, a major power with colonial ambitions of her own, had suffered a blow.

The involvement of France's ally, Russia, in a disastrous war in the Far East tipped the delicate balance of power in Germany's favor and made the moment seem propitious for vigorous self-assertion. At the urging of Chancellor Bernhard von Bülow, the Kaiser interrupted a voyage to the Mediterranean for a call at Tangier on Morocco's Atlantic coast. In well-publicized speeches to the Sultan's representative and the diplomatic corps on March 31, 1905, he hailed the Sultan as a fully independent monarch, with whom he chose to deal directly in safeguarding German interests in Morocco. This obvious challenge to France Germany followed up with advice to the Sultan which led him to reject French demands for supervision of his finances and to appeal for an international conference to settle Morocco's relations with other powers. Talk of a Franco-German war was widespread. As a conciliatory gesture, the French Premier, M. Rouvier, dropped his aggressive Foreign Minister, Théophile Delcassé, chief proponent of the Moroccan policy, but the question of foreign rights and interests in Morocco remained undetermined.

Through the late winter and spring of 1905, both before and after his visit to Tangier, the Kaiser was in frequent communication with Roosevelt through his ambassador and Roosevelt's friend, Baron Speck von Sternburg. Germany, the Kaiser insisted, wanted no special privileges in Morocco, only equality of treatment with all other powers. Germany, in other words, was asking in Morocco only the open door, the very principle which the United States had so recently championed in China. The Kaiser intimated plainly that French refusal of his demands might mean war—a war in which France would probably be joined by England. He tried to alarm Roosevelt further by predicting that if in such a war England and France should succeed in destroying German sea power, they would join with Russia to partition China, putting an end to the cherished American policy in the Middle Kingdom. Roosevelt, therefore, the Kaiser urged repeatedly, should put pressure on France and England to consent to a conference on Morocco, thus removing danger of a war that might have such disastrous consequences. In an indiscreet letter to Roosevelt, Speck von Sternburg promised that if the conference was arranged, the Kaiser would agree to any solution that Roosevelt might propose. He had been authorized to say merely that von Bülow would urge the Kaiser to accept Roosevelt's advice.

Roosevelt received the Kaiser's appeals and warnings with a combination of skepticism and sympathy. He doubted the

German disclaimer of a desire for any special privileges in Morocco, feeling confident that Germany would gladly accept a sphere of influence there if it were offered. The warnings of sinister French and British designs on China gave him no worry. On the other hand, he was quite willing to cooperate in bringing about a conference on Morocco. Such a conference, above all, might prevent a European war of incalculable magnitude. It might improve Anglo-German relations. And it might, through minor concessions to Germany, preserve the essentials of the French and Spanish position in Morocco, which Roosevelt believed to be generally correct. Through the French ambassador, J. J. Jusserand, whose friendship with Roosevelt was even more intimate than Speck's, the President promised that if France agreed to a conference, the United States would participate (on the basis of its commercial treaty of 1880 with Morocco) and would support France against any German demands that Roosevelt might consider unreasonable.

With this assurance France agreed (June 25, 1905) to a conference to be held at Algeciras, near Gibraltar, beginning in January 1906. The participants, those who had attended an earlier conference on Morocco in 1880, included the principal European powers and the United States. The United States was represented by Henry White, now ambassador to Italy, and Samuel R. Gummere, United States minister to Morocco. It was agreed by all that the Sultan's sovereignty was and must continue to be a fiction; that in government finance and in policing the seaports his government needed supervision from outside. Like some backward nations of the Caribbean, Morocco was a second-class state. The chief disagreement among the delegations was over control of the police. A plan introduced by Austria-Hungary and favored by Germany would have assigned supervision of the police at different ports to officers nominated by different governments—French, Spanish, Dutch, and Swiss. This plan was acceptable to most of the delegations at the conference, but Roosevelt backed French objections to it. It would, he argued, facilitate the creation of spheres of influence by the powers controlling the police in the respective ports, and he saw the possibility of Germany's gaining control of one such sphere. He proposed an alternative plan for joint French and Spanish control over police in all the ports, with a supervisor-general from some small power (Switzerland was eventually agreed upon) to reside at Tangier. When Germany objected to this plan, Roosevelt invoked Speck's promise that the Kaiser would accept his guidance. Not, however, until he had threatened to publish the correspondence, including Speck's indiscretion, did the Germans yield.

The international Algeciras Convention, signed on April 7, 1906, paid lip service to the independence of Morocco and the sovereignty of the Sultan and endorsed the open door principle. It provided for a native police force under French and Spanish instructors, who were to be appointed by the Sultan upon nomination of the French and Spanish governments, all under a Swiss inspector-general. A State Bank of Morocco, set up at Tangier, with shares owned by the signatory powers, was to handle government finance, including provision for payment of the police. The arrangement was so close to what Germany had professed to desire that Roosevelt tactfully congratulated the Kaiser on a diplomatic triumph, in having brought France to the conference table and having secured acceptance of the open door principle for Morocco. Roosevelt's important role had been played in secret and was not revealed till many years later.[4]

[4] Roosevelt told the story of his role before and during the Algeciras Conference in a long confidential letter to Whitelaw Reid of April 28, 1906, which was first published by Joseph Bucklin Bishop in his *Theodore Roosevelt and His Time Shown in His Own Letters* (2 vols., New York: Charles Scribner's Sons, 1920), I, 467–503; also in E. E. Morison, ed., *The Letters of Theodore Roosevelt*, V, 230–251. This account is confirmed in virtually all details by the published German documents.

The United States Senate approved the convention subject to a reservation declaring that American participation in the conference had been for the sole purpose of preserving and promoting commerce, protecting American citizens in Morocco, and alleviating international friction, "and without any purpose to depart from the traditional American foreign policy which forbids participation by the United States in the settlement of political questions which are entirely European in their scope."

There was less contradiction than might at first appear between the language of the Senate's reservation and the role that Roosevelt had actually played at Algeciras. He was the first American President to realize that war between major powers anywhere was of vital concern to the United States. Questions as serious as that between France and Germany over Morocco were no longer "entirely European in their scope," and Roosevelt had acted decisively to get this one settled.

Believing as he did that "something was done for peace" at the First Hague Conference, Roosevelt was anxious to see the effort resumed at a second meeting. In 1904, in fact, he had tried to steal the initiative from the Russian Czar by suggesting, through the State Department, that the time would soon be ripe for a second conference. The time, in reality, was disappointingly unripe for such an undertaking. Russia and Japan had just gone to war, ignoring the possibility of arbitration through the Hague tribunal. In reply to Roosevelt's suggestion, Japan stipulated that a new conference, should one be called, should take no action relating to the existing war; Russia declined to participate until that war was finished.

Upon the conclusion of the Russo-Japanese War in 1905, the Czar passed the word to Roosevelt that he himself preferred to sponsor a second conference as he had sponsored the first in 1899. Again, therefore, the invitation went out from St. Petersburg. Proposed originally for 1906, the Second Hague Conference was postponed for a year to avoid conflict with the Inter-American Conference at Rio de Janeiro. It sat from June 15 to October 18, 1907. Forty-four nations were represented, including, at Secretary Root's suggestion, all the states of Latin America.

The hoped-for limitation of armaments fared no better at the second conference than at the first. British and American public opinion favored limitation. Roosevelt suggested limiting the size of battleships to fifteen thousand tons displacement; but the British *Dreadnought* had already started the escalation in battleship size which was to reach forty-five thousand tons in the *Missouri* class of World War II. Root suggested reducing the term of enlistment in standing armies. Neither of these ideas was laid before the conference. The only official proposal was one for an agreed limitation of military and naval budgets, offered without conviction by the British and perfunctorily endorsed by the United States. Nothing came of it. Germany, Russia, France, and Austria-Hungary were in no mood for arms limitation of any kind.

Secretary Root's instructions to the United States delegation directed it to work for two principal objectives—adoption of the Drago Doctrine on the collection of international debts, and conversion of the Permanent Court of Arbitration into a genuine international court of justice.

The Drago Doctrine, as originally proposed by the Argentine Foreign Minister during the Venezuela crisis of 1902–03, declared inadmissible armed intervention by a European power to enforce payment of the public debt of an American nation. Root, during his South American tour of 1906, had warmly endorsed the doctrine. As part of his "good neighbor policy," he undertook to gain general acceptance of it at The Hague. The European delegations were not ready to yield so much, and Root sponsored what he thought a reasonable compromise. By the convention adopted at the conference the signatory powers agreed not to use armed force "for the recovery of contract debts" owed by the government of one country to the nationals of another; the promise was not applicable, however, if the debtor government refused arbitration or failed to carry out an arbitral award when one had been made. These exceptions left important loopholes for the use of force, which Latin Americans wished to outlaw entirely in the collection of debts. Of the larger Latin American countries only Mexico ratified the convention, and Mexico withdrew her consent some years later. As a gesture of friendship to Latin America, Root's obeisance to Señor Drago was a failure.

The creation of a genuine international court of justice with permanent, full-time judges, who should reach their decisions on a basis of law and not by compromise or adjustment (as was common in arbitration) was a favorite project of Elihu Root, the lawyer.

> It should be your effort [he told the American delegation] to bring about in the Second Conference a development of The Hague Tribunal into a permanent tribunal composed of judges who are judicial officers and nothing else, who are paid adequate salaries, who have no other occupation, and who will devote their entire time to the trial and decision of international cases by judicial methods and under a sense of judicial responsibility. . . .

There was general agreement at The Hague upon the need for such a court as Root proposed, but as to how many judges there should be, how they should be chosen, how the respective rights and interests of large and small nations should be safeguarded—on these questions agreement could not be reached. Root's statesmanlike proposal failed in 1907. It was to be realized in the "World Court" of later years.

The Hague Conference of 1907 did adopt a convention for the creation of an International Prize Court of Appeals, to serve as a court of last resort in wartime prize cases. To provide it with a body of agreed-upon law to apply in its deliberations, an international conference in London in 1908–09 undertook to codify the laws of maritime war. Its conclusions were issued as the Declaration of London (1909), but neither the Declaration nor the International Prize Court Convention had received the necessary ratifications when World War I began in 1914; nor was either ratified later.

Apart from these failures and illusory successes, the Second Hague Conference had little to show for its labors, other than the continued existence of the Permanent Court of Arbitration (so-called) and the extension of most of the conventions on arbitration, the conduct of war, respect for Red Cross, etc., subscribed to eight years before. Its achievements, though disappointing, seemed worthwhile at the time. Sixty years and two world wars later, they evoke respect for certain good intentions and little more.

The same can be said for some twenty-five arbitration treaties negotiated by Root in his last years in office. Root's arbitration treaties were in a sense unfinished business inherited from his predecessor, John Hay. Hay in 1904 and 1905 had negotiated a dozen treaties following the pattern of an Anglo-French treaty of 1903. They bound the signatories to submit to arbitration questions of a legal nature not affecting their vital interests, independence, or honor, or the interest of third parties. Each such arbitration was to be preceded by a special agreement defining the matter in dispute, the nature and authority of the tribunal, and the like. The Senate, in giving its advice and consent to Hay's treaties, provided that the special agreement in every case must, like a treaty, be given Senate approval. This Senate action, in Roosevelt's eyes, made the treaties "an absurdity. We say," he wrote, "that now we conclude an arbitration treaty to the effect that whenever we hereafter choose we shall conclude another arbitration treaty on any subject which we regard as fit. Surely this makes the present arbitration treaties the veriest sham." He refused to ask the other parties to accept the Senate amendment, and the Hay treaties died.

Root took a more optimistic view. He was impressed by the swelling popular demand for arbitration treaties, stimulated in part by the activity of numerous peace societies. He persuaded Roosevelt that even treaties rendered "an absurdity" by the Senate's amendment were better than none, and with the President's consent negotiated twenty-five such treaties in the form that the Senate had prescribed. What effect they had (if any) is difficult to determine, though in the opinion of one distinguished authority on international relations they made it "in actual practice more difficult to secure international arbitration than it was in the early days of our independence!"

One important Anglo-American arbitration did in fact follow, though it was hardly the result of, the signing of the new arbitration treaty with Great Britain. On January 27, 1909, Root's last day as Secretary of State, he signed with James Bryce, the British ambassador, a treaty submitting to arbitration a group of questions concerning the rights of American fishermen in the harbors and other inland waters of Newfoundland, Labrador, and the Magdalen Islands. The Northeastern Fisheries question went back to the boundary treaty of 1818 or even to the peace treaty of 1783, and had been a perennial source of controversy. As far as Canada was concerned, a *modus vivendi* of 1888, extended from time to time, had removed nearly all causes of friction, but the Newfoundland authorities, irritated at the Senate's rejection of a treaty admitting their fish to the United States duty free, did all that the law allowed (and Americans said more) to harass American fishermen who exercised their rights in Newfoundland waters under the treaty of 1818.

Arbitration of the entire question was discussed between

Root and Bryce while the Hague Conference was in session in 1907, but the British found it expedient to wait until Sir Robert Bond, the Newfoundland Premier, could be conciliated. This was finally accomplished, and Root had the satisfaction of signing the treaty on the day before he left the department to become a United States Senator from New York. The treaty submitted the fisheries controversy to a tribunal of five judges chosen from the Hague Court panel —one each from the United States and Canada, the others from Austria, The Netherlands, and Argentina. The Argentine judge was the famous former Foreign Minister, Luis M. Drago.

The decision, handed down on September 7, 1910, favored the United States on nearly all counts. Most important was the ruling that all regulations imposed by local authorities on American fishermen must be "reasonable" and that the question of their reasonableness should be determined by a mixed commission. The award settled the longest-standing controversy in American diplomacy. The outcome was doubly gratifying to Elihu Root. As Secretary of State he had signed the treaty providing for arbitration. As senior counsel for the United States before the tribunal, he had spent, as he said, "the hardest three months work" of his life in presenting the American case.[5]

[5] Root served as chief counsel for the United States without pay. As a United States Senator, he could not receive compensation for other service to the government.

CHAPTER V

Friends and Rivals
in Eastern Asia

Theodore Roosevelt's dramatic relations with Japan—his role in ending the Russo-Japanese War, his handling of the San Francisco school crisis, his sending of the battleship fleet to Tokyo, his understanding with Japan on Korea and Manchuria—have tended to overshadow his less spectacular and less successful dealings with China. These concerned principally the maintenance of the open door in China and issues arising from American restrictions on Chinese immigration. With Japan Roosevelt was happy to deal as with an equal; by its efficiency in both peace and war the Nipponese government had shown itself worthy of respect. China, on the other hand, had displayed an incapacity to defend itself in war or to keep order and promote progress in peace, which stamped it in Roosevelt's mind as a second-class power. Its independence and territorial integrity required protection by others, as did the keeping open of its doors to commerce and industry. Individual Chinese, scholars and businessmen, enjoyed Roosevelt's full respect; not so their government. The rule of the decadent Manchu dynasty no doubt merited his scorn. He was apparently unaware of the stirrings of a new nationalism among the younger Chinese which before very long was to remake China.

In Roosevelt's early years as President, the only serious challenge to the open door in China as propounded by John Hay came from Russia. Russian troops remained in Manchuria, where they had been brought to help quell the Boxer Rebellion, and Russia obstructed the proposed opening by China of new "treaty ports" in Manchuria. American pressure, supported by the retention of three battleships in Far Eastern seas and linked with parallel pressure from Britain and Japan, induced Russia in 1903 to consent to China's opening of several Manchurian cities to foreign trade and traders. Russia, however, until she was subdued by Japan in the war of 1904–05, continued to be regarded as the chief threat to the open door, and United States navy men made contingent plans for a Pacific war in which the United States, Britain, and Japan would confront Russia, France, and Germany.

In a different aspect of open door policy Roosevelt took a personal hand, but without success. An American corporation, the American China Development Company, had earlier secured a contract to build a railroad from Hankow on the Yangtze River to the southern Chinese port of Canton. The company had violated provisions of its contract and in six years had built only twenty-eight miles of a proposed eight hundred. Foreign railroad building was becoming anathema to budding Chinese nationalists, and the Chinese government generously offered to buy back the concession. To Roosevelt surrender of the contract seemed a sacrifice of American prestige and a discouragement to further American enterprise. He did his best to persuade J. P. Morgan, chief financier of the company, to refuse to sell; but Morgan had had enough of the attempt to do business with unbusinesslike and antagonistic Chinese, and not even Roosevelt's appeal to his patriotism could induce him to refuse China's offer to buy him out.

While endeavoring to hold the Chinese door open to American business, Roosevelt went along with Congress in keeping the American door closed to would-be Chinese immigrants of the working class. Since the 1880s, Chinese laborers (coolies) had been excluded by law from entry into the United States. Students, tourists, businessmen, and government officials were admitted for temporary residence, but were often subjected to outrageous indignities by immigration officials. China had consented by treaty to the exclusion policy, but when the treaty expired in the spring of 1904, the Chinese government declined to renew it without modification. Congress thereupon reenacted the exclusion laws without time limit.

Roosevelt approved of the exclusion of Chinese of the coolie class but deplored the mistreatment of qualified Chinese visitors. With a politician's eye on the voters of the West Coast, he gave both encouragement and official signature to the new exclusion act, but in turn issued drastic orders for courteous and considerate treatment of Chinese entitled to admission. When, however, the Chinese people, resentful at the reenactment of the exclusion laws without China's consent, organized a boycott against American trade and traders in China, Roosevelt became angry. The boycott reached its peak in the summer of 1905. In northern China, imperial and provincial officials held it in check, but in Shanghai and Canton, American goods went unsold, American employers lost their Chinese clerks and workmen and found their homes without servants. So intense was the anti-American feeling that "Princess Alice," Roosevelt's elder daughter, traveling with an official party in the Far East, was warned away from Canton. Roosevelt held the Peking government responsible for the boycott, which threatened American business in China with disaster. When Peking failed to take effectual measures to halt the agitation, the President ordered the Navy to concentrate a force of warships off the Chinese coast and made preparations to land an expeditionary force of fifteen thousand men on the Chinese mainland. Such drastic measures were not necessary. The Peking government submitted to Roosevelt's "gunboat diplomacy." An imperial edict of March 6, 1906, condemned anti-foreign sentiment and activity. The boycott, which injured Chinese as well as Americans, had already lost the support of the merchant class and now came quickly to an end.[1]

In February 1904, a smoldering conflict between Japanese and Russian ambitions in the Far East burst into flame. Since ousting China from Korea in the war of 1894–95, Japan had aspired to dominate that nominally independent but misgoverned kingdom. Japan also had an eye on Manchuria. She had, in fact, secured the cession of its southernmost point, the Liaotung Peninsula, from China in 1895, but had been forced to return it by a coalition of Russia, France, and Germany. Russia had then cynically secured a long-time lease for herself on the same area and had built a great naval base at Port Arthur at its tip. Germany had anticipated Russia by securing a foothold in Shantung, and France and Great Britain had obtained compensating concessions elsewhere in China's coastal provinces.

In both Korea and Manchuria, Japanese and Russian ambitions clashed. In 1902, Japan took out insurance in the form of a defensive alliance with Great Britain. A year later she sought a diplomatic settlement with Russia. When the Czar's government insisted not only on primacy in Manchuria but also on a sphere of influence in northern Korea, Japan broke

[1] A goodwill gesture to China toward the end of Roosevelt's second administration was the remission of nearly one-half of the Boxer indemnity (over twenty-four million dollars) assigned to the United States to cover losses suffered in the Boxer uprising of 1900. There were further remissions later. The sums thus returned to China were applied toward the education of young Chinese in the United States.

off the negotiations. Without awaiting the formality of a declaration of war, the Japanese Navy inflicted heavy damage in a surprise attack on Russia's Far Eastern fleet, carelessly riding at anchor outside the defenses of Port Arthur.

The reaction of Theodore Roosevelt to this attack without warning was very different from that of the later Roosevelt to the surprise attack on Pearl Harbor. Far from labeling February 5, 1904, "a date that will live in infamy," the President wrote confidentially to Theodore, Jr.: "I was thoroughly well pleased with the Japanese victory, for Japan is playing our game." "For several years," he explained in the same letter, "Russia has behaved very badly in the Far East, her attitude toward all nations, including us, but especially toward Japan, being grossly overbearing."

Russia, then, was the chief threat to American interests in the Far East. Japan, in fighting Russia, was "playing our game." Japan, if victorious, must not this time be cheated of the fruits of victory by a coalition of the powers, as she had been in 1895. This Roosevelt made plain in a conversation with Secretary Hay in January 1905. That he warned Germany and France to that effect, adding that he would "proceed to whatever length was necessary" in Japan's behalf, is doubtful. He so stated in a letter to his British friend Cecil Spring Rice, in July 1905, but no record of such a warning has ever been discovered in the diplomatic archives of Germany, France, or the United States. Roosevelt did, however, in a conversation with the German ambassador, endorse Japan's claim to Korea; and in July 1905 he permitted William H. Taft, his Secretary of War, to assure the Japanese Premier that an extension of Japanese suzerainty over Korea would meet with no objection from the United States.

Taft's confidential conversations with Premier Count Katsura in Tokyo and parallel exchanges with the British government brought about such a close understanding with those two powers that some scholars have seen the United States as a *de facto* member of the Anglo-Japanese Alliance (which was, incidentally, renewed in stronger terms in August 1905). While this may be an overstatement, there is no doubt that Roosevelt believed American interests in the Far East to be so nearly identical with the interests of the two allies that he assured them both of American sympathy and cooperation. The exchanges with England throw interesting light on Roosevelt's diplomatic methods. With the British ambassador in Washington, Sir Mortimer Durand, his relations were never comfortable. Consequently he arranged to have Cecil Spring Rice, at the time attached to the British embassy in St. Petersburg, brought to Washington in February 1905 for confidential talks. Spring Rice carried verbal messages between Roosevelt and Foreign Secretary Lord Lansdowne. Back in St. Petersburg he continued to channel Roosevelt's ideas to the British Foreign Office. They reached him through the American ambassador to Russia, George von L. Meyer, another of the President's intimates.

But despite Roosevelt's admiration for the Japanese and his satisfaction at the trouncing they were giving the Russians, he did not wish to see their success too complete. He could not avoid a suspicion, as he wrote Spring Rice, that "down at bottom" the Japanese lumped "Russians, English, Americans, Germans, all of us, simply as white devils inferior to themselves." In any event, Japanese domination of the Far East was little more to be desired than Russian domination. American interests would be best served by a preservation of the balance of power. "Upon conclusion of peace," he told the German ambassador in May 1904, "an effort ought to be made to leave points of friction as they were before the war between the two powers." He spoke in similar terms to the French ambassador a few months later, and to Henry Cabot Lodge he wrote (June 16, 1905):

... for the rest of us, while Russia's triumph would have been a blow to civilization, her destruction as an eastern Asiatic power would also in my opinion be unfortunate. It is best that she should be left face to face with Japan so that each may have a moderating action on the other. . . .

If the military events of the war did not threaten Russia's "destruction as an eastern Asiatic power," they seemed likely to leave her so weakened that she could no longer offer effective opposition to Japan. Her Far Eastern naval forces were destroyed piecemeal. Her naval base at Port Arthur fell to Japan, after a long siege, in January 1905. In February and March her armies were turned back in the great battle of Mukden. Her Baltic fleet, after the long voyage from Europe, was annihilated in Tsushima Straits, May 27, 1905. Foreseeing that if the war continued Japan might occupy Vladivostok and Eastern Siberia, Roosevelt was glad to act upon the confidential request of Japan—to whom the war was proving embarrassingly expensive—that he take the initiative in proposing a peace conference. Upon ascertaining—also confidentially—that Russia would accept such a proposal, the President, on June 8, 1905, invited the belligerents to begin negotiations, offering his own services in arranging for the meeting. In his efforts for peace, Roosevelt received more cooperation from Berlin than from London. The Kaiser suspected—at least he so told Roosevelt—an Anglo-French scheme to arrange a peace and to profit from it in new accessions of Chinese territory. He was anxious, therefore, to see Roosevelt's initiative succeed, and used his influence with the Czar for that purpose. The British government, engaged in negotiating a renewal of the alliance with Japan, was reluctant to ask any sacrifice of its ally.

The peace conference, originally set for Washington, was shifted to Portsmouth, New Hampshire, far from the heat and humidity of the capital. There the Russian and Japanese commissioners—Baron Rosen and Count Serge Witte, Foreign Secretary Count Komura and Baron Takahira, minister to the United States, met on August 9, 1905. Roosevelt had introduced them to one another and entertained them at luncheon on the presidential yacht *Mayflower*, and from his Oyster Bay home he kept in close touch with the negotiations during the weeks that followed.

The delegates agreed without difficulty upon acceptance of Japan's major demands—a free hand for Japan in Korea; transfer to Japan of Russia's lease of the Liaotung Peninsula with the port of Dairen and the Port Arthur naval base; cession to Japan of the southern two-thirds of the South Manchuria Railway, with the appurtenant rights of policing and economic exploitation; otherwise, Manchuria to be restored to China with full right to develop its commerce and industry. Trouble came over Japan's demand for a war indemnity of six hundred million dollars and cession of the island of Sakhalin. The Czar's government refused either to pay indemnity or to cede territory. Here Roosevelt's pressure upon both governments for concessions was helpful; but the conference was actually saved from failure by Count Witte's disobedience to an order from St. Petersburg to break off negotiations and by Tokyo's yielding in its demand for indemnity, contrary to the advice of chief delegate Komura. Agreement was finally reached August 29, on cession to Japan of the southern half of Sakhalin and no indemnity. The Treaty of Portsmouth was signed a week later. For his part in bringing the war to an end Roosevelt was in 1906 awarded the Nobel peace prize.

Despite Roosevelt's friendly attitude to Japan during the war and his immediate acquiescence when Japan, in November 1905, assumed control of Korea's foreign relations, a marked deterioration in American-Japanese relations followed the war. Minor irritants were Japanese popular resentment at Roosevelt's supposed role in persuading Japan to forego a war indemnity, and the killing by United States revenue officers of a number of Japanese seal poachers in the Pribilof Islands; but the chief cause of friction was the manifestation of anti-Japanese sentiment in California. Unlike the Chinese, Japanese subjects had never been excluded by law from entering the United States, and although Japan since 1900 had voluntarily withheld from laborers passports to the continental United States, Japanese were entering West Coast ports via Hawaii, Canada, and Mexico at the rate of a thousand or more per month. Resentment at their presence in such numbers sometimes took the form of riotous attacks upon Japanese persons or establishments, but the action most resented in Japan was an order of the San Francisco school board in October 1906, requiring that all Japanese school children attend a segregated Oriental school. The implication of inferiority in this order was infuriating to a nation that prided itself upon its high civilization and had just shown itself militarily more than a match for one of Europe's great powers. The Japanese ambassador made strong representations to the State Department, and Japan's jingo press indulged in bitter attacks on the United States and even talked of war.

Roosevelt deplored the San Francisco action, but since public schools were entirely under state or local jurisdiction, there was little that the President could do about it except through persuasion.[2] Denunciation of the school board's order in his annual message to Congress merely stiffened the Californians in their stand. Their reaction led Roosevelt to take a different approach. Recognizing that the uncontrolled immigration was at the root of the trouble, he proposed to halt or restrict the immigration—by means inoffensive to Japan—in return for abandonment of the seg-

[2] The 1894 treaty with Japan assured Japanese in the United States of most-favored-nation treatment with respect to residence and travel. Most legal authorities were of the opinion that this guarantee did not cover education.

regation policy by San Francisco. The school board, the superintendent of schools, and the mayor of the city were brought to Washington and in conferences of several days were persuaded to accept this arrangement. Roosevelt then obtained from Japan a promise to continue its policy of refusing passports to mainland United States to Japanese laborers, while agreeing to make no objection if the United States forbade their entry from Hawaii or other intermediate points, which the President promptly did. This was the so-called Gentlemen's Agreement of 1907. It was not consummated at one stroke but required conversations with Japan extending over several months, as well as further pressure on the school board, before it was fully implemented. The American position vis-à-vis Japan was strengthened by an outbreak of anti-Japanese rioting in Vancouver, British Columbia, demonstrating that the prejudice of the Californians was shared by subjects of Japan's ally, Britain. At any rate, by August 1908 Japanese leaving the United States were outnumbering arrivals, and the San Francisco school front was calm. Roosevelt and Secretary Root would have preferred to settle the issue with Japan by treaty. They learned, however, that Japan would accept only a treaty that gave Japanese complete most-favored-nation status, including immigration and naturalization, and this the United States was not able to offer.[3]

Desegregation of the San Francisco schools did not end racial tensions in that city. There were, in fact, serious anti-Japanese riots in May 1907. The injured Japanese were compensated for their losses by the city authorities, and their grievances did not become an issue between the two gov-

---

[3] Japanese, like other Asiatics, were not eligible for naturalization in the United States. Roosevelt and Root would gladly have conceded that privilege, but most-favored-nation status in immigration would have meant opening the gates to Japanese of the coolie class. This was unacceptable to Roosevelt and would certainly have been so to the Senate.

ernments. The riots did, however, result in much loose war talk in the sensational press of both countries. Even in Europe, rumors of impending war were current. The German Kaiser relayed to Roosevelt reports of the arrival of Japanese reservists in Mexico and actually offered the President military aid should the United States be attacked through Mexico or Canada.

The Kaiser's offer of military assistance was part of a plan for enlisting the support of the United States in opposition to what the nervous German monarch assumed to be a scheme for the dismemberment of China without regard for the interests of Germany or America. Japan had allied herself with England and had reached understandings with Russia and France in regard to their respective spheres of influence in China, and now England and Russia had settled their Asian differences. Germany and the United States, as well as China, the intended victim, were omitted from all these arrangements. Why should not the three draw together to defend their common interests?

With this end in view, the Kaiser began an ardent wooing of Roosevelt. The President declined the offer of military assistance against invasion but gave guarded encouragement to Wilhelm's proposal of a German-American-Chinese alliance in defense of China's integrity and the open door. Roosevelt was on the point of launching the battleship fleet on a cruise around the world. In an intimate conversation with Ambassador Speck von Sternburg in November 1907 he intimated—at least so the German reported—that the fleet's arrival in the Far East might be an appropriate occasion for announcing the proposed alliance. The hint, though Roosevelt later substituted "understanding" for "alliance," raised false hopes in the Kaiser's mind, and he saw to it that German diplomats and German naval vessels showered the fleet with attentions during the early phases of its cruise.

It was in June 1907, when rumors of war with Japan were at their peak, that Roosevelt had resolved to send the fleet on its round-the-world cruise. The original announcement on July 4 stated simply that the fleet would visit San Francisco, and the full plan was not revealed until the following March when the "Great White Fleet" of sixteen battleships had reached Magdalena Bay on the west coast of Mexico. Publicized at the time as a practice cruise, the venturesome voyage was undoubtedly designed also to advertise the Navy to the American people and Congress and to enhance America's prestige as a world power. There seems no reason, however, to doubt Roosevelt's later statement that he wished at the same time to demonstrate to the Japanese that the United States had a battle fleet which would be a formidable opponent, not a pushover such as Japan had found in the Czar's navy. In accord with this purpose was the accompanying flirtation with Germany.

Whether the expensive naval demonstration actually had the desired effect upon Japan is debatable. It is true that Japanese war talk ceased and that the two governments reached an accord in an atmosphere of renewed cordiality, enabling the President to claim later that the voyage of the fleet had been a great stroke for peace. But the accord was on terms that were actually at least as favorable to Japan as to the United States, and it followed an occasion on which impressive naval might was brandished by both sides.

Roosevelt, with some misgivings, had accepted Japan's invitation to have the fleet visit Tokyo Bay, following its festive stops in New Zealand and Australia. For a week, October 18 to 25, 1908, the fleet and its personnel were royally entertained by the Japanese. The welcome was said to have surpassed even that accorded Admiral Togo after his great victory over the Russians in 1905. Known only to the initiated was the fact that while the Japanese had

retained a number of old ships in Tokyo Bay to welcome
the visitors, the main Japanese fleet was at sea on maneuvers
in the area between the Japanese islands and the Philippines.
Had a showdown come, Roosevelt's sixteen battleships, with
their white paint and high visibility, unattended by cruisers
or destroyers—the six torpedo boats that had begun the
voyage had been left behind at San Francisco—would have
confronted an opposing fleet in battle trim, comprising ten
battleships, twenty-nine armored cruisers, and fifty destroyers, to say nothing of numerous torpedo boats and submarines. The Japanese were in home waters, the Americans
thousands of miles from an adequate base and unaccom-
panied by colliers or repair ships. Under these circumstances,
who scared whom is perhaps an open question.[4]

Five weeks after the fleet left Tokyo Bay, Secretary Root
and Ambassador Takahira in Washington signed an agreement, in the form of an exchange of notes, which undoubtedly helped to relieve tension between the two countries
but whose precise import was ambiguous. The notes of
November 30, 1908, declared that it was the wish of the
two governments "to encourage the free and peaceful development of their commerce on the Pacific Ocean"; that
their policy was directed "to the maintenance of the existing
status quo" in the region mentioned; that they were
"accordingly firmly resolved reciprocally to respect the territorial possessions belonging to each other in said region";
and that they were "also determined to preserve the common interest of all powers in China by supporting by all
pacific means at their disposal the independence and integrity of China and the principle of equal opportunity for
commerce and industry of all nations in that Empire."

On the surface the Root-Takahira agreement appeared to

[4] This interpretation of the American fleet's visit to Japan follows Robert
A. Hart, *The Great White Fleet: Its Voyage around the World, 1907–
1909* (Boston, 1965).

be a clear-cut diplomatic victory for the United States. The pledge of mutual respect for the territorial possessions of the two parties was in effect a repetition of Japan's disclaimer of designs on the Philippines, made to Secretary Taft on visits to Tokyo in 1905 and 1907. The statement on China seemed an acceptance by Japan of America's open door policy. The agreement was acclaimed in the United States at the time, except by certain pro-Chinese members of the State Department, who thought it to be a surrender to Japan on Manchuria. In this contention they were probably right. Root had sought to include a pledge of respect for the "administrative entity" of China. Japan had refused, the Foreign Minister explaining to Takahira that the phrase might be interpreted as compromising Japan's administrative and policing rights in the Liaotung leased territory and the railroad zone acquired from Russia. There is no evidence that Takahira passed on this explanation to Root. Had he done so, Root's acquiescence would have been no more than a recognition by the United States of rights that Japan had acquired by treaty from Russia with the subsequent consent of China. However, on the day the notes were signed, Root received from Tokyo a report of an unofficial conversation in which Foreign Minister Komura had declared "that South Manchuria constituted Japan's outer line of defense and that Japan no longer considered the principle of China's integrity to include Manchuria." [5] Unfortunately, it is impossible to determine whether Root read this report before or after signing the note to Takahira. If he knew of Komura's statement before signing, his acceptance of the status quo

[5] For this and a number of other details I am indebted to Raymond A. Esthus, whose book, *Theodore Roosevelt and Japan* (Seattle: University of Washington Press, 1966), I was privileged to read in manuscript. In Esthus' view, neither the omission of "territorial" (before integrity) nor the inclusion of "industry" (with commerce) in the statement on China was significant. The latter had appeared in earlier statements and presumably referred to light industry such as textiles.

in the region could be interpreted as giving Japan a green light in South Manchuria. That this had actually been done is indicated by contemporary events in the Far East and in Washington.

The exchange of amenities in Tokyo Bay signaled the end of the Kaiser's "pipe dream" of a German-American-Chinese alliance or understanding. After a week of basking in profuse Japanese hospitality, the fleet administered what could only be viewed as a snub to China. The Chinese government had urged a visit to Chefoo (facing Japanese Port Arthur across the Gulf of Chihli) or to the great port city of Shanghai. These invitations were declined. Instead, a single squadron of four ships paid a call at the minor port of Amoy. There the Chinese government prepared a "Pleasure City" for the entertainment of the visitors, but no imperial prince or Chinese of the highest rank was on hand to greet them. A special Chinese envoy who had been dispatched to Washington to seek support for the Chinese cause in Manchuria arrived just in time to witness the signing of the Root-Takahira agreement and was promptly recalled by Peking. It was clear to the Chinese that they could not count on Roosevelt to back them against Japan in Manchuria.

To the Kaiser, Roosevelt excused his defection on the ground that governmental instability in China made that country undependable as an ally and that he could not risk being drawn into war in the Far East unless in defense of purely American interests. For whatever reason, the President had resolved to avoid a confrontation with Japan at the cost of conceding Tokyo a free hand in Manchuria.[6] Hoping that this conciliatory policy might be carried on after

[6] After the conclusion of the Root-Takahira agreement, the U.S. Navy abandoned its long cherished plan for a major base in the Philippines and undertook the development of Pearl Harbor as its advanced Pacific base. Roosevelt, the imperialist of 1898, was now eager to give independence to the Philippines lest they become the "Achilles' heel" of the United States in a possible war with Japan.

he left the White House, he warned President Taft, his successor, not to give the Japanese in Manchuria any reason to feel that the United States was "a menace—in however slight a degree—to their interests." This was advice that Taft and his Secretary of State failed to heed.

CHAPTER VI

The Epigoni

William Howard Taft, first civil governor of the Philippines and Roosevelt's Secretary of War (1904–08), was also Roosevelt's handpicked Republican candidate for the presidency in 1908. He had an excellent record as an administrator and as a man of unimpeachable high principle, but he lacked Roosevelt's talent for leadership and also Roosevelt's luck. His four years as President (1909–13) present a sad record of mistakes and misfortunes in both domestic and foreign policy. Philander C. Knox, his Secretary of State, a corporation lawyer, for three years (1901–04) a "trust-busting" Attorney General under Roosevelt, and from 1904–09 a Senator from Pennsylvania, lacked the appreciation of the sensitivities of other governments and peoples which had distinguished Elihu Root. His heavy-handed diplomacy in the Far East and the Caribbean met with rebuff in the former area and frustration in the latter. General arbitration treaties with France and Britain, so amended by the Senate as to be unacceptable, and a reciprocity agreement with Canada, rejected by the Canadian electorate, round out the picture of failure.

If, as seems clear, Roosevelt had resolved to avoid opposing Japan in Manchuria, Taft and Knox lost little time in reversing his policy. They took their inspiration from Willard Straight, an ambitious young man who had been consul general at Mukden from 1906 to 1908 and had then been brought home to serve briefly as acting chief of the Division of Far Eastern Affairs in the State Department. As a member of the United States legation at Seoul, Straight had witnessed the Japanese assumption of the protectorate over Korea in 1905. Resenting Japan's action in Korea, he hoped to prevent her further encroachment in Manchuria and elsewhere in China. His remedy was the injection of American capital into China, especially investment in the construction of railroads. Only through possession of a material stake in China, he believed, could the United States attain sufficient influence to thwart Japanese plans and preserve China's territorial integrity. He found converts in the State Department in Assistant Secretary Huntington Wilson and William Phillips of the Far Eastern Division, and their influence prevailed with the new administration. "Dollar diplomacy" became the Taft-Knox policy for the Far East. The open door, which under Hay and Root had been a door to trade, became in the eyes of Taft and Knox, a door also to investment in China.

While still in Mukden, Straight had been in touch with the American railroad king, Edward H. Harriman. At the time of the Portsmouth Peace Conference, Harriman had conceived the idea of purchasing the South Manchurian Railway as part of a round-the-world system of transportation. The Japanese had first encouraged him but had finally withheld approval. A later plan for a railroad paralleling the South Manchuria line, promoted by Straight and Chinese officials in Manchuria, had also enlisted Harriman's interest. It had collapsed following changes in the Chinese government and the conclusion of the Root-Takahira agreement, which Straight held responsible for its failure. Interest in

Manchurian railroad plans was soon to revive, but when Taft and Knox took office, their immediate problem in China was the proposed Hukuang railroad loan being negotiated by British, French, and German capitalists.

Originally designed to connect Hankow in Hupeh province with Canton in Kwangtung (whence the name Hukuang), the project had been broadened to include a line from Hankow westward to Szechuan province on the upper Yangtze. A group of American capitalists, including Harriman and J. P. Morgan, wished to participate with the Europeans in the loan but found their entry obstructed by both the Europeans and the Chinese officials in charge of the deal. In this situation President Taft took the unusual step of appealing directly to the Chinese Prince Regent for the admission of the American group. He based his appeal partly on promises made by the Chinese government in 1903 and 1904, when Morgan had surrendered his railroad contract,[1] but he added a sentence which clearly set forth the idealistic side of dollar diplomacy.

> . . . I have an intense personal interest [Taft wrote, July 15, 1909] in making the use of American capital in the development of China an instrument for the promotion of the welfare of China, and an increase in her material prosperity without entanglements or creating embarrassments affecting the growth of her independent political power and the preservation of her territorial integrity.

Taft's appeal succeeded. The American bankers' group was admitted to a share in the Hukuang project on equal terms with the bankers of Britain, France, and Germany, thus taking its place in the four-power consortium. In the spring of 1911 the consortium authorized a loan of six million pounds for the Hukuang project and also, on American initiative, a loan of fifty million dollars to the Chinese govern-

[1] See p. 55.

ment for currency stabilization. Both loans were held up, however, because of the outbreak in October of the same year of the revolution which overthrew the Manchu dynasty.

In the meantime Knox had undertaken a still more ambitious scheme, which grew directly out of the ideas of Straight and Harriman. This was no less than to enable China, by means of an international loan, to acquire the Russian- and Japanese-owned railroads in Manchuria—the Chinese Eastern and South Manchurian lines—and thus to bolster her slipping sovereignty in the three Manchurian provinces. Knox was apparently unaware that Japan and Russia in 1907 had composed their rivalry by delimiting their respective spheres of influence in Manchuria, that both were resolved to hold what they had, and that they could count upon support from Europe, where Britain and France were allies of the two powers respectively, and where Britain had also come to terms with Russia in the entente of 1907. Knox's initial feeler to the British government (November 9, 1909) brought from Foreign Secretary Sir Edward Grey a cautious statement of approval "in principle" coupled with a suggestion for delay in attempting to put the plan into practice. Early in 1910 Japan and Russia warned China of their disapproval. Later in the year they signed new treaties, reaffirming their respect for each other's spheres of influence in Manchuria and in effect serving notice upon the United States that they would submit to no interference with their exploitation of those spheres. The Taft-Knox program of neutralizing the Manchurian railroads had been rudely rebuffed.

Following the downfall of the Manchu dynasty, Yüan Shih-k'ai, president of the shaky republican government, sought a three hundred million dollar "reorganization loan" from the four-power consortium. Before this request could be acted upon, the four powers involved yielded to pressure from Russia and Japan and admitted bankers of those nationalities to the group, which thereby became a six-power consortium. The American bankers, in the meantime, had become disillusioned with regard to the prospects of profitable business in China and were prevented from withdrawing from the consortium only by the urging of Secretary Knox. When the new administration of Woodrow Wilson, in March 1913, took a negative attitude to the whole concept of dollar diplomacy in the Far East,[2] the American group left the consortium with evident relief. They had been serving the former administration's concept of the national interest rather than their own business instincts, and that concept had now been discarded.

In their relations with the small states of the Caribbean area, Taft and Knox took over the policeman's role that Roosevelt had created, but with a difference. Roosevelt had (with the exception of the Panama episode) respected the sovereignty of the states in which he had intervened. The customs receivership in Santo Domingo had been instituted at the request (even though the request had been suggested from Washington) of the Dominican President. The intervention in Cuba in 1906 had similarly been undertaken at the request of the harassed President of Cuba. Elihu Root had made it a basic principle to treat the Latin Americans as equals and their states as sovereign. President Taft, on the other hand, told Knox, at the end of nine months in office, that he would never be satisfied until he had "some formal right to compel the peace between those Central-American governments." He yearned for the "right to knock their heads together until they should maintain peace between them." Such expressions, of course, were not made public, but actions in accord with their spirit led understandably to an increase in "Yankeephobia" in Latin America.

An illustration of the new attitude was seen in American relations with the Dominican Republic, though the issue

[2] See pp. 84–85.

here was not international strife but domestic anarchy. For
four years after 1907 the customs receivership had worked
well. It had maintained service on the foreign debt and had
supplied the Dominican government under President Ramón
Cáceres with revenues adequate for the promotion of useful
public works over and above the ordinary expenses of government. But Cáceres was assassinated in 1911, and months
of factional strife resulted in a condition of virtual anarchy
and in the contraction of a floating debt in violation of the
convention of 1907 with the United States. The United
States thereupon, by simply directing the receiver general to
withhold funds, compelled the resignation of the incumbent
President and helped to bring about the choice as his successor of Adolfo A. Nouel, Catholic archbishop of Santo Domingo.

The Archbishop-President was beyond his depth from the
outset. Torn between the demands for patronage of contending leaders and with his palace occupied by the ragged
soldiery of one faction, he silently stole away and boarded a
ship for Europe, sending his resignation to the Dominican
congress from his port of embarkation. His "reign" had extended from December 1912 to March 1913, and his abdication left a basket of headaches on Woodrow Wilson's
doorstep.[3]

President Taft's yearning to knock together the heads of
unnamed Central American leaders certainly had reference,
among others, to the dictator José Santos Zelaya of Nicaragua. In his ambition to dominate the region, Zelaya
had repeatedly picked quarrels with his neighbors and had
continued to do so even after signing the Central American
peace treaties of 1907, sponsored by the United States and
Mexico. He had also canceled concessions of American citizens in Nicaragua and had contracted a loan in England
which might conceivably become an excuse for British inter-

[3] See p. 92.

vention. Consequently, when a revolt (seemingly instigated in part by American interests) broke out against Zelaya in 1909, Taft and Knox looked with favor upon the rebels. Zelaya's execution of two Americans, serving as technicians in the rebel forces, gave Knox an excuse to denounce Zelaya and all that he stood for. Zelaya resigned, turning over the government to José Madriz, elected provisional President by the Nicaraguan Congress. The civil war continued. The United States was nominally neutral, but the landing of American Marines, ostensibly for the protection of foreign lives, prevented government forces from attacking the rebel stronghold at Bluefields and saved the day for the revolution. The Madriz regime collapsed, and in August 1910 the revolutionary leaders entered Managua, the capital.

The success of the revolution brought into power leaders of the Conservative party. This was the minority party in Nicaraguan politics, and several of its leaders, in order to remain in power, were willing to accept from the United States the kind of guardianship that it had instituted in the Dominican Republic. Since Taft and Knox were convinced that customs receiverships on the Dominican model were the remedy for the ills that beset all the little countries of the area, it was easy for them to come to terms with the new Nicaraguan leaders.

Juan J. Estrada, who had taken over the presidency from Madriz, was an anti-Zelaya Liberal, who had joined the Conservatives in their revolt. He was soon at odds with his erstwhile allies and found it expedient to leave the country without the formality of resigning. His departure brought the vice-president, Adolfo Díaz, to the presidential office. Unlike most of the Nicaraguan politicians of the day, Díaz was a civilian, a businessman with a contempt for militarism and also with important connections with American interests. What he wanted most for Nicaragua, as he stated in a letter in December 1911, was "lasting and stable peace, order, economy, moderation, and liberty." These blessings, in his opinion, could not come "through our own means," but only "by means of more direct and efficient assistance from the United States, like that which resulted so well in Cuba." It was his hope, therefore, through a treaty with the United States, so to amend the Nicaraguan constitution as to permit "the United States to intervene in our internal affairs in order to maintain peace and the existence of a lawful government, thus giving the people a guaranty of proper administration."

Such a treaty as Díaz proposed was not feasible at this time. In fact, the Senate proved unwilling to consent to a much less radical one which had been signed in the preceding June by Secretary Knox and Castrillo, the Nicaraguan minister. The Knox-Castrillo Convention (signed June 6, 1911) provided that the government of Nicaragua should obtain a loan in the United States (the amount proposed was fifteen million dollars) to be used in refunding existing external and internal debts, paying claims, and for other purposes. The loan was to be secured by customs receipts, and these were to be administered by a collector general appointed by the Nicaraguan government from a list submitted by the bankers making the loan and approved by the President of the United States. Nicaragua would not change the rates of her duties during the existence of the loan without the consent of the United States. Nicaragua promised to afford full protection to the collector general, and the United States agreed to furnish further protection to that official if circumstances should require.

The convention represented the type of agreement which Taft and Knox wished to make with as many as possible of the Central American republics. Knox had previously signed one with Honduras and had tried in vain to sell the idea to the dictator of Guatemala. In sending the Nicaraguan convention to the Senate (June 7, 1911), Taft recommended both it and the still unratified agreement with Honduras not only as promising to contribute to the peace of Central America, but also as meeting the responsibilities of the United States under the Monroe Doctrine.

> Much of the debt of Nicaragua [he observed] is external and held in Europe; and, while it may not be claimed that by the Monroe doctrine we may be called upon to protect an American Republic from the payment of its just foreign claims, still complications might result from the attempted enforced collection of such claims, from the involutions of which this Government might not escape. Hence it should be the policy of this Government, especially with respect to countries in geographical proximity to the Canal Zone, to give them when requested all proper assistance . . . in the promotion of peace, in the development of their resources, and in a sound reorganization of their fiscal systems . . .

Thus Taft brought the proposed conventions clearly under the philosophy of the Roosevelt Corollary, as did Knox in an address a few months later. "It would not be sane," remarked Knox, "to uphold a great policy like the Monroe Doctrine and to repudiate its necessary corollaries and neglect the sensible measures which reason dictates as its safeguards." Both men, furthermore, stressed the special danger to the United States in permitting disorder and financial irresponsibility to flourish in the region of the Canal Zone. Their policy, like that of Roosevelt, was clearly designed to safeguard the national security.

But Taft and Knox were fated to meet with serious rebuffs in their endeavor to broaden the application of the Roosevelt Corollary. The 1910 congressional elections had gone against the Republicans, and Democrats and Progressives found this variety of dollar diplomacy an eligible target. In May 1912 a motion to report the Nicaraguan and Honduran treaties to the Senate from the Committee on Foreign Relations lost by a tie vote. No further action was taken on them. The Honduran treaty, furthermore, was rejected by the Honduran

Congress. A canal treaty negotiated with Nicaragua in February 1913, just before Knox left office, was not acted upon by the Senate. It paved the way, however, for the Bryan-Chamorro Treaty, negotiated by the next administration.[4]

But though the results of Knox's negotiations with Nicaragua were rejected by the Senate, they bore fruit nevertheless. The plan for a collector general of customs, though lacking treaty status, was put into effect by agreement between Nicaragua, the American bankers with whom the proposed loan was to be negotiated, and the State Department. It functioned successfully until the eve of World War II. A claims commission consisting of one Nicaraguan and two Americans, set up during Estrada's brief tenure, also carried out its purpose. In three years of labor it passed upon nearly eight thousand claims against the Nicaraguan government, allowing a mere 1,750,000 dollars out of 13,750,000 dollars presented. Worthy of note was the fact that about two-thirds of the awards were for small claims presented by natives; American concession holders received under 540,000 dollars of 7,500,000 dollars claimed.

An unfortunate consequence for Nicaragua of the Senate's failure to approve the loan convention was the bankers' refusal to advance the projected fifteen million dollar loan. One-tenth of that sum was advanced while the convention awaited action; after its failure, the bankers (Brown Brothers & Company and J. and W. Seligman & Company) continued to make small hand-to-mouth loans that meant little profit for them and were insufficient to enable Nicaragua to liquidate her European debt or to engage in needed public works.

One more episode completes the story of the Taft administration's relations with Nicaragua. In July 1912 President Díaz, facing a formidable revolt led by his Secretary of War,

[4] See p. 89.

General Luis Mena, appealed to Washington for aid. In an effort to discourage the revolt, the State Department equated Mena's program with Zelayaism and announced:

> The government of the United States will, therefore, discountenance any revival of Zelayaism, and will lend its strong moral support to the cause of legally constituted good government for the benefit of the people of Nicaragua, whom it has long sought to aid in their just aspiration towards peace and prosperity under constitutional and orderly government.

When moral support proved inadequate, President Taft sent in the marines, who not only quelled the revolt but deported General Mena to the Panama Canal Zone, where he was held for a while in custody, meanwhile receiving needed medical attention at U.S. expense.

With the Mena revolt put down, the United States thought it expedient to leave a detachment of about one hundred marines at Managua, the capital, as a legation guard. The guard continued to be stationed there for thirteen years. It is perhaps significant that throughout that period Adolfo Díaz and his successors of the minority Conservative party retained the reins of power.

Relations of the United States with its stable neighbor on the north were completely different from those with the states of the Caribbean and the mid-continent.[5] Yet even in his policy toward Canada Taft suffered an exasperating defeat. The promises of Taft and the Republican platform in 1908 to revise the tariff (downward, as the country understood it) had had at best an ambiguous fulfillment in the

[5] The overthrow of President Porfirio Díaz of Mexico by Francisco Madero in May 1911 confronted Taft and Knox with new perplexities. The United States recognized the Madero government and took a forbearing attitude toward the disorders that followed. When Madero was overthrown and assassinated by General Huerta in February 1913, Taft left the decision as to the United States attitude to the incoming Wilson administration. See pp. 104–5.

Payne-Aldrich tariff of 1909, and the country expressed its dissatisfaction by electing a Democratic House of Representatives in 1910. Taft sought to redeem campaign pledges and to win favor with the electorate by negotiating a tariff reciprocity agreement with Canadian Premier Sir Wilfrid Laurier. The agreement, signed in January 1911, provided for general free trade between the two countries in raw materials and reduction of duties on a long list of manufactured products. It was not a treaty but an agreement to be put into effect by concurrent legislation by Congress and the Canadian Parliament. In Congress the measure encountered opposition especially from the western farm belt, but Taft succeeded in getting it enacted with the support of Democrats and Eastern Republicans. Unfortunately, Canadian patriotic antagonism was aroused by indiscreet hints from American newspapers and politicians that reciprocity was a step toward annexation. Laurier was forced to dissolve Parliament and appeal to the electorate with reciprocity as the principal issue. A sweeping victory at the polls of the opposition Conservative party over Sir Wilfrid's Liberals sealed the fate of reciprocity. A statemanlike proposal had fallen victim to chauvinism on both sides of the border.

Another variety of chauvinism, combined with partisanship, personal antagonism, and special interests, brought to naught another high-minded Taft enterprise—a brace of new arbitration treaties with France and Britain. In 1910 Taft accepted the honorary presidency of the newly organized American Society for the Judicial Settlement of International Disputes. In a speech in New York in March of that year he called for a permanent court of arbitration to which "all questions" should be submitted—even questions of "national honor." "I do not see," he observed, "why questions of honor may not be submitted to a tribunal supposed to be composed of men of honor who understand questions of national honor."

This and similar pronouncements brought Taft wide acclaim. The period was one of widespread optimism for the abolition of war. It was the year of the publication of Norman Angell's *The Great Illusion,* which argued persuasively that in modern war even the victor loses. Andrew Carnegie, the retired steel king, found in Taft's speeches the inspiration for the creation of his ten million dollar Endowment for International Peace. "You will note," he wrote the President, "that your noble note of leadership among Rulers prompted me to create the fund." From French ambassador Jusserand came an offer to make such a general arbitration treaty as Taft had proposed. The most significant dissent came from Theodore Roosevelt. The colonel, now in private life, but as voluble as ever, had fallen out with his erstwhile protégé on several grounds. He now attacked the proposed agreement to arbitrate all disputes as hypocrisy—as making promises that clearly would not be kept.

In spite of Roosevelt's criticism, Taft instructed Secretary Knox to negotiate general arbitration treaties of the kind proposed with the governments of France and Great Britain. The two were signed on August 3, 1911. They provided for submission to the Hague Court or other suitable tribunal of all "justiciable" questions (that is, questions "susceptible of decision by the application of the principles of law or equity") which could not be settled by ordinary diplomacy. To determine whether a given question was or was not justiciable each treaty provided for a six-man commission, three members from each country, with the stipulation that no question should be submitted to arbitration unless at least five of the six held it to be justiciable.

The treaties had widespread popular support—they were endorsed, for example, by almost three hundred chambers of commerce in as many cities—but the opposition of Roosevelt was serious, and in the Senate they encountered jealousy of the Senate's cherished prerogative, concern for selfish local interests, and some Democratic opposition that was primarily partisan. Senators objected to delegating the identification of justiciable questions to a commission; they took that right from the commission and reserved it to themselves. West Coast Senators, with recent Japanese troubles in mind, feared arbitration of questions relating to the rights of aliens. Southerners were apprehensive that their repudiated state debts might be submitted to arbitration. Many Senators would never consent to arbitration of any question involving the Monroe Doctrine. The treaties were amended to exclude all these issues, whether justiciable or not, from the obligation to arbitrate. In this mutilated form they received the Senate's consent. President Taft refused to ask the British and French governments to accept the treaties with the Senate's amendments. "So I put them on the shelf and let the dust accumulate on them," he related some years later, "in the hope that the senators might change their minds, or that the people might change the Senate; instead of which they changed me."

The last clause alluded, of course, to Taft's disastrous defeat in the three-cornered race with Roosevelt and Woodrow Wilson in 1912. On March 4, 1913, Taft and Knox surrendered their offices to Wilson and William Jennings Bryan.

CHAPTER VII

The Policeman Turned Democrat

The triumph of the Democratic party in the presidential and congressional elections of 1912 seemed, upon all the evidence, to foretell a new policy toward the Latin American neighbors of the United States. The Democrats had been, consistently since 1900, opponents of Republican "imperialism." Not only had they favored early independence for the Philippines, but Democratic Senators had blocked for two years Theodore Roosevelt's Dominican treaty and had killed Secretary Knox's similar treaty with Nicaragua. William Jennings Bryan, the new Secretary of State, had been an outspoken critic of the "dollar diplomacy" of Knox and Taft.

Woodrow Wilson, as a professor of political science, had been concerned with the domestic rather than the foreign applications of constitutional government. As a university president and as governor of New Jersey he had had little occasion to give attention to foreign policy, and he had left that subject virtually unnoticed in his campaign for the presidency. But as President, his early pronouncements on foreign policy seemed consistent with the Democratic record. He promptly repudiated the Taft-Knox venture in dollar diplomacy in China. When the American bankers participating in the consortium inquired whether the new administration wished them to continue, they were told that it did not. After discussion in two cabinet meetings but without consulting either the State Department or the other governments concerned, Wilson issued a statement disassociating the United States from the proposed loan. Its conditions, he remarked, seemed "to touch very nearly the administrative independence of China," and his administration did "not feel that it ought . . . to be a party to those conditions." The American bankers promptly withdrew from the consortium. Their elimination and the engulfment of Europe in war in 1914 left China increasingly dependent on a self-seeking Japan for financial aid. Wilson later realized his mistake and tried ineffectually to correct it.

In a public statement of March 11, 1913, a bare week after taking office, Wilson described his proposed policies toward Latin America. "One of the chief objects of my administration," he declared, "will be to cultivate the friendship and deserve the confidence of our sister republics of Central and South America, and to promote in every proper and honorable way the interests which are common to the peoples of the two continents." Seven months later, in an address at Mobile, Alabama, the President assured the peoples to the south "that the United States will never again seek one additional foot of territory by conquest"; and in the same speech he promised the Latin American countries relief from what he described as "the harder bargains driven with them in the matter of loans than with any other people in the world." By such words he sought to dampen the suspicion and dislike of the United States, which had grown appreciably south of the border under the administrations of Taft and Knox.

Several policies pursued by the new administration were consistent with these declarations. Bryan negotiated a treaty with Colombia by which the United States proposed to pay

Colombia twenty-five million dollars for the loss of Panama and expressed regret for the American part in that transaction. The treaty, however, was blocked in the Senate by senators loyal to Theodore Roosevelt. Wilson sponsored a proposal, first suggested by Colombia, for an inter-American treaty guaranteeing the independence and territorial integrity under republican governments of all the signatories—an idea which eventually bore fruit in Article Ten of the League of Nations Covenant.[1] Wilson welcomed the cooperation of the more stable Latin American governments in dealing with the troubles that soon arose in Mexico. He advocated and signed legislation that brought about notable advances in self-government in both Puerto Rico and the Philippines and committed the United States to the early independence of the latter.

All these moves were in line with a policy of anti-imperialism, but they show only one side of the picture. In his famous statement of March 11, 1913, in which he dedicated his administration to cultivating the friendship and confidence of the sister republics, Wilson also declared: "Co-operation is possible only when supported at every turn by the orderly processes of just government based upon law, not upon arbitrary or irregular force. . . . We can have no sympathy with those who seek to seize the power of government to advance their own personal interests or ambition." This was a public hint of disapproval to would-be revolutionists in Latin America. To members of his cabinet he spoke more plainly. "The agitators in certain countries," he was reported to have said, "wanted revolutions and were inclined to try it on with the new administration. . . . he was not going to let them have one if he could prevent it." To an official British visitor he asserted later: "I am going to teach the South Americans to elect good men."

These statements are highly indicative of what was to

[1] See p. 183.

come. They signify that Wilson and Bryan (and to a less degree Robert Lansing, Bryan's successor) had such faith in democracy and in the human capacity for it that they believed that a little persuasion and pressure could make real democracies out of even the strife-torn states of Central America and the Caribbean. Persuasion could take the negative form of withholding recognition from governments that attained office by force. Pressure could be financial, or, if need be, military. In the application of such modes of pressure the Wilson administration went far beyond its predecessors in intervening in the affairs of its neighbors. And when pressure failed, as it usually did, to induce resort to democratic procedures, Wilson and his advisers substituted their own authority for that of "the people." Thus, to take the chief cases in order of ascending degrees of severity, the Nicaraguans were told whom they must elect; the Haitians were required by treaty to place direction of their affairs in the hands of American advisers; the Dominicans, who refused to do the same, were subjected to American military government. In all three the United States enforced the doctrine which Bryan stated to the Dominicans: "The period of revolutions is past." The new policy produced order but not democracy. It was ironic that a policy motivated by a desire to promote democracy promoted instead authoritarian rule by an external hand.

As Wilson's biographer, Arthur Link, has remarked: "It goes without saying that such conclusions were possible because Wilson, Bryan, and Lansing assumed that the ordinary rules of international comity did not apply when small republics had demonstrated their incapacity to govern themselves." [2]

The promotion of democracy, or at least its negative side, the prevention of a chronic state of revolution, seems with

[2] A. S. Link, *Wilson: The Struggle for Neutrality* (Princeton: Princeton University Press, 1960), p. 550.

little question to have been the principal motive in Wilson's policy of intervention. Associated with it was the desire, as with Roosevelt and Taft, to remove excuse or opportunity for European intrusion. This motive probably weighed more heavily with Bryan and Lansing than with Wilson. After August 1914 there was little to justify it. American citizens with economic axes to grind urged intervention from time to time, most persistently in Haiti. There is no reason to believe that such pressures led the administration to do what it would not have done anyway. In not one of the states where it intervened did the administration ask or receive special economic privileges for its nationals.

In Nicaragua Bryan and Wilson accepted, apparently with few qualms, the situation passed on to them by Taft and Knox. Adolfo Díaz, they assumed, was to be sustained as President, his financial needs met as far as possible, his rivals intimidated by retaining the guard of marines at the American legation. Bryan tried to get for Díaz more generous terms from the bankers whose repeated small loans had kept his leaky regime afloat. He even suggested to Wilson that the United States government itself initiate a policy of lending money to such governments at a rate of interest slightly above that at which the United States could borrow. The difference would go into a sinking fund to discharge the debt, and the needy republics would be enabled to pay off their obligations to Europe and engage in needed public works at home. When Wilson rejected this early version of foreign aid, Bryan could only turn again to the bankers. Thus the policy of dollar diplomacy was carried forward by one of its former leading critics.

Knox, it will be recalled, had negotiated a canal treaty with the Díaz regime, on which the Senate had failed to act. It gave the United States, at the price of three million dollars, perpetual and exclusive right to the canal route through Nicaragua and the further right to establish naval bases on

the Corn Islands and the Gulf of Fonseca, near the eastern
and western termini of the canal route respectively. The
treaty was designed to alleviate Díaz' financial troubles on
the one hand and, on the other, to assure the United States
that no rival power—rumor had it that both Germany and
Japan had shown interest—would acquire canal or base
rights in this sensitive area. These merits seemed to Bryan
adequate justification for the treaty, and he took the matter
up where Knox had left it. At Díaz' suggestion, however, he
added provisions closely resembling those of the Platt
Amendment. These would have bound Nicaragua neither to
declare war without the consent of the United States nor to
make any treaty that would impair its independence or territorial integrity, and would have empowered the United
States to intervene in Nicaragua to preserve its independence or to protect life and property. "I believe," Díaz
cabled President Wilson, "that revolutions will cease if your
Government can see its way clear to grant the addition of
the Amendment as requested."

Wilson and Bryan were willing, but they met opposition in
two quarters. When Bryan consulted the Senate Foreign Relations Committee, he found opinion cool to the whole treaty
but actively hostile to the Platt Amendment clauses. In Central America, Nicaragua's neighbors, especially Costa Rica
and El Salvador, objected strongly, the more so in view of
press reports that the United States contemplated similar
Platt Amendment treaties for other Central American republics. To meet such criticism Bryan dropped the Platt Amendment features, and thus modified the canal treaty was signed
by Bryan and Emiliano Chamorro, the Nicaraguan minister,
on August 5, 1914.

The Senate was still to delay a year and a half in approving the treaty, which it finally accomplished on February
18, 1916. Nicaragua's neighbors were not satisfied by the
elimination of the protectorate articles from the treaty. Costa

Rica claimed that Nicaragua was bound by treaty not to grant canal rights without her consent. El Salvador laid claim to proprietary rights jointly with Nicaragua and Honduras in the waters of the Gulf of Fonseca and asserted that these were violated by Nicaragua's concession of naval base privileges to the United States. Bryan attempted to conciliate this opposition. His envoy to El Salvador, Boaz Long, after touring the Central American capitals, proposed that the United States purchase canal rights from Costa Rica and naval base rights from El Salvador and confer other material benefits upon them and other Central American states, including a school to introduce North American know-how in agriculture and business. Nothing came of this plan. The Senate in approving the treaty stipulated that nothing therein should impair the rights of the protesting states. Not satisfied with this safeguard, Costa Rica and El Salvador appealed separately to the Central American Court of Justice, asking that the treaty be declared null and void as violating their rights. The United States and Nicaragua took a somewhat cavalier attitude toward the court. Both denied its jurisdiction in the matter, and Nicaragua refused to appear as a party. When the court held that Nicaragua had violated the treaty rights of the plaintiffs, Nicaragua abrogated her treaty of adherence to the court, and the tribunal soon thereafter went out of business. Though the court had shown itself during its short life on the whole a political rather than a judicial body, it was regrettable that the United States, which under Elihu Root had presided at its birth, played an important part in its demise.

In 1916 the four-year presidential term of Adolfo Díaz ended. The United States had picked Emiliano Chamorro, the minister in Washington, as the best man to succeed him. It put pressure upon a reluctant Díaz to accept Chamorro as the Conservative candidate, expressing its confidence by sending the minister home on board a naval vessel. The

Liberals nominated Julián Irías, a former lieutenant of Zelaya. Though Irías gave assurance that if elected he would cooperate with the United States, the State Department made it plain that it would recognize no *zelayaista* as President of Nicaragua. Irías withdrew from the contest, the Liberals boycotted the election, and Chamorro received virtually all votes cast. He served until 1920. Prevented by the Nicaraguan constitution from succeeding himself, he secured the Conservative nomination for a relative, Diego Manuel Chamorro. On this occasion the United States made a genuine attempt to secure a free and fair election, but with the Chamorro forces in control of the electoral machinery, the result was not in doubt. Diego Chamorro was the victor by a substantial majority.

In 1917, under Emiliano Chamorro, American control over Nicaraguan finance was strengthened. The collector general of customs, installed during the Taft regime, was given provisional control also over the collection of internal revenue, and a new High Commission, with one member named by the President of Nicaragua and two by the Secretary of State, controlled government expenditures over a stated minimum. Under the new arrangement, aided by a war-induced rise in prices, substantial progress was made on the payment of the foreign debt, and for the first time in many years Nicaragua attained financial solvency.

Such controls as the United States exercised over Nicaragua were not formalized in treaties. They were in part based on contracts between Nicaragua and its creditors, in which a role was assigned to the State Department; in part they comprised "advice" transmitted at election time and supported by the presence of the legation guard in Managua and visits of naval vessels to Nicaraguan ports. Far different were the controls that in the same years the Wilson administration had instituted over the two republics on the island of Hispaniola.

The Dominican Republic, as noted earlier, was left without a President by the flight of Archbishop Nouel in March 1913. The Dominican Congress chose General José Bordas Valdés as provisional President for a year, but by the time the new United States minister arrived in the fall of 1913, Bordas was facing rebellion by rival politicos, especially on the northern coast. The new minister, James M. Sullivan, a Democratic lawyer from New York, was one of the more regrettable examples of Bryan's injection of the spoils system into the State Department and the diplomatic service, which stripped the Latin American Division and the Caribbean missions of knowledgeable men. Sullivan had an unsavory past, exposure of which led to his removal after two years at Santo Domingo. His comprehension of the Dominican scene is suggested by his prediction to Bryan that baseball was about to replace revolutionary activity as the favorite national sport!

Sullivan, speaking for Bryan and Wilson, lectured the dissident leaders on the virtues of fair elections and the vices of revolution, and warned them that the United States would "employ every legitimate means to assist in the preservation of order and in the prevention of further insurrection." With the aid of several U.S. naval vessels, Bordas was able to suppress his rivals, but when through fraudulent elections in June 1914, he got himself reelected for a new term, rebellion threatened anew. President Wilson then proposed a plan of settlement, a suggestion for which had come to him from the State Department. Following a cease-fire and a dispersal of all armed forces, the principal leaders should agree on a man for provisional President. If they failed to agree, the United States would make the choice, and in either case the United States would recognize and support the man selected. The provisional President would hold elections, in which he must not be a candidate. The United States would send observers, and if satisfied that the elections were free and fair, would recognize and support the President and Congress so chosen. This accomplished, the United States would feel free to insist that insurrectionary movements cease and that all future changes in government take place by peaceful and constitutional procedures.

This "Wilson Plan," though phrased in the form of advice, was presented as an ultimatum. For the first time, as one authority has written, "the establishment of a quasi-protectorate by the United States over the Dominican Republic was unmistakably asserted." [3]

The Dominican leaders had little choice but to accept Wilson's proposal. They chose for provisional President Dr. Ramón Báez, son of a dictator who had once negotiated with President Grant for annexation of his country to the United States. Bordas resigned. Elections were held in October 1914, with two American observers at each polling place and with American naval vessels present at several ports. For the most part the elections were fairly conducted. Juan Isidro Jiménez, former President and leader of one of the two principal parties, won by a small margin over two opponents. The United States promptly made it clear that it would recognize Jiménez. When certain rivals meditated resistance, Bryan sent word that the United States "will not tolerate insurrections. The period of revolutions is past," declared the Secretary; "law and order will be supported; necessary reforms will be urged through legislation."

Prominent among the reforms which the State Department now asked of Jiménez were the appointment of an American financial adviser with full control over expenditures, and the creation of a constabulary to be trained and initially commanded by officers of the United States. A financial adviser (or comptroller of finances) had been provisionally accepted by Bordas, and Jiménez had promised to retain

[3] Sumner Welles, *Naboth's Vineyard: The Dominican Republic, 1844–1924* (2 vols. New York: Payson & Clarke, Ltd., 1928), II, 739.

him, but when he undertook to do so in defiance of a resolution by the Congress, the latter body threatened to impeach him. The impeachment proceedings were dropped at the insistence of Washington. The United States, though arguing that the reforms demanded were covered by the receivership treaty of 1907, hesitated to press them upon the aging and irresolute Jiménez.

In April 1916 Jiménez faced a new crisis. He had owed his election in part to the support of General Desiderio Arias, a semi-independent chieftain of the northwestern corner of the republic, whose strength and isolated position in a land almost without roads had enabled him to blackmail one president after another. Jiménez had paid for Arias' support by making him Secretary of War. When Arias' exactions became intolerable and Jiménez undertook to dismiss him, Arias seized the fortress in the city of Santo Domingo and threatened to take over the government.

To the United States Arias was wholly objectionable. He had repeatedly stirred up trouble in the republic; he was reported to have instigated armed resistance to current American policy in that part of Haiti that adjoined his stronghold; he and his followers were reputed to be pro-German at a time when German-American relations were worsening. The United States could not tolerate an Arias regime in the Dominican Republic any more than a *zelayaista* regime in Nicaragua. To prevent such a misfortune (and to carry out its warning against revolutions), the United States landed marines from ships at Santo Domingo, forced Arias to withdraw, and extended the military occupation to all strategic centers. Jiménez resigned. A new provisional President failed to accept the American program for reform. Warned that new elections might return a pro-Arias Congress, a high-level conference in Washington concluded that nothing short of temporary military government by the United States could bring peace and order to the Dominican

Republic. President Wilson gave his consent to the decision, as he wrote, "with the deepest reluctance," but "convinced that it is the least of the evils in sight in this very perplexing situation." On November 29, 1916, a proclamation by Captain Harry S. Knapp, U.S.N., placed the Dominican Republic in "a state of military occupation." For the next six years the Dominican Republic was governed by the Navy and the Marine Corps of the United States.

The Dominican Republic was Spanish in language and tradition, and in race predominantly mestizo. Haiti, its neighbor on the west, was African with a thin veneer of French culture. In the eighteenth century it had been a profitable French colony. During the French Revolution the slaves had revolted, murdered or expelled their French owners, and founded an independent nation. A century later, the affluence of colonial days had long since vanished. Of Haiti's population some ninety-five percent were poverty-stricken and illiterate Negro peasants; the remainder, the so-called élite, were mulattoes. Their language and their education were French, and their livelihood was largely derived from office-holding or government employment. There were no such political parties as those of the Dominican Republic; instead, rival politicians were backed by bands of mercenary soldiery known as *cacos*. Elections were empty formalities, determined by *caco* votes. The leader who had won the battle could count on winning the ensuing election.

Like other states of the Caribbean area, Haiti had lived beyond its means and contracted a sizable foreign debt. Much of this was held in France, and French interests also controlled the Banque Nationale, or National Bank, of Haiti. In 1910, however, French, German, and American banking firms joined in floating a new loan and in reorganizing the National Bank. In both the loan and the stock of the new bank, the French took fifty percent, the Americans forty,

and the Germans ten. The bank was made the sole deposi-
tory for government revenues and was given the responsibility of paying monthly service on the foreign debt before
making funds available for governmental expenses.

An American syndicate held a concession for a railroad to
connect Port au Prince, the capital, with Cap Haitien on
the north coast. The railroad was only partly built, and the
mutual obligations of government and railroad company
were often in controversy.

In Port au Prince there were a number of German
merchants. They were not only active in trade but also made
loans at profitable rates, sometimes to the government, sometimes to revolutionary leaders who sought to overthrow the
government. Loans of the latter type became obligations of
the government when the revolution succeeded. Thus each
revolution added to the national debt.

French and German investments in Haiti gave the governments of France and Germany an excuse to take an official
interest in Haitian affairs. Prior to August 1914, visits of
French and German cruisers were not uncommon, and
French and German marines were now and then put ashore
to protect their nationals in time of disorder. More disturbing to the United States than these minor intrusions were
rumors of French and especially German designs to acquire
Môle St. Nicolas at the northwestern tip of the island for a
coaling station. The United States occasionally coveted the
Môle for its own use but for the time being was content with
assurances that Haiti had no intention of alienating it.

When the Wilson administration began to contemplate
the possibility of a customs receivership for Haiti like that in
Santo Domingo, both the French and German governments
served notice that they would expect to share in any such
control. The United States politely acknowledged the
French claims; to such a German demand it responded with
a strong negative. After the outbreak of war in Europe,

neither France nor Germany was in a position to press its claims.

The period from 1910 to 1915 was one in which Haitian revolutions followed one another at intervals of only a few months. No sooner was one President elected (by the National Assembly) and installed in the palace at Port au Prince than a rival betook himself to the north coast, collected a *caco* army, and began a march on the capital with a better than even chance of success. Such chaotic conditions were alarming to Haiti's creditors and to enterprises such as the bank and railroad. Spokesman for the New York banks which owned stock in the Banque Nationale d'Haiti, and also for the railroad, was one Roger L. Farnham. A vice-president of the National City Bank and the Banque Nationale and president of the Haitian National Railroad, Farnham saw salvation for his enterprises in the establishment of an American financial protectorate over Haiti. As a friend of Boaz Long, now chief of the State Department's Latin American Division, Farnham had no difficulty in getting Bryan's ear. He seems to have played skillfully upon Bryan's fear of French or German intervention; yet the course adopted by the United States for Haiti was so consistent with its policy in Nicaragua and the Dominican Republic that the importance of Farnham's influence is debatable.

At any rate, early in 1914 the State Department began angling with the Haitian government, then briefly headed by Oreste Zamor, for an invitation to institute a customs receivership. Zamor was at first unresponsive, and by the time he had begun to see advantage in such an arrangement, he was on his way out. Davilmar Théodore, who overthrew and succeeded him in November 1914, provided a new argument for intervention when he violated the government's contract with the bank and the bondholders by directing that government revenues be deposited with local merchants instead of with the bank. Bryan had hopefully sent him a

copy of the "Wilson Plan," which then seemed to be working in the Dominican Republic; but no headway had been
made with Théodore when in February 1915 he was in turn
overthrown by Vilbrun Guillaume Sam.

Attempts to arrive at an agreement with Guillaume Sam
came to naught. A special agent sent to talk with him in May
1915 suggested a treaty giving some supervision of Haitian
finance to the United States minister. That failing, the agent
advised President Wilson, the United States should intervene by force and impose on Haiti a treaty on the lines of the
Platt Amendment. The report gave Wilson, as he said, "a
great deal of concern." As it turned out, conditions were
soon favorable for imposing on Haiti the substance of the
Platt Amendment, and more.

Before Guillaume Sam had been in office four months, a
new revolution was afoot, led by Dr. Ronsalvo Bobo. While
Bobo's *cacos* approached from the north, Guillaume Sam,
fearing conspiracy in the capital, filled the jail with political
suspects. On the night of July 26 he took refuge in the
French legation, but before leaving the palace he or a lieutenant gave orders for execution of the prisoners. Over one
hundred and sixty of these, many of them members of prominent families, were massacred in cold blood. The barbaric
act evoked a barbaric response. On July 28 a Haitian mob
violated the French legation, dragged the President from
concealment under a bed, and threw him into the street,
where he was hacked to pieces.

At that moment—some would call it psychological—the
U.S. cruiser *Washington,* bearing Rear Admiral W. B. Caperton, entered Port au Prince harbor. At the urging of the
local American, French, and British representatives, and on
timely orders from Washington, the admiral that afternoon
landed enough marines and bluejackets to guard the foreign
legations. In Washington Wilson and Lansing, the new Secretary of State, agreed that the United States must assume

responsibility for establishing a stable government and a sound financial system in Haiti. Admiral Caperton was authorized to extend his control over the city and the customhouses and to encourage the Haitian National Assembly to elect a suitable man as President. Caperton and the United States minister were directed to make clear to the National Assembly that the United States would recognize as President only a man who could be expected to put an end to factional strife; they were also to make clear to any candidate for the office "that the United States expects to be entrusted with the practical control of the customs and such financial control over the affairs of the Republic of Haiti as the United States may deem necessary for efficient administration."

In the normal Haitian course of events, the National Assembly would have elected the victorious Dr. Bobo for President while his armed *cacos* looked on. Sheltered by the marines from *caco* intimidation, the Assembly chose Philippe Sudre Dartiguenave, then serving as president of the Senate. Dartiguenave had been interviewed by Caperton. He had promised to accept the American program and had received Caperton's endorsement backed by that of Washington. Unquestionably the candidate of the United States, he received 94 of 116 votes in the Assembly.

Installed in office and recognized by the United States, Dartiguenave was asked to sign a treaty which went considerably beyond the earlier proposals, combining the substance of the Platt Amendment and the Dominican receivership and adding features found in neither. It provided for a general receiver of customs and a financial adviser to be appointed by the President of Haiti upon nomination by the President of the United States. Appointed in like manner would be an engineer or engineers to supervise measures for sanitation and public improvements, and American officers to train a new constabulary and command it until replaced by qualified Haitians. The treaty provided that all debts of the government should be classified and arranged, that service upon them should be paid from the revenues, and that Haiti should not increase its debt without the consent of the United States; nor should it in any way impair its independence or alienate any of its territory. Finally, the United States would lend any necessary assistance to preserve Haitian independence and to maintain "a government adequate for the protection of life, property and individual liberty." The treaty was to remain in force for ten years and might be extended for a like period should either party hold such extension necessary for the attainment of the treaty's purposes.

The Haitian government was not pleased with the treaty, but since the United States held the customhouses and hence the purse strings, it had the choice of yielding or abdicating, and abdication meant almost certainly, as in Santo Domingo a year later, military government by the United States. Dartiguenave chose to yield. He signed the treaty September 16. In the bicameral National Assembly, the Deputies gave their approval early in October. The Senate held out until warned by Caperton that the United States would retain control until its desires were met and would "forthwith proceed to the complete pacification of Haiti." The Senate finally gave its consent on November 11. A *modus vivendi* put the treaty terms into effect pending ratification by the United States. The United States Senate approved the treaty without debate, and it was proclaimed May 3, 1916.

The treaty of 1915 removed any danger that may have existed of European intervention in Haiti. It removed one incentive to revolution by placing government funds beyond the reach of native politicians. An American general receiver of customs controlled the government's access to income from revenue, and an American financial adviser controlled all government expenditures. There was little chance left for graft. Any attempt at revolt, furthermore, would have to contend with the American-trained constabulary or *gendarmerie* backed if necessary by U.S. marines. A *caco* revolt of 1918 was a protest against forced labor on the roads (the corvée), not a manifestation of traditional political ambitions. Aside from that revolt, the treaty brought greater peace and order to Haiti than it had known for generations.

The treaty also brought financial stability, though lack of funds delayed resumption of full service on the debt and kept the public works program within narrow limits. Even after the life of the treaty was extended ten years (to 1936), new loans were slow in coming. The treaty made no provision for education of the illiterate masses. Neither the treaty nor the protectorate which it established made any contribution to the promotion of democracy in Haiti. A new constitution, mainly American in origin, approved in a well-chaperoned plebiscite in 1918, contained democratic features, but these were conveniently postponed to a date to be determined by the President of Haiti. In the meantime (actually until 1930) the functions of government were exercised, subject to the American controls, by the President and a Council of State, which was named by him and empowered to name his successor. Neither in Haiti nor in Nicaragua or the Dominican Republic did American intervention advance the cause of those democratic ideals that Wilson and Bryan professed. It merely replaced chronic revolution with varying degrees of authoritarian control.

CHAPTER VIII

Mexico—The Intractable Revolution

More troublesome and much more dangerous to the United States than the disorders in Hispaniola or Nicaragua was the long period of civil war and near-anarchy in Mexico. In May 1911 the long reign of President Porfirio Díaz came to a sudden end. He had attained the presidency in 1877 and except for one short interval had held it continuously by dictatorial methods. He had given Mexico the first period of real stability that it had enjoyed since independence and had promoted its material prosperity by encouraging investment of foreign capital in Mexican land, mineral resources, and railroads. He had thus won the admiration not only of American businessmen but of conservative American statesmen like Taft and Root. Root predicted after Díaz' downfall: "The time will come again when Mexico lauds him as the greatest of her sons."

But the prosperity which Díaz had brought to Mexico was confined for the most part to foreigners and a few privileged Mexican families. Little of it had seeped down to peasants and laborers, and many Mexicans of the upper class resented the transfer to foreign ownership of much of the nation's agricultural land and mineral wealth. Assorted resentments, anti-Díaz and anti-foreign, were brought to a focus in 1910 in the person of Francisco I. Madero. Madero, the diminutive (five feet, four inches) scion of a wealthy family of Coahuila, of partly Portuguese-Jewish ancestry, had completed his education in France and the United States and apparently settled down to the routine life of a *hacendado* on the family estates when a spiritualistic experience turned his mind to Mexico's need for reform. As a candidate against Díaz in the elections of 1910, he was considered sufficiently dangerous to be imprisoned and then allowed to escape to the United States. In the carefully controlled election he was credited with 196 votes against millions for Díaz. From his foreign sanctuary Madero called for revolt against the tyrant Díaz, to begin with mass uprisings on May 20, 1911. Proclaiming himself provisional President of Mexico, he promised honest elections and a variety of political, social, and economic reforms.

The success of a movement thus fantastically begun on a shoestring—Madero's armed supporters numbered not over 17,500—shows that the once powerful Díaz regime was now nothing but an empty façade. The senile President could not cope with the seemingly insignificant displays of opposition. On May 25, 1911, he resigned and sailed for Europe on the German steamer *Ypiranga*. New elections were held. Madero became President of Mexico and was recognized as such by the United States and other powers.

Madero's reform program made him powerful enemies—including foreign economic interests and the Catholic Church—and failed to unite his followers. He maintained his position amid growing perplexities for a year and a half. In February 1913 Felix Díaz, nephew of the exiled dictator, led a revolt in Mexico City. The general whom Madero had named to command his troops in the capital, Victoriano Huerta, connived with Díaz. The two generals had the encouragement of the United States ambassador, Henry Lane

Wilson, who had conceived a violent antagonism for Madero. Meeting with Wilson at the American embassy, they
signed (February 18, 1913) the "Pact of the Embassy."
Huerta, they agreed, should immediately assume the office
of provisional President; Díaz might become a candidate at
the next election. Madero and his vice-president, meanwhile,
had been arrested and induced to resign by promises of immunity. Madero's disloyal Foreign Minister thereby became
President. By naming Huerta Secretary of Gobernación, and
then resigning, he brought Huerta "constitutionally" to the
presidency. Ambassador Wilson then presented Huerta to
the diplomatic corps as "the savior of Mexico" and urged
that all foreign governments recognize him as President.

Wilson's actions had been taken on his own responsibility
without authority from his government. He neglected, furthermore, to transmit to Huerta a telegram from Secretary
Knox urging that no harm come to Madero and Vice-
President Pino Suárez. He was not blameless, therefore,
when the two were shot on the transparent pretext that their
friends were attempting a rescue.

President Taft had but a few days to remain in office when
word of these events arrived in Washington. Though urged
by Ambassador Wilson to give immediate recognition to
Huerta's government, he thought it best to leave decision
in that matter to his successor.

Woodrow Wilson's dedication to orderly processes of government, and his belief that such processes could be made
to prevail in Latin America, were described in the preceding
chapter. These ideas were no less applicable to Mexico than
to the Caribbean. Indeed, a part of his statement of March
11, 1913, may well have had direct reference to Huerta.
"We can have no sympathy," he said, "with those who seek
to seize the power of government to advance their own personal interests or ambition." Feeling for Huerta, as Arthur
Link remarks, a "deep revulsion," Wilson was not moved

by clamorous demands for the recognition of Huerta's government. Such demands reached him from the American colony in Mexico City and from American businessmen with investments in Mexico. Huerta, these groups believed, would be another Díaz, the "strong man" who could enforce order in Mexico and protect foreign interests from radical dreamers like Madero. Their demands were enthusiastically endorsed by Ambassador Henry Lane Wilson and by specialists on Latin America in the State Department.

Had President Wilson followed well-established precedent, he would have extended *de facto* recognition to Huerta as soon as the latter seemed firmly in the saddle. This was, in fact, the course followed by the British and by other European governments. But Wilson postponed a decision, and meanwhile Huerta's *de facto* authority was challenged by a formidable uprising. In March a group of former Madero supporters from northern Mexico met at Guadalupe, organized under the name of Constitutionalists, and chose Venustiano Carranza, Governor of Coahuila, as "First Chief" of their Constitutionalist Army. On March 30, Carranza proclaimed himself provisional President of Mexico. To his support came other northern leaders: Alvaro Obregón, a former schoolteacher who was to show rare military talent; Pancho Villa, semi-bandit and adept at guerrilla fighting; while in the South Emiliano Zapata, a radical agrarian reformer, joined the rebellion. In three years Mexico had suffered revolution, counterrevolution, and now civil war.

To Woodrow Wilson in Washington there appeared to be a simple solution for Mexico's ills: a cease-fire, free elections, and a popularly chosen government that would govern constitutionally! Was not that the American way? To critics who questioned whether such techniques would work in Mexico he replied: "When properly directed, there is no people not fitted for self-government." But since neither he nor Secretary of State Bryan had any sound knowledge of

Mexico, and since he distrusted Ambassador Wilson (whom he recalled in July 1913) and the State Department's experts, Wilson sent a procession of personal representatives to Mexico to report on conditions and in some instances to negotiate informally with Mexican leaders. They were novices in the field, most of them spoke no Spanish, and their labors were not very helpful.

By one such agent, ex-Governor John Lind of Minnesota (Democrat and friend of Bryan), Wilson sent a proposal to Huerta: an immediate cease-fire; a guarantee of early and free elections; Huerta not to be a candidate; all parties to agree to abide by the results. Huerta appeared to agree (the Constitutionalists did not), setting elections for October 26, 1913; but when Huerta, on October 10, dissolved Congress and arrested over one hundred opposition Deputies, Wilson resolved that Huerta must be got rid of. He made this clear in a circular note to foreign governments of November 24, 1913. Usurpations such as Huerta's, he wrote, "menace the peace and development of America as nothing else could." It was therefore the purpose of the United States "to discredit and defeat such usurpations whenever they occur. The present policy of the Government of the United States," the President continued, "is to isolate General Huerta entirely; to cut him off from foreign sympathy and aid and from domestic credit, whether moral or material, and so to force him out." If such "peaceful" measures failed, the President threatened, others would be used, with due notice to other governments. He gave assurance that the United States would not "seek any special or exclusive advantages" for its citizens but would "seek here as elsewhere, to show itself the constant champion of the open door."

Here was an extraordinarily frank statement of a Wilsonian policy—a policy altruistic in purpose but unabashedly interventionist in method. Mexico, for her own good, said the President, must have a government that conformed to Wilsonian norms.

Rather surprisingly, the British government eventually fell in line with Wilson's policy. British oil concerns had large holdings in Mexico, and these vitally affected the national interest, since the British Navy had converted from coal to oil for fuel. Britain had recognized Huerta soon after his coup, and the new British ambassador, Sir Lionel Carden, was ostentatiously friendly to the dictator. He was reported by the American chargé d'affaires as working to counteract American policy. Wilson's diatribe, in his Mobile speech of October 27, against foreign exploitation of Latin America[1] was certainly aimed in part at European policy in Mexico. But Wilson did not stop there. He himself typed a draft of a note to be sent to all the major powers. Huerta's usurping government, he charged, was sustained only by recognition and financial aid granted by other nations, contrary to the policy and wishes of the United States, the nation with the weightiest responsibility for Mexico. Would European governments now cooperate with the United States, he asked, or would they continue "to antagonize and thwart us and make our task one of domination and force"?

Cooler heads dissuaded Wilson from sending this ill-tempered communication, but the substance of it leaked to the newspapers. It alarmed the British, who in the face of growing tension in Europe could not afford a quarrel with the United States. Foreign Secretary Sir Edward Grey sent his private secretary, Sir William Tyrrell, to America for confidential talks with Wilson and his advisers. An unwritten but satisfactory agreement resulted. Britain would not oppose American policy in Mexico. After a decent interval Ambassador Carden was sent elsewhere and British recognition of Huerta was withdrawn. Wilson, in return, undertook to protect British persons and property in Mexico and

[1] See p. 85.

agreed (whether explicitly or not) to seek repeal of the article in the Panama Canal Act exempting American coastwise shipping from the payment of canal tolls. The exemption, the British argued, violated the Hay-Pauncefote Treaty, which stipulated that the canal should be open to the ships of all nations "on terms of entire equality." Though the Democratic platform of 1912 had endorsed the exemption, Wilson now went before Congress and asked its repeal, "in support," he said, "of the foreign policy of the administration." He did not mention Mexico, but there is no doubt of the connection. Congress repealed the exemption article, much to the satisfaction of the British. In protecting British persons and property in Mexico Wilson was less successful. Revolution and civil war were destructive of life and property regardless of nationality.

Wilson's resolve that Huerta must be driven out was reiterated in his first annual message to Congress (December 2, 1913). Such "pretended governments" as Huerta's, he said, "will not be countenanced or dealt with by the Government of the United States." For the time being, however, he was content to follow a policy of what he called "watchful waiting," leaving the active role in ousting the dictator to the Constitutionalists. In October Carranza's forces had captured the important railroad center of Torreón and seemed well on the road to the capital; but in the following months, conservative groups rallied to give Huerta increased moral and material support. Banking and commercial interests, landholders, and the Roman Catholic Church, all feared the radical economic and anticlerical program of the Constitutionalists. With their renewed support Huerta regained strength and the Constitutionalist drive faltered.

Wilson now turned to more active measures. First, on February 3, 1914, he revoked the embargo on the shipment of arms to Mexico, which President Taft had imposed (with exceptions for the Mexican government) early in the revolution. The revocation permitted the flow of arms to the Constitutionalists, whose northern stronghold gave them easy access to the American market. Before taking this step, however, Wilson got from the Constitutionalist leaders assurance that their reform program, with which Wilson felt much sympathy, would be pursued by "constitutional and legal methods."

But when the stubborn dictator still held his own, Wilson apparently welcomed an excuse for armed intervention. He found it in a trivial incident at the port and oil refining center of Tampico. On April 9, 1914, a paymaster and seven sailors from the U.S. gunboat *Dolphin* were loading oil into a whaleboat at a wharf which, unknown to them, was in a prohibited area. They were arrested, two of the sailors being required to leave the boat, which flew the American flag, and marched to a nearby police station. There they were promptly released, and the commander of Huerta's forces in the area offered an apology and punishment of the subordinate officer responsible for the arrest. The United States consul at Tampico considered the apology ample amends for an understandable mistake, but Admiral Henry T. Mayo, commanding the United States naval squadron at Tampico—where the navies of half a dozen powers were showing the flag to protect their interests—was convinced that the United States flag had been insulted. He demanded amends in the form of a twenty-one gun salute to the stars and stripes. Wilson and Bryan supported the admiral, and when Huerta, who had already expressed regret for the incident, refused the salute (except in exchange for a simultaneous salute to the flag of Mexico), Wilson ordered the entire Atlantic Fleet to Mexican waters. Appearing before a joint session of the two Houses of Congress on April 20, he asked approval of the use of the armed forces to obtain from General Huerta "the fullest recognition of the rights and dignity of the United States." In justification of his request, he coupled with the Tampico affair two even more trivial incidents: the arrest, and immediate release, of an American sailor at Veracruz—a clear case of mistaken identity; delay of less than an hour in the delivery of a telegraphic dispatch to the embassy in Mexico City—the result at worst of a careless error in the censor's office. To those three unconnected incidents Wilson attached a significance far beyond their true character. They betrayed, he indicated, a deliberate intent on Huerta's part to affront the United States in retaliation for its refusal to recognize his government.

Congress passed the requested resolution two days later, but in the meantime the President had acted on his own authority. He and his advisers had planned tentatively to occupy Tampico and Veracruz, to blockade both coasts of Mexico, and possibly to send an expedition to Mexico City. This was not to be war against Mexico but merely what might be called a police action against a man who, in Wilson's view, was an enemy of the Mexican people as well as of the United States.

Wilson's hand was forced by news of the approach to Veracruz of the German steamer *Ypiranga,* bearing a cargo of military supplies for Huerta. By a midnight decision in Washington Admiral Mayo, who was preparing to occupy Tampico, was ordered to take his ships to Veracruz instead. There on April 21, 1914, sailors and marines from the American warships occupied the customhouse and later the city. There they, or their successors from the Army, remained until November.

Wilson, who had expected the occupation to be peaceful, was shocked when the Mexicans resisted, inflicting and suffering serious casualties. He was shocked further when the Constitutionalists vied with Huerta in denouncing this invasion of the sacred soil of Mexico.[2] He abandoned plans

[2] An exception was Pancho Villa, who sought to ingratiate himself with the United States by applauding the occupation of Veracruz.

for further warlike measures and readily accepted an offer of mediation by the "ABC Powers"—Argentina, Brazil, and Chile.

The Mediation Conference met at Niagara Falls, Ontario, from May 20 to July 1, 1914. Wilson dropped his demand for a salute—the ostensible purpose of the intervention. He hoped to use the conference for the elimination of Huerta and the creation of a provisional government under Constitutionalist leadership, which should then hold free elections. But since Carranza, an intense nationalist, refused to participate in the conference or to agree to an armistice, the mediation failed to produce a settlement. It succeeded, however, in easing the tension between the United States and Mexico while Huerta's difficulties increased. Cut off from the revenues of Veracruz, his chief port, and under constant pressure from the Constitutionalists, Huerta found his position impossible. On July 14, 1914, he resigned the presidency and soon thereafter, like Díaz before him, sailed for Europe on a German steamer. On August 20 the Constitutionalists occupied the capital.

Wilson had had his way with Huerta, but his troubles with Mexico were far from over. Friction between Carranza and Villa, smoldering for some time, broke out into open conflict soon after the fall of Huerta. Zapata also rebelled against the First Chief, who abandoned Mexico City and set up his government in Veracruz. Villa ruled the North, where his military talent and his professions of democratic principle for a time persuaded Wilson and his advisers that he might be the man who could redeem Mexico. This belief was short-lived. During the spring of 1915 General Obregón won impressive victories for Carranza, driving Villa back into the state of Chihuahua. But since there seemed little prospect of an early end to the civil war, certain members of the State Department considered a plan to support a refugee group in the United States in an attempt at counterrevolution. This scheme can hardly have had Wilson's approval, but the President was slow in surrendering a faith that he might still play a constructive role in putting Mexico on the road to peace and order. On June 2, 1915, he called upon the leaders of all the contending factions to act together and "act promptly for the relief and redemption of their prostrate country." Otherwise, he warned, the United States government would "be constrained to decide what means should be employed by the United States in order to help Mexico save herself and serve her people."

Wilson's admonition produced no result. The State Department, under Lansing, the new Secretary, devised a plan calling for the retirement of all the contending chiefs—Carranza, Villa, Zapata—and cooperation of their factions, under United States and Latin American guidance, in the formation of a provisional government that the United States and the Latin American states could recognize and support. For this purpose Lansing called in the ambassadors of the ABC governments and the ministers of Uruguay, Bolivia, and Guatemala. These six and the Secretary of State proposed to all the chiefs and sub-chiefs in Mexico that they stop fighting and meet to agree on a new provisional government. Carranza, in response, made it clear that he would neither have any dealings with Villa nor accept guidance from outside Mexico. His reply apparently confirmed Lansing and his Latin American collaborators in the belief that the First Chief's staunch rejection of any compromise required his elimination as a contender for the presidency.

At this point President Wilson played a key role in the drama. He came to the rescue of Carranza. He had been thoroughly exasperated with Carranza and had originally endorsed Lansing's plan, but at some time in July or early August 1915, he changed his mind. In telegrams of August 8 and 11 from his summer retreat in New Hampshire he advised Lansing that it would be unwise for the conference "to take for granted or insist upon the elimination of Carranza," and that early elections—hitherto an indispensable item in the American program—were not so important after all. It seemed necessary, he said, that "a provisional government essentially revolutionary in character should take action to institute reforms by decree before the full forms of the constitution are resumed." Wilson had decided, in the words of Arthur Link, to "accept the Revolution on its own terms."

Why Wilson changed his attitude at this particular time is not at all clear. Obregón's military successes against Villa must have impressed him, but at the same time he evidently had a growing faith in the aims of the revolution. A year before, Carranza had sent his chief "brain truster," Luis Cabrera, to explain those aims to Wilson, and the President soon thereafter had avowed his concern for the "submerged eighty-five percent" of the Mexican population. Carranza and Obregón, in their quest for popular support in the winter of 1914–15, had issued a series of decrees on agrarian reform, labor reform, and other subjects—precursors of the revolutionary Constitution of 1917. These reform measures must have impressed the President as moves in the right direction; and it seems probable too that he had been disturbed by the counterrevolutionary plots nurtured in the United States in the winter and spring of 1915, and a suspicion that they were backed by self-seeking economic interests. At any rate, from now on he was for the revolution in Mexico. Ten months later, when war with Mexico seemed unavoidable, Wilson stated emphatically in a draft of a proposed message to Congress that the United States would not take advantage of military success to interfere with the institutions of the Mexican people.

As a result of Wilson's about-face, the seven-nation conference, which had been on the point of calling for Carranza's retirement, ended by recommending that his regime be recognized as the *de facto* government of Mexico. Wilson took this step for the United States on October 19, 1915, undeterred by a barrage of protests from the Roman Catholic clergy in the United States, who objected strenuously to the anticlerical principles of the Constitutionalists and to their alleged desecrations of churches, convents, and monasteries. In Mexico City there was rejoicing. Mexican newspapers appeared in United States colors on October 20. At Veracruz on the same day American battleships fired a twenty-one-gun salute to the Mexican flag, and a Mexican gunboat returned the courtesy. There seemed hope for peace and even for cordiality in United States-Mexican relations.

But such harmony as there was soon vanished. Pancho Villa, now reduced to bandit status in the Chihuahua mountains, was bent on revenge against Carranza and against the United States for recognizing Carranza. His method was to embroil his intended victims in hostilities with one another. In January 1916 one of his lieutenants removed seventeen American mining engineers from a train near Santa Ysabel and shot all but one. While newspapers and Congressmen in the United States were crying for intervention to punish this outrage, Villa pulled off his master stroke. In the early hours of March 9, his mounted guerrillas crossed the border and shot up the peaceful town of Columbus, New Mexico. The town was left in flames. Nineteen Americans had died, some of them civilians, the others cavalrymen from a troop that pursued Villa a few miles into Mexico.

It was obvious that Carranza, with the best of intentions could not maintain order along the international border. In the United States, so great was the popular clamor for the punishment of Villa that Wilson had to act. Brigadier General John J. Pershing, with two brigades of cavalry and one of infantry, was ready to cross the border but was held up several days while Lansing sought Carranza's consent to the expedition. Carranza was willing to accept a mutual agreement for "hot pursuit" in the event of future incidents like that at Columbus. He insisted that this agreement was not retroactive, but Mexican troops made no resistance when Pershing crossed the border on March 15. The Punitive Expedition, as it was called, eventually numbered nearly seven thousand men and penetrated three hundred and fifty miles into Mexico. It fought some skirmishes with units of Villa's forces, killed some of his guerrillas and one of his "generals," but failed to catch the elusive chieftain.

Pershing had been given strict orders to cooperate with Mexican national forces if opportunity should occur, and to avoid any appearance of hostility to Mexico. Friction was inevitable, however, and Carranza grew more and more resentful of this invasion by foreign troops. He continued to insist that he had never actually consented to Pershing's entry. He proposed to limit future "hot pursuit" strictly in time and space; and finally he withdrew his consent even to such limited pursuits and demanded that Pershing's troops withdraw. An agreement for gradual withdrawal had almost been reached when new raids into American territory, this time in Texas, led to new border crossings by United States troops. Wilson mobilized the National Guard of Texas, New Mexico, and Arizona and sent additional Regular Army units to the border. Carranza sent a provocative note, charging the United States with bad faith and sinister purposes, and again demanding immediate withdrawal of Pershing's expedition.

The Mexican attitude grew increasingly threatening. On June 16, the Mexican commander at Chihuahua notified Pershing that he had orders to attack any United States troops that undertook to move in any direction but northward. Five days later a company of cavalry, attempting to enter the town of Carrizal in defiance of a Mexican warning, clashed with Mexican troops. Both commanding officers and twelve United States enlisted men were killed in the fray, and twenty-three American troopers were captured and sent to Chihuahua.

The shots fired at Carrizal, in what initial reports interpreted as a Mexican ambush, seemed for some days to betoken war. Wilson had already decided to mobilize the entire National Guard, and Mexico moved thousands of troops toward the border. Wilson demanded immediate release of the prisoners. Bowing to new outcries for intervention, he prepared an address to Congress calling not for a declaration of war but for authority to use the armed forces to clear northern Mexico of bandits—war in all but name. Then, on June 28, came news that the Carrizal prisoners had been released and were being transported to El Paso. Tension eased. Individuals and groups opposed to war became active and vocal. Wilson declined a new offer of mediation by the ABC governments, but on July 4 Carranza, dropping his bellicose tone, inquired whether the United States would prefer to settle the controversy by mediation or by direct negotiation. With great relief the President agreed to negotiate, and a Joint High Commission representing the two governments met at New London, Connecticut. Here and elsewhere they argued from September to January, keeping the two countries out of war and tiding over the national elections in the United States. Carranza insisted upon withdrawal of Pershing's troops as a preliminary to agreement on other points. This condition was unacceptable to the United States. A compromise tentatively agreed upon by the commissioners in November was rejected by Carranza. No agreement proved possible, but when the commission adjourned, January 15, 1917, the American members recommended to their government an almost complete acceptance of the Mexican demands: withdrawal of the Punitive Expedition, assumption by each government of responsibility for guarding its side of the border, and reestablishment of full diplomatic relations.

Wilson accepted the advice of his commissioners. Impressive victories of Carranza's forces over the ever troublesome Villa provided convenient justification for withdrawing the Punitive Expedition. The decision to that effect was publicly announced on January 28, and the last of Pershing's troops crossed the border eight days later. Lansing attributed Wilson's yielding to Mexico to his expectation of war with Germany, but Wilson's decision was made while he was still hopeful of bringing peace to Europe.

Restoration of regular diplomatic relations followed the removal of the soldiery. The new Mexican Constitution of 1917, in Article 27, declared subsoil rights in minerals, petroleum, etc., to be the property of the nation. American proprietors of oil and mineral lands in Mexico, with support in the State Department, proposed that a guarantee against retroactive application of Article 27 be exacted as a precondition of restoring normal relations. Wilson ignored the proposal, and an American ambassador presented his credentials in Mexico City on March 3. Later in the month Carranza was regularly elected to the Mexican presidency under the new constitution. He was inaugurated on May 1, and regular *de jure* recognition followed.

Talk of intervention and war subsided. Friction of many kinds still lay ahead, but never again were the two countries brought so close to war as they had been in the summer of 1916. Wilson had avoided war when pressures for it seemed almost irresistible; he had given the Mexican revolution a chance to succeed; he had made it plain that the United States had no selfish axes to grind in Mexico and desired to work there in harmony with the governments of other Latin American countries. A policy marked by glaring mistakes, vacillations, and inconsistencies had been in the end redeemed by statesmanlike decisions.

CHAPTER IX

War and Neutral Rights

As the Mexican problem overshadowed the problems of the Caribbean, so, after August 1914, the war in Europe raised issues far more vital to the United States than the quarrels with Huerta and Carranza. Taken together this ascending series of problems meant that President Wilson, espouser of the New Freedom on the home front, found it necessary to devote an increasingly large share of his time and energy to foreign relations. "It would be the irony of fate," he remarked soon after taking office, "if my administration had to deal chiefly with foreign affairs." This was precisely the irony which fate had in store for him.

In spite of his lack of experience in the conduct of foreign relations, and his inadequate intellectual preparation for it, Wilson was, perhaps more than any President before him, his own Secretary of State. William Jennings Bryan, who first occupied that office, was ill equipped for it by experience and temperament.[1] He was, furthermore, so often absent on profitable lecture tours that much of the business of

---

[1] Apart from his promotion of protectorates in the Caribbean, Bryan took pride in having negotiated a score of bilateral conciliation treaties, none of which was ever applied. His substitution of grape juice for wine at diplomatic dinners brought him the sobriquet of "Grape-juice Billy."

his department gravitated to the White House. Wilson, in any case, had little confidence in Bryan's judgment. When Bryan resigned in June 1915, Wilson replaced him with Robert Lansing, who had served for a year as counselor in the department. A trained and experienced international lawyer, Lansing was technically well qualified for the post, but he lacked imagination and had little sympathy with Wilson's broader aims. Consequently Wilson, with Lansing as with Bryan, made virtually all important decisions. He even typed out on his portable Hammond typewriter many of the crucial diplomatic notes that went out over the signature of the Secretary of State.

Much more influential with Wilson than either Bryan or Lansing was his confidential friend and unofficial adviser Colonel Edward M. House. An affluent Texan with no ambition for office and no selfish material ends to serve, House ("Colonel" by grace of honorary appointment to the staff of the governor of Texas) attached himself to Wilson before inauguration. The two became close friends. House was a frequent visitor at the White House and enjoyed Wilson's confidence to such a degree that he was allowed to go on a series of unofficial but delicate confidential missions to Europe; one just before the outbreak of war and two during the period of American neutrality. Later he represented Wilson officially in Europe after American entry into the war and served as a member of the American delegation at the peace conference. House always (until their break in 1919) had Wilson's ear; but it should be added that the President never followed House's advice uncritically. He made his own decisions.

The "guns of August," 1914, took the administration, no less than the American public, by surprise. The growing international tension in Europe had been no secret to informed Americans. Colonel House and Walter Hines Page, Wilson's ambassador in London, had been quite aware of it and had racked their brains to find ways to alleviate it. But not even they seem to have dreamed that the Sarajevo assassinations of June 28 might trigger a major war. That possibility became plain when Austria-Hungary, on July 28, declared war on Serbia. At this juncture the American ambassador in Paris, Myron T. Herrick, urged that Wilson appeal to the governments in the opposing alliances for "delay and moderation"—an appeal which he believed "would meet with the respect and approval of Europe." This was a suggestion which Theodore Roosevelt, in a similar situation, would probably have heeded; but Wilson and Bryan, after a perfunctory but well-received sounding of the British Foreign Office, took no further steps. Such an appeal would have been at best a forlorn hope.

Russian mobilization on July 30 was followed by declarations of war in quick succession: Germany against Russia, August 1; Germany against France, August 3; Germany against Belgium, August 4. When Britain responded, also on August 4, with a declaration of war against Germany, all the major powers of Europe save Italy were at war. On August 23, Japan entered the fray. An ally of Great Britain, she saw a chance to seize German holdings in China and the islands of the North Pacific. In 1915 Italy deserted her former partners, Germany and Austria-Hungary, and entered the war on the side of Britain, France, and Russia—"the Allies" as they were called in the United States. Rumania followed a year later. Meanwhile, Turkey and Bulgaria joined Germany and Austria-Hungary in the grouping known to Americans as "the Central Powers."

Wilson issued the inevitable proclamations of neutrality as between the belligerents. On August 19, at the suggestion of Counselor Lansing, he published an appeal to the American people to be "neutral in fact as well as in name . . . impartial in thought as well as in action." For most Americans "impartiality in thought" was impossible. As the horrifying orgy of bloodshed and destruction dragged on in Europe with no sign of an ending, it was natural for Americans to take sides, though rarely to the extent of wishing to participate. Both groups of belligerents sought to capture American sympathy through slanted propaganda; both groups had their American champions; but Germany's mode of warfare, from the violation of Belgian neutrality to the ruthless submarine campaign, and the spirit of Prussian militarism behind it, gradually alienated Germany's American sympathizers. Revelations of the activities of German secret agents in the United States and in Mexico contributed to the same result. In the United States such agents subsidized pro-German publications and the activities of German-American societies, supported efforts for an embargo on the export of munitions, and instigated labor trouble in munitions plants. In Mexico they worked to keep the civil war alive and to stir up troubles for the United States which would keep it occupied in its own back yard. In the end the German government had few defenders in the United States outside groups of German and Irish descent. The hatred of England cherished by most Irish-Americans made them natural allies of Britain's enemies.

Sympathize as they might with the Allied cause, few Americans wished to fight for it. To the time of Wilson's war message in April 1917 it is probable, as Arthur Link has written, that "the majority of people were still firmly for peace." There were some, indeed, who believed with Theodore Roosevelt that the United States should join the war against Germany in defense of national honor and international morality. There were others, like Elihu Root and Robert Lansing, who saw the war in ideological terms: as a struggle between Western democracy and Prussian autocracy and militarism. Such men believed that the United States should intervene if necessary to prevent a German victory. A German victory must be prevented, in still an-

other view, because it would upset the balance of power in
Europe and thereby present a threat to the Monroe Doctrine.
But such ideas were confined to a small élite. For most Americans the maintenance of peace outweighed any issues of
the war in Europe, and whatever their sympathies, they saw
neutrality as the proper official attitude of the United States.

Neutrality was a matter of governmental policy, which
could be adhered to in spite of sentimental or ideological
preferences for one side or the other. For two and a half
years Wilson attempted to follow a neutral course: to conform to neutral obligations and to defend neutral rights.
About the first there was no great difficulty. The recognized
rules of neutrality permitted sales of munitions to belligerents by private enterprise in a neutral country. Sales to
Britain and France, starting with a trickle, grew to a flood
by 1916. That such sales were made to Britain and France
(the Allies) and not to Germany resulted not from American
choice but from Allied control of the sea. The right to make
such sales, wholly one-sided though they were, was stoutly
defended by the State Department. A neutral government
had no obligation to prevent them.

The same was true of loans to the Allies by American
bankers; such loans soon became necessary to support the
purchase of munitions. Secretary Bryan at first took the
opposite position, declaring that money was "the worst of
contrabands" and that loans by bankers to belligerent governments were "inconsistent with the true spirit of neutrality." But historical precedent said otherwise. Bryan's stand
was reversed, tacitly by him, explicitly later by Lansing.
Before the United States entered the war in 1917 the Allies
had borrowed over two and one-quarter billion dollars
through American banks. Loans and munitions sales vital
to the Allied war effort were sanctioned by international law.
To have forbidden them during the war because only one
side had the means of using them would have been in itself

an unneutral act. The government's neutral obligations were limited for the most part to the prevention of recruiting for belligerent armed forces on American soil and of the use of American waters as bases of operation by belligerent navies. Early in 1916 the United States assumed the obligation of denying the use of its ports to armed belligerent merchant vessels, but only if their armament was offensive in purpose.

The defense of neutral rights as conceived by the United States was a more difficult matter. It produced heated arguments with both England and Germany and finally led to war with the latter. As in the Napoleonic Wars of a century earlier, the United States was confronted with a duel of giants who would use any weapon that seemed to promise victory. Each struck at trade as the jugular vein of its antagonist. Great Britain, with her superior surface fleet, undertook to cut off all German trade, direct or indirect, with the transoceanic world. Germany with a growing fleet of submarines, or U-boats, attempted to throttle Britain by sinking as many as possible of the ships that approached her ports. Both programs violated recognized rights of neutrals under international law, with the significant difference that the British measures infringed upon neutral property rights only, while the U-boat campaign took the lives of neutral passengers and seamen.

Both British and German campaigns developed only gradually. It was the good fortune of the United States that during the first two years of the war the policies of both major belligerents were controlled by moderate statesmen who set great store upon maintaining good relations with the United States. In England, Sir Edward Grey, Foreign Secretary, kept interference with American commerce within bounds, contrary to the urgings of more ruthless colleagues and coteries. Thus he contained American wrath until German offenses overshadowed Britain's. In Germany, the civilian Chancellor, Theobald von Bethmann-Hollweg was able

for over two years to restrain the naval and military ex-
tremists. These, as the available submarines grew in number,
were convinced that, given a free hand, they could starve
England into submission before American military intervention could become effective. Bethmann believed that the
capabilities of the U-boat were overrated and that American
participation in the war would be fatal to the German cause.
His eclipse by the militarists early in 1917 was to prove him
right.

In the meantime, the United States had engaged in long
arguments with both sides, had twice won concessions from
Germany by threatening to break off diplomatic relations,
and had utilized the respite by making minimal preparations
for war.

We may now glance at the oft-told tale of these events in
chronological sequence. A few days after the war began,
Secretary Bryan proposed to the belligerents that they agree
that in the war at sea they would be bound by the terms
of the Declaration of London of 1909.[2] This declaration,
tentatively agreed to at the London Conference of that year,
had never received the ratifications (including the British)
necessary to make it binding. If accepted, it would have
limited severely the activities of the power controlling the
sea. Specifically, it would have defined rigidly the commodities constituting contraband, non-contraband, and conditional contraband,[3] and would have safeguarded belligerent
commerce in non-contraband goods carried in neutral ships
and through neutral ports. Germany and Austria-Hungary

[2] See p. 51.
[3] "Conditional contraband" comprised commodities susceptible of both
military and non-military uses, which became contraband (and so subject
to confiscation) when consigned to the armed forces or a government department of an enemy state. Contraband proper, "absolute contraband,"
comprising obviously military supplies, was subject to confiscation if destined to any point within enemy territory or under enemy control.

replied to Mr. Bryan that they would abide by the declaration if their antagonists would do so. The British government agreed only with qualifications and reservations that virtually nullified the declaration. In the end, Britain set it aside altogether, though professing to observe such features of it as constituted generally accepted principles of international law.

Since the Declaration of London had in itself no legal validity, the United States could only acquiesce when Britain declined to be bound by it. Serious grounds of complaint against the British arose when an order-in-council of March 11, 1915, undertook to stop all seaborne trade with Germany, whether through German or neutral ports. The British were at the same time committing other acts that offended the American sense of justice: they declared food to be conditional contraband; they carried American ships into British ports for examination at the cost of long delays; they interfered with American mails; they protected British ships from attack by disguising them with American flags. The United States complained to the British government of all these practices as violations of American rights under international law. In the meantime, however, a far more serious crisis with Germany had arisen.

The British order-in-council of March 11, 1915, was, in fact, a response to the German initiation of submarine warfare against commerce with Britain. On February 4, 1915, the German government announced that the waters around the British Isles would thenceforth be considered "within the seat of war." Enemy merchant vessels encountered in this area after February 18 would be destroyed, "although it may not always be possible to save crews and passengers." In other words, such vessels would risk being torpedoed and sunk without warning. Furthermore, because the British had adopted the practice of disguising their ships with neutral flags, Germany warned that she could not guarantee the safety of neutral vessels that chose to enter the war zone.[4]

The new German policy represented a temporary victory for the Admiralty and its chief, Grand Admiral Alfred von Tirpitz, over the Chancellor and Foreign Office. The belief that Britain could be quickly subdued by a submarine blockade was encouraged by a bit of prewar science fiction by the creator of Sherlock Holmes. In a story in *Strand* magazine A. Conan Doyle had pictured England as brought to the edge of starvation by a fleet of hostile submarines. Though Germany possessed at that time only twenty-one U-boats, of which fewer than half could reach the Atlantic sea-lanes, the admirals persuaded the Kaiser to let them try this shortcut to victory.

The proposal to sink enemy merchant vessels without warning, since it allowed little chance for saving the lives of passengers and crew, was clearly contrary to international law. It called forth an immediate protest from Washington. In a note composed jointly by Wilson and Counselor Lansing, the United States warned the Kaiser's government that for any American lives or American ships destroyed under the new and illegal policy, Germany would be held "to a strict accountability." Was this a threat of war or merely a warning that the United States would claim monetary damages? Was Germany to be held accountable for loss of American lives on Allied ships or only on American ships? On neither point was the note clear; on both, there were sharp differences between Wilson's advisers; Bryan and Lansing stood respectively for mild and stern interpretations of the American position.

---

[4] The Germans, early in the war, had begun laying mines in the North Sea. The British had asserted the right to retaliate and on November 2, 1914, had proclaimed the entire North Sea to be a "war area," which merchant vessels would enter at their own risk. The United States had refrained from joining the Scandinavian countries in protesting the British action.

Ambiguous though the American protest was, it enabled Bethmann-Hollweg in Berlin to recover partial control of German policy. The German reply to Wilson defended the U-boat policy as justified retaliation for Britain's illegal blockade,[5] but U-boat commanders were ordered to avoid attacks on American ships. The German government had reasons, however, for not taking the American warning too seriously. Wilson's contemporary indecisiveness toward Mexico suggested that he would be unlikely to act vigorously against Germany. Furthermore, when Colonel House, in a quest for peace terms in European capitals, came to Berlin in March, he failed to raise the issue of the submarine campaign. Instead, he talked of future German-United States cooperation to secure "freedom of the seas," giving the impression that England was the chief culprit. U-boat commanders grew careless. An American seaman died when the British steamer *Falaba* was torpedoed in March 1915, and the American tanker *Gulflight* was sunk early in May. While Washington debated on what response to make to these incidents, the submarine *U-20* on May 7 torpedoed and sank the giant Cunard liner *Lusitania*. This tragedy, which took the lives of 1,198 persons, including 128 American citizens, was a result of chance and error. The U-boat commander was homeward bound, his cruise presumably completed, when the *Lusitania* appeared in his periscope. Steaming slowly and on a straight course, in violation of the Admiralty's precautionary instructions, the big ship was a tempting target.

The sinking of the *Lusitania* brought on governmental crises in both Washington and Berlin. In Washington it led

[5] The United States proposed a compromise under which Britain should discontinue use of neutral flags and allow food for civilian use to enter Germany freely, and Germany should desist from illegal use of the submarine against merchant vessels. The proposal failed when Germany insisted that she be allowed to import raw materials as well as food.

to Bryan's resignation as Secretary of State and his replacement by Lansing. When Wilson determined to demand that Germany disavow the sinking, indemnify the sufferers or their heirs, and give guarantees against repetition, Bryan consented to sign the note embodying these demands only "with a heavy heart." Such a course, he feared, would lead to war. In order to alleviate the warlike tendency of the note he proposed that the United States express willingness to accept arbitration of Germany's liability for the sinking; that it prevent American citizens from traveling on ships carrying munitions (the *Lusitania* had carried many tons of rifle ammunition); and that it protest with equal vigor against British violation of neutral rights. When Wilson rejected Bryan's advice and reiterated his demands after an initial German evasion, Bryan resigned, June 8, 1915, and the two men parted with expressions of mutual esteem and affection. Lansing served as Secretary *ad interim* until June 23, when Wilson named him as Bryan's successor.

In Berlin the American demands produced a new struggle between the Chancellor and the Foreign Office on one side and the Admiralty on the other. Again the Chancellor won and succeeded in appeasing the United States, but only after an exchange of notes between Berlin and Washington which dragged on through the summer and into the fall of 1915. The Germans contended, with considerable logic, that enemy ships loaded with munitions of war should not be immune from submarine attack simply because a few Americans chose to travel on them. Lansing, speaking for Wilson, asserted the right of American citizens to travel in safety on peaceful Allied merchant vessels, whatever their cargo, and declared that the United States could not "consent to abate any essential or fundamental right of its people because of a mere alteration of circumstance."

The assumption by the United States of the right to protect its citizens when sailing under foreign flags was, like its later claim of immunity for defensively armed merchant-men, open to question under international law. But Wilson and Lansing adhered consistently to the former position and, except for a brief interval, to the latter.[6]

The correspondence over the *Lusitania* was interrupted by the torpedoing on August 19 of another British steamer, the White Star liner *Arabic*. Two Americans were among the dead. Wilson had already warned the Germans that a repetition of the *Lusitania* tragedy would be regarded as "deliberately unfriendly." He was now advised by both House and Lansing to break off relations with the German government. A further argument for a break was found just at this time in the dramatic exposure of the promotion of propaganda and sabotage in the United States by German agents, notably Dr. Heinrich Albert, commercial attaché, whose briefcase, loaded with incriminating documents, was snatched by a Secret Service agent on a New York elevated train.[7] A severance of relations with Germany would have been easy, and also popular in many quarters in the United States.

In this tense situation, a break was averted by the vigorous independent action of Count Johann von Bernstorff, German ambassador in Washington. Twice he went well beyond his instructions in response to American demands. On September 1 he assured Lansing in writing: "Liners will not be sunk by our submarines without warning and without safety of the lives of non-combatants, provided that the liners do not try to escape or offer resistance." This promise was in accord with the ambassador's knowledge of the latest orders

[6] On the armed merchantmen controversy see pp. 138–9.

[7] Some months later, further revelations of German and Austrian espionage and sabotage in the United States led the government to request the recall of the German military and naval attachés, von Papen and Boy-Ed, and the Austrian ambassador, Dr. Constantin Dumba. Von Papen had been involved, among other things, in an attempt to promote counterrevolution in Mexico by the exiled General Huerta.

given to submarine commanders, but he had not been au-
thorized to publicize the German retreat. A month later,
October 5, with the *Arabic* crisis again threatening a break,
Bernstorff exceeded his instructions even further, avowing to
Lansing, as he had not been empowered to do, that his
government regretted and disavowed the sinking of the
Arabic and was "prepared to pay an indemnity" for the
American lives lost on that ship. Furthermore, the ambassador declared, orders to submarine commanders had been
made so stringent "that the recurrence of incidents similar
to the *Arabic* case is considered out of the question."

The German Foreign Office did not repudiate the ambassador's assurances, although Gottlieb von Jagow, the Foreign
Minister, made it plain to Lansing that the indemnity would
be paid "out of friendly consideration" without acknowledging any legal liability.[8]

With grudging though substantial concessions from Germany to its credit, the State Department went through the
motions, at least, of demanding equivalent concessions from
Great Britain. Both House in his conversations in Berlin and
Wilson in talks with Bernstorff had spoken of a common
German-American interest in "freedom of the seas" and had
given assurances that if Germany would respect American
rights under international law, England would be pressured
to do the same. German concessions had, in fact, been
grounded on the assumption that England too would yield.
Ambassador Bernstorff assured the Foreign Office in Berlin:
"I have always stressed that we would reserve complete

[8] The German government never acknowledged the illegality of the sinking of the *Lusitania*. From November 1915 to February 1916 Lansing
persistently pressed Bethmann-Hollweg for such admission. Feeling in
Germany against further yielding to the United States was so intense
that Bethmann could not give in without precipitating his fall and the
accession of the militarists. The United States was about to accept a
watered-down acknowledgment of "liability" but not illegality when a
new crisis over armed merchantmen (see pp. 138–9) led to its rejection.

freedom of action in case England does not meet us half-way."

To carry out these commitments to Germany, and also to appease domestic resentment against the British blockade, the State Department drafted a seven thousand word note to be presented to the British government. Dated October 21, 1915, and described by pro-British Ambassador Page as "an uncourteous monster of 35 heads and 3 appendices," the note was a detailed indictment of various features of the British blockade of Germany. It described the blockade itself as "ineffective [in a legal sense], illegal, and indefensible;" and it denounced British technique in searching neutral ships as "without justification," and the procedure of British prize courts as "inherently defective for the purpose." The note sounded like an ultimatum and stirred up, when published, a storm of anti-American sentiment in England. In reality, its harsh tone was designed to impress domestic complainants and to convince Germany that the United States was acting impartially. The note was not an ultimatum; there was no threat of retaliation (such as an embargo on munitions); and Lansing was writing House: "In no event should we take a course that would seriously endanger our friendly relations with Great Britain, France, or Russia . . ."

In England, the government took the American protest more calmly than did the public. Sir Edward Grey did not reply until April 24, 1916, when the torpedoing of the *Sussex* had involved the United States in a new crisis with Germany. He then defended most of the practices complained of as justified either by American Civil War precedents or by the argument that altered circumstances require modifications in international law. The latter argument, incidentally, was the same that the Germans used in defending U-boat warfare.

The British had already, before Lansing's note, taken one

important step to quiet American criticism. Upon declaring cotton to be absolute contraband (August 19, 1915), British agencies launched a purchasing program designed to hold the price of cotton at eight to ten cents a pound, compared to the four cents to which it had dropped in the early months of the war. This went far toward quieting anti-British feeling in the South, a region with heavy influence in a Democratic administration. After the note of October 21, the British found means of reducing the long delays involved in the search of neutral ships for contraband or for other goods of "enemy destination, ownership, or origin." In other respects British practices continued as before. The United States had asserted its neutral rights impartially against both belligerents. Obviously, however, the degrees of pressure behind the assertions were not impartial.

CHAPTER X

"The Right is
More Precious than Peace"

From the time of the *Lusitania* crisis in the spring and summer of 1915, there was an evident possibility that the United States might be drawn into war with Germany. On the issue of the *Lusitania*, and the later issue of the *Arabic*, Wilson approached close to a severance of diplomatic relations, and such a breach might well have been but a prelude to war. At the close of 1915, as we shall presently see, Wilson dispatched Colonel House on a mission to Europe with authority to offer, upon certain conditions, participation by the United States in the war on the Allied side. It is not surprising, therefore, that from July 1915 onward the President was giving some thought to the means of fighting a war if the necessity arose. Wilson, in fact, not only joined but led a military preparedness movement which he had originally discouraged.

Theodore Roosevelt had sparked the movement with articles in *The Outlook* in November and December 1914. On December 1 of that year one hundred and fifty prominent citizens, meeting in New York, organized the American Security League, explicitly dedicated to preparing the nation for a possible war with Germany. Articles, books, and motion pictures, in growing numbers after the *Lusitania* sinking, called attention to the glaring military weakness of the United States, its unreadiness even for self-defense, to say nothing of participation in a war in Europe. The preparedness movement was for the most part confined to the Northeast. It had little support in the agrarian South and West and was anathema to many of the liberal leaders who supported Wilson's domestic program. It required courage, therefore, for the President to espouse a cause so alien to the thinking of great numbers of his followers.

In July 1915 Wilson requested his Secretaries of War and Navy, Lindley M. Garrison and Josephus Daniels, to recommend programs for such expansion and reorganization of the armed services as would adapt them to the needs of national security. On November 4, in a speech in New York, he supported the ambitious programs submitted by the Secretaries. When Southern and Western Democrats in the House of Representatives balked at what they considered a needless bowing to militarism, the President defended his proposals on a speaking tour in cities ranging from New York to Topeka, Kansas. He was handicapped in his appeal by being inhibited from speaking in more than guarded terms of what must have been most on his mind—possible war with Germany. He came nearest to revealing his thinking in his speech at Des Moines, February 1. "If these breaches of international law which are in daily danger of occurring should touch the very vital interests and honor of the United States," he asked, "do you wish to do nothing about it? Do you wish to have all the world say that the flag of the United States, which we love, can be stained with impunity?" Elsewhere he warned: ". . . there may at any moment come a time when I cannot preserve both the honor and the peace of the United States."

The President made few converts on the trip. Nevertheless, by exerting to the full his influence on Congress and

with ardent support in the Senate, he succeeded by the summer of 1916 in getting most of his program enacted. The
Regular Army was more than doubled; the National Guard
was increased threefold and thoroughly federalized; for the
Navy Congress provided an unprecedentedly large building
program calling for the construction within three years of
four battleships, four battle cruisers, and well over fifty
smaller craft. The principal casualty in the program was
Secretary Garrison's proposal of a Continental Army of four
hundred thousand men, to be raised by volunteering and to
replace the National Guard as the principal reserve force to
back up the Regular Army. When Wilson bowed to congressional opposition to this innovation, Garrison resigned and
was succeeded as Secretary of War by Newton D. Baker,
appointed March 7, 1916.

While Congress was battling over the preparedness program, Colonel House was engaged in an extraordinary mission to Europe. Beginning in the fall of 1914, House, with
Wilson's approval, had tried repeatedly to bring the belligerents into mutual discussion of terms of peace. His mission of
1915 to London, Paris, and Berlin was mentioned earlier.
Any faint hope of peace that House may have found on that
occasion was snuffed out by the sinking of the *Lusitania.*

By the early fall of that year House had come to believe,
and apparently had convinced Wilson, that a German victory in Europe would be a threat to the security of the
United States. He proposed, therefore, that the United States
make an effort to end the war on reasonable terms, and if
Germany rejected the overture, that the United States enter
the war on the side of the Allies; all this on the assumption
that the Allies were willing to make peace on terms that the
United States (meaning President Wilson) would deem
acceptable. As the plan took shape, it contemplated that
House should go to Europe and secure the consent of the
Allies to the proposal. That accomplished, the President

would issue a call for a peace conference. The Allies would accept. If Germany accepted and if peace resulted, well and good. If Germany refused to attend or attended and then rejected reasonable peace terms, the United States would enter the war and assist in the defeat of Germany.

This was the shape of the plan in House's mind. Wilson had reservations. In agreeing to House's proposal (October 18, 1915) he qualified with the word "probably" House's statement that if the Central Powers were obdurate "it would be necessary for us to join the Allies and force the issue." In his final instructions to House, furthermore, he indicated that if *either* side showed a willingness to discuss peace on the terms that he outlined, it would be the duty of the United States to "use our utmost *moral* force to oblige the other to parley" (italics added). Thus Wilson was willing to assume that Germany might be the party deserving American support, and in this communication at any rate he envisaged that support as moral rather than military. There was less than a perfect understanding on essential details of the plan between the President and his agent. But Wilson gave House a free hand in Europe and eventually underwrote the proposal that his envoy submitted to the British government.

Wilson named only two conditions of peace as being indispensable: a guarantee of military and naval disarmament and the creation of a league of nations to prevent aggression and maintain freedom of the seas. With the apparently reluctant consent of Sir Edward Grey, House set out on his travels in January 1916.

House divided his time between London, Paris, and Berlin. In Berlin he quickly learned that the German government was not ready to discuss peace on any terms that the Allies or the United States could accept. In Paris he exceeded his instructions in promising France American aid if it were needed to avert defeat. The crucial conversations were in London, before and after House's visit to the Continent.

In these meetings Grey and other British leaders outlined peace terms which House deemed acceptable and gave him the impression that the British government welcomed his proposal and would act upon it. The supposed understanding was set down in a memorandum initialed by Grey on February 22, 1916. This House-Grey memorandum was submitted to President Wilson for his approval. This he gave, though again as in his earlier correspondence with House, he inserted the word "probably" in a key sentence in the memorandum, making it read: "If it [the proposed peace conference] failed to secure peace, the United States would probably leave the Conference as a belligerent on the side of the Allies, if Germany was unreasonable."

House returned to Washington in March in the belief that his plan was accepted and that at a propitious time the Allies would signify that they were ready for the President to act. His summons to a peace conference would then, unless the Germans were unexpectedly conciliatory, lead to American participation in the war—all on the somewhat dubious assumption that Congress would declare war at the President's behest. As a matter of fact, if we may accept the conclusions of Arthur Link's meticulous study, the British never took House's proposals seriously. As the spokesman of the President of the most powerful neutral nation, House had to be treated with respect; his well-meant scheme could not be given a flat negative. But presumably skepticism about what the President would really do, coupled with their own and their allies' distaste for his idealistic conception of peace terms, deterred the British from acceptance. Some British and French cynics, indeed, viewed the whole enterprise as a gambit to ensure the President's reelection in November. Whatever the reason, House and Wilson waited in vain for the anticipated signal. Not until August did Grey tell House finally not to expect it.

While House was in Europe, Lansing, with Wilson's ap-

proval, made a new proposal for compromise in the submarine war. The British were arming their merchant vessels
and instructing them to attack enemy submarines either by
gunfire or by ramming. Under these circumstances, the
Germans complained, the U-boats could not surface and
give warning without risking destruction; the only safe procedure was to torpedo their victims without exposing themselves to attack. The German contention struck Lansing as
reasonable. He suggested, therefore, that the Allies should
disarm all merchant vessels and that the Germans in return
should agree not to sink such ships until after conventional
visit and search and provision for the safety of crew and passengers. Lansing added that his government was impressed
with the argument that an armed merchantman should be
treated by both neutrals and belligerents as an auxiliary
cruiser and was "seriously considering instructing its officials
accordingly."

The suggestion met such violent criticism in Allied countries, and such adverse reaction from Ambassador Page and
Colonel House in London, that Lansing withdrew it, though
continuing to insist that merchantmen armed *offensively* forfeited their right to immunity from attack. In the meantime,
however, the Germans had announced that in harmony with
the American proposal, their submarines, after February 29,
would treat all armed enemy merchantmen as ships of war—
liable, that is, to be sunk without warning. Unarmed merchantmen, Bernstorff assured Lansing, would be treated in
accordance with the promises given in connection with the
Lusitania and *Arabic*.

Wilson rejected the new German policy. When spokesmen
of the agrarian and neutralist South and West, Representative Jeff McLemore of Texas and Senator T. P. Gore of
Oklahoma, proposed that American citizens be warned not
to travel on armed ships, the President spoke out in emphatic
tones. In a letter to Senator Stone of Missouri, chairman of

the Committee on Foreign Relations, he wrote: ". . . I cannot consent to any abridgment of the rights of American citizens in any respect. The honor and self-respect of the nation is involved. . . . To forbid our people to exercise their rights for fear we might be called upon to vindicate them would be a deep humiliation indeed." The legal right of any armed merchantman to immunity from attack as a ship of war was at best open to question. Nevertheless, Wilson's strong stand, qualified by Lansing's assurance that the administration's claim pertained only to ships armed *defensively*, quelled the rebellion in Congress. The Gore and McLemore Resolutions were tabled.

On March 24, 1916, the unarmed French passenger steamer *Sussex* was torpedoed without warning in the English Channel. The ship remained afloat and made port; no American lives were lost, but several American passengers were seriously injured. The attack on the *Sussex* was, as was subsequently proved, the result of an error on the part of the U-boat commander, who with some justification mistook her for a mine-layer. Submarine commanders were still under orders not to attack liners, and the *Sussex*, though not in the liner class, was an unarmed passenger boat. The incident came at a time, however, when Bethmann-Hollweg had been forced to agree to a "sharpened" U-boat policy, which permitted enemy merchantmen (not liners) to be sunk without warning, anywhere if armed, in the war zone whether armed or not. Sinkings under these orders of British ships, with resulting death of several American crewmen, were reported within a few days of the *Sussex* incident. In American eyes they seemed to add up to a policy of unrestricted submarine warfare in glaring violation of the promises of 1915.

To both Lansing and House it seemed that the time had come to break off relations with the German government. Lansing drafted a note recalling Ambassador Gerard from Berlin and dismissing Bernstorff. But Wilson, still hoping to play a mediator's role in the war and aware of the strong anti-war spirit in Congress, resolved to give Germany one more chance to wage sea war in accordance with the rules of law and humanity. He himself composed the note that was sent to Ambassador Gerard on April 18. In temperate language it related the history of the past year's controversy over the use of the submarine and announced the conclusion reached by the United States, that use of that weapon for the destruction of an enemy's commerce was incompatible with the established principles of law and humanity. Unless the German government should immediately abandon "its present methods of submarine warfare against passenger and freight-carrying vessels," the President concluded, "the Government of the United States can have no choice but to sever diplomatic relations with the German Empire altogether."

Again Germany yielded. After days of debate between the civilian and military authorities, the Kaiser once more ruled that a break with the United States must be avoided. The Foreign Office's reply of May 4 to Wilson's ultimatum gave considerable space to indictment of Britain's illegal practices and the alleged leniency of the United States toward the Allies; but at the same time it promised that merchant vessels, both within and without the war zone, would "not be sunk without warning and without saving human lives, unless these ships attempt to escape or offer resistance." This promise, it is true, was made conditional upon Great Britain's also abandoning her illegal practices, and the note closed with a warning that unless the United States exacted equivalent concessions from Britain, the German government would reserve to itself "complete liberty of action."

Wilson, after some hesitation and upon the advice of House, accepted the German reply as meeting his demands. He rejected, however, the attempt to make the German concession contingent upon his winning concessions from Great

Britain. "Responsibility in such matters," he warned Germany, "is single, not joint; absolute, not relative."

The *Sussex* settlement marked the beginning of nine months of relatively friendly relations with the German Reich. But as relations with Germany improved, those with Great Britain worsened. It seems clear, for one thing, that Wilson felt aggrieved at Grey's ignoring of his offer to call a peace conference, with American intervention probable if the move failed to bring peace. The German response to Wilson's *Sussex* ultimatum had alluded to the German government's "readiness to make peace on a basis safeguarding Germany's vital interests." This seemed to Wilson a hint that should be followed up. He had House write Grey urgently to that effect. When this approach brought no response, Wilson used an address (May 27, 1916) to the League to Enforce Peace to expound the peace aims which Grey and other British leaders had outlined to House, including "an universal association of the nations," in which the United States would willingly participate. "The entire speech," writes Ernest R. May in *The World War and American Isolation,* "was so constructed as to draw the Allies into negotiation on the basis of the House-Grey understanding." This overture likewise was overlooked.

To this negative attitude to Wilson's invitation Britain added positive provocations. The ruthless suppression of the Easter Rebellion in Ireland, including the execution of Sir Roger Casement, was a matter wholly within British jurisdiction, but it antagonized millions of Americans. The war against German commerce, instead of being relaxed, was intensified. In the spring there was new interference with American mails. In June an order-in-council set aside all that remained of the Declaration of London. In the same month the British government published a "blacklist" of some fifteen hundred commercial firms in neutral countries, nearly one hundred of them in the United States, with which, because of their alleged business connections with the Central Powers, British subjects were forbidden to trade. No British action during the war had so deeply offended American opinion. The staunchly pro-British *New York Times* described it as "quite the most tactless, foolish, and unnecessary act of the British government during the war," and the State Department condemned the practice as "inconsistent with that true justice, sincere amity, and impartial fairness which should characterize the dealings of friendly governments with one another."

The rejection of his plan for ending the war and the harsh measures adopted during the spring and summer of 1916 shook Wilson's faith in the purposes of the Allies, particularly in their war aims. With Germany now on good behavior, Wilson reverted to that impartiality of thought which he had counseled in 1914 but from which he had been diverted by German actions on land and sea. Having won substantial concessions from Germany, he now asked and got from Congress authority to retaliate for such discriminations against American businessmen as were inherent in the British blacklist—authority which, it must be added, he never used. As Congress neared enactment of the monster naval bill in September, he remarked to House, apropos of relations with Britain: "Let us build a navy bigger than hers and do what we please."

The summer and fall of 1916 saw a decline in the influence of moderate statesmen in both Germany and England. In Germany Field Marshal Paul von Hindenburg replaced General Falkenhayn as chief of staff and brought with him General Erich Ludendorff as first quartermaster general, the two constituting the Supreme Command. Falkenhayn, earlier a supporter of Bethmann against the admirals, had reversed his position. Bethmann expected support from Hindenburg, but he and Ludendorff soon joined the advocates of unrestricted submarine warfare. At the same time Bethmann's support in the Reichstag was dwindling. It was clear that he could not long hold Germany to the policy of the *Sussex* note.

For Wilson a return to unrestricted submarine warfare, abandonment of the *Sussex* policy, would mean either severance of diplomatic relations with Germany (with probable war to follow), or a humiliating retreat from the position taken in the *Sussex* ultimatum. Reelected in November in a campaign in which the popular Democratic slogan was "He kept us out of war," Wilson would find the choice a distressing one. The only way to avoid the dilemma would be to end the war, and, even before his reelection, Wilson was again contemplating a move for peace, though now from a neutral rather than a pro-Allied position. He was encouraged, in fact urged, by Bethmann-Hollweg, who was as anxious as Wilson to end the war before it involved the United States.

But a new obstacle to peace was the ebbing of moderate statesmanship in England. Grey, like Bethmann, was succumbing to extremist pressure and would soon retire. David Lloyd George, destined to become Prime Minister in December, had succeeded General Lord Kitchener as War Minister in the Asquith cabinet, upon Kitchener's death in a sea tragedy. In an interview with an American correspondent on September 28, 1916, he declared that the fight with Germany "must be to the finish—to a knockout. The whole world," he continued, "including neutrals of the highest purposes and humanitarians with the best motives, must know that there can be no outside interference at this stage." The allusion to the United States and to Wilson was unmistakable. Though the words perhaps needed not to be taken literally, they nevertheless portended difficulty for the would-be peacemaker.

Beginning in September 1916, Bethmann-Hollweg, and even the Kaiser, pressed Wilson to call for a peace conference, warning that if peace were not made soon, Germany must resume the "liberty of action" reserved in the *Sussex* note. Wilson thought it inexpedient to make such a move before the November election. He was also advised against it by Colonel House, who feared, as did Lansing, that it might produce a rift with the Allies. Though not persuaded by these arguments, the President procrastinated further, as a consequence of illness and preoccupation with post-election patronage problems. He delayed until the Germans, tired of waiting, took the initiative themselves. German armies had been repulsed in their costly attempt to take the French fortress of Verdun. On the other hand, they had won a quick and complete victory over Rumania, which had rashly entered the war in August. Bucharest fell December 6. The Germans had also won impressive victories against Russia and had repulsed an Allied offensive on the Somme. Holding, as they believed, good cards, they were ready for a game at the conference table. On December 12 they announced their readiness to meet their opponents to discuss terms for peace.

The Allies eventually rejected the German invitation in indignant language. Meanwhile Wilson, taken aback by the German initiative, altered his plan. Instead of the contemplated call for a peace conference with its intimation that the United States might align itself with the side that showed itself more cooperative, he merely invited both belligerent groups to state their peace terms. Both camps, he observed, in notes of December 18, professed to be fighting for similar ends. If both would specify what those ends were, perhaps they would prove to be "not so irreconcilable as some have feared. . . . It may be that peace is nearer than we know," said the President, with a show of optimism.

At this point, if we accept Arthur Link's persuasive interpretation, Secretary Lansing intervened clandestinely to sabotage the peace plans of his chief. Convinced that German autocracy and militarism must be crushed, he opposed any compromise peace and apparently believed it essential that the United States should come to the aid of the Allies. After a public hint that the United States was on the brink of war had been rebuked by the President, Lansing held confidential interviews with the French and British ambassadors. He assured them of American sympathy in their struggle with Germany. He then suggested that in replying to Wilson's request for a statement of war aims, "they were free [in Link's words] to draw up their most extreme demands as they saw fit." Such a response, presumably, would end peace talk, ensure Germany's resumption of unrestricted submarine warfare, and bring the United States into the war as a partner of the Allies.[1]

The German government, in answer to Wilson's request, declined to state its terms, declaring its preference for "a direct exchange of views" with its antagonists. The Allies, in their reply of January 10, 1917, listed terms which by either design or coincidence, were nearly identical with those that Lansing had suggested. They would have meant the return of Alsace-Lorraine to France, the dismemberment of Austria-Hungary and Turkey, expulsion of the latter from Europe, and the saddling of an indefinite amount of indemnities upon the Central Powers. That the Allies considered these ends attainable only by complete victory was implicit in the final paragraph of the note, in which they expressed their joint determination to bring the conflict to a victorious close.

The President, if we may believe Bernstorff's report of a confidential conversation with House, considered the Allies' terms "impossible of acceptance" and actually "a bluff." He was evidently confident that under such pressure as he could apply they would take much less. He challenged their underlying assumption in his famous address to the Senate on Jan-

[1] Arthur S. Link, *Wilson* [V]: *Campaigns for Progressivism and Peace* (Princeton, 1965), pp. 221–225.

uary 22, 1917. A peace that America could support, he declared, must be "a peace without victory." His other specifications called for recognition of the equality of all nations, acceptance of the principle "that governments derive their just powers from the consent of the governed," provision of an outlet to the sea for every great people, freedom of the seas, and a general reduction of armaments. Could peace be made on such terms, said Wilson, the United States would be ready to join with other nations in "formal and solemn adherence to a League for Peace."

Four days later occurred the conversation between House and Bernstorff in which the colonel represented Wilson as considering the Allies' terms "a bluff." If Germany would now submit terms "of a moderate nature," the President hoped that he could bring about a peace conference "at such an early date that unnecessary bloodshed in the spring offensive would be avoided."

Bernstorff urged his government to meet Wilson's wishes and to postpone the launching of unrestricted submarine warfare, which as the ambassador had been confidentially informed on January 19, was scheduled for February 1. The last hope for peace now rested with the German authorities. Had Germany consented to defer the submarine campaign and to submit moderate peace terms, Wilson was ready, it seems clear, to put pressure on the Allies to consent to a conference; and so great was their dependence upon the United States, for supplies and especially for credit, that they could hardly have refused to engage in peace discussions or to qualify their extravagant demands. Bethmann, indeed, hastened to Imperial Headquarters at Pless to make a final plea for acceptance of Wilson's proposals. But the Kaiser had made his decision and brushed off the Chancellor's entreaty with annoyance. There was to be no turning back. Bernstorff, therefore, notified Lansing on January 31 that beginning on the following day all ships encountered in the war zone would be sunk, with the exception of neutral ships that had sailed prior to the announcement. Provision would also be made for the safety of one American passenger steamer each week to and from the English port of Falmouth. At the same time the ambassador handed the Secretary confidentially a summary of the terms that Germany and her allies *would have* asked if the proposed conference had met. They amounted to a return to the *status quo ante bellum* with certain deviations in Germany's favor and provision for "indemnification of German undertakings and private persons who have been injured by the war."

Unless he were to repudiate the unequivocal threat in his *Sussex* note, Wilson now had no choice but to sever diplomatic relations with Germany. Yet Wilson hesitated. He had promised Senator Stone, chairman of the Foreign Relations Committee, that he would consult him before taking any drastic action. While he waited for Stone to return from Missouri, he weighed the question of whether he should break relations on the basis of the German declaration of policy alone or await an overt act against an American ship. He would have been willing, believes Arthur Link, to let Germany have her way with armed merchantmen, even with unarmed belligerent merchantmen, so long as they were not passenger ships. Such was his deep anxiety to avoid war. But the German announcement made no exceptions. Armed and unarmed, belligerent and neutral, all ships encountered in the war zone were to be sunk without warning. This relentless character of the German declaration was stressed by the Senators with whom Wilson talked after Stone's return. With two exceptions, they urged an immediate break in relations. This step the President took on February 3.

And yet Wilson still hoped to avoid war—a war which, he said to Lansing, might mean the destruction of "white civilization." Perhaps Germany, seeing that Wilson's threats were not empty, would refrain from carrying out her ruthless policy. Perhaps Austria-Hungary, if she could be guaranteed against dismemberment, would agree to make a separate peace. All such hopes proved vain. The Austrian government had already endorsed the German U-boat policy. The young Emperor, Karl, who had succeeded the aged Franz Josef upon the latter's death, was anxious for peace. But the Vienna Foreign Office replied to American secret inquiries that Austria could negotiate only in conjunction with her allies. In Germany, the Supreme Command had weighed the danger of war with the United States and had convinced itself that it had nothing to fear from such a war: the expanded U-boat fleet would bring England to submission and the war to an end before an ill-prepared America could mobilize. Sinkings began at once, without regard for unarmed ships or for neutral flags.

Wilson asked Congress for authority to arm American ships for defense and to take other defensive measures. "A little group of willful men," as Wilson termed them, defeated the proposal by a Senate filibuster in the closing days of the Sixty-fourth Congress, but Wilson's legal advisers discovered that the President already had the authority he needed. He announced on March 9 that American ships were being armed with naval guns.

In the meantime Wilson's indignation against the German government had been newly aroused by revelation of a German attempt to involve the United States in war with Mexico. British intelligence had intercepted and decoded an instruction of January 16 from German Foreign Secretary Arthur Zimmermann to the German minister in Mexico. The minister was to inform the Mexican President of the impending change in submarine policy and to propose that, if the United States responded by going to war, Mexico should ally herself with Germany against the United States. Germany would provide "generous financial support" for the reconquest by Mexico of "the lost territory in Texas, New

Mexico, and Arizona." The note suggested, further, that Mexico seek to detach Japan from the Allies and to bring her into alliance with Mexico and Germany.[2]

The Zimmermann telegram enraged Wilson, not only because of its content but perhaps even more because Zimmermann had taken advantage of American courtesy to send it—as one of three routes—over the State Department cable from Berlin to Bernstorff in Washington. The whole transaction, instituted at a time when the President was making every effort to bring about peace in Europe, blackened the German image in Wilson's mind and went far to convince him that war was necessary. He promptly gave the note to the press. Its publication raised a country-wide storm of indignation; in particular, it aroused the Southwest —hitherto lukewarm on the submarine issue—against a Germany that proposed to hand it back to Mexico. The Zimmermann telegram and the death of two American women when a U-boat sank the Cunard liner *Laconia*, February 25, contributed to a swelling popular conviction that war was inevitable.

For a week, March 12 to 19, Wilson secluded himself in the White House, debating inwardly whether to maintain the status of armed neutrality already adopted or to proceed to outright war with Germany. Precisely what reasoning led him to decide on the second course we shall never know, for he left no definite clues to his thinking in this Gethsemane period. For two years or more, advisers like House and Lansing had argued that a German victory, destroying the bal-

---

[2] The real author of the Zimmermann telegram was one von Kemnitz, Latin American specialist in the German Foreign Office. The idea, however, had its origin in Mexico. In November 1916 Carranza had proposed that Mexico and Germany cooperate and had actually offered to provide Mexican bases for German U-boats. The proposal was declined on that occasion, but after the German government decided upon unrestricted submarine warfare, von Kemnitz drew up the telegram and persuaded Zimmermann to send it. See Link, *op. cit.*, pp. 433–436.

ance of power and constituting a triumph for the forces of authoritarianism and militarism, would endanger not only American security but the cause of free government throughout the world. Wilson rarely talked in such terms. He certainly did not contemplate the possibility of a German victory with equanimity. But on the basis of his knowledge in March 1917 a German victory was no immediate threat. His preference was still for a "peace without victory." But since Germany had blocked the road to a negotiated peace, the next best hope was to shorten the war through American participation on the Allied side. Trusting the aims of neither camp, he had found the ruthlessness and deception of the German government more obnoxious than any traits displayed by the Allies. The Allied image, furthermore, was now suddenly brightened by the overthrow of the Russian Czar and the creation of a provisional government that seemed destined to make Russia one among the democratic states—"a fit partner for a League of Honor," as Wilson was to say in his war message.[3] American participation, furthermore, would not only shorten the war; it would give America—and Wilson—a voice at the peace conference and an opportunity to shape the peace in a Wilsonian mold.

Yet it is difficult to believe that Wilson, hating war with an intensity that neither House nor Lansing shared, would have brought himself to recommend American participation on such rational and idealistic grounds alone. The submarine war, after all, was a challenge, a defiance, to Wilson and to the United States. This aspect of the matter was brought vividly to his and the country's attention on March 18 by reports of the sinking of three American freighters, two without warning, and the death by drowning of fifteen American

[3] A useful analysis of the voluminous literature on the reasons for America's entry into World War I is Daniel M. Smith, "National Interest and American Intervention, 1917: An Historiographical Appraisal," *Journal of American History*, LII, 5–24 (June 1965).

crewmen. After this there could be no doubt of Germany's complete repudiation of the *Sussex* pledge. Speaking for the United States in 1916, the President had said his country would not accept this violation of international law and the laws of humanity. He had committed the prestige, the honor, of the United States to resisting what, in his mind, was a great wrong. To stand aside, or to take only half measures, now that the wrong was made deliberate policy, would compromise the prestige of the American government, at home and abroad. A time might come, he had warned a year before, "when I cannot preserve both the honor and the peace of the United States." That time had come, and the President chose to preserve honor at the expense of peace.

Wilson emerged from his week of seclusion and on March 20 held a meeting of his cabinet. Any doubt that lingered in his own mind must have been dispelled when he found the cabinet, even its formerly pacifist members, unanimous for war. Promptly he called Congress to meet, April 2, and on that day delivered his well-known address asking Congress to accept the status of belligerent thrust upon the nation by act of Germany. Describing German submarine warfare as "a warfare against mankind," the President called upon the nation "to exert all its power and employ all its resources to bring the Government of the German Empire to terms and end the war." But that was not enough, and the idealistic President went on to enumerate the more positive ends for which Americans would fight and shed their blood: "for democracy, for the right of those who submit to authority to have a voice in their own governments, for the rights and liberties of small nations, for a universal dominion of right by such a concert of free peoples as shall bring peace and safety to all nations and make the world itself at last free."

Congress responded on April 6, 1917, with a declaration "that the state of war . . . which has been thrust upon the United States is hereby formally declared."

CHAPTER XI

Wartime Diplomacy

The United States had declared war on Germany alone. It was not at war, and had no wish to be, with Germany's allies. Of these, Austria-Hungary and Turkey severed diplomatic relations with Washington but did not declare war. Bulgaria did not even break relations. In December 1917, after Italy's military disaster at Caporetto, Wilson was advised that an American declaration of war against Austria would bolster sinking Italian morale. Upon the President's recommendation Congress passed a war resolution on December 7. Pleas from American educational and religious groups with schools and missions in Turkey and Bulgaria persuaded the President to omit these states from his proposal to extend the war. Hence the United States remained at peace with Turkey and Bulgaria and even maintained formal diplomatic relations with the latter. Though at war with Austria-Hungary after December 1917, the United States only slowly abandoned hope of persuading the Vienna government to desert Berlin and make a separate peace.

Having gone to war in defense of neutral rights and for the preservation of democracy, the United States hoped that states with similar interests, especially the nations of Latin

America, would follow its example. The Department of State, indeed, attempted to bring about a Pan-American united front against Germany. But in Latin America there was no unanimity of sentiment toward the belligerents. Violation of neutral rights caused less concern than in the United States. While culture and tradition in the main favored the Allies, especially France, there were in some of the countries influential groups of German blood and a German tradition in military circles. Furthermore, though Wilson's gestures of friendship to Latin America had done something to check the "Yankeephobia" induced by United States assumption of guardianship over its neighbors, distrust of the "Colossus of the North" still persisted, especially in Colombia and Mexico.

Pulled both ways by these conflicting forces, the Latin American states separated into three groups. Brazil, traditionally friendly to the United States despite a large German minority, declared war against Germany and sent a squadron of destroyers to the Mediterranean. All the small states of the Caribbean and Central America (except El Salvador)—five of them American protectorates and one under American military rule—also declared war but made no tangible contribution to the cause. A second group—Bolivia, Ecuador, Peru, and Uruguay—lent moral support by breaking off diplomatic relations with Germany. The other seven states of the twenty—Argentina, Chile, Colombia, El Salvador, Mexico, Paraguay, and Venezuela—remained neutral. Of these only Argentina and Mexico displayed an attitude otherwise than benevolent toward the United States and the Allies, and in Argentina it was the President, Hipólito Irigoyen, rather than Parliament or the public, who took a critical view of the Allied cause. His attempt to organize a Latin American "third force," to act wholly independently of the United States, met with no encouragement except from Mexico.

Of all the states of the hemisphere only Mexico gave Washington real cause for concern during the war years. Here, in the fertile soil left by the recent friction with Wilson's government, German agents were busy attempting to make trouble for the United States. The climax of the German bid for Mexican support was the Zimmermann note of January 1917 promising a return of Mexico's lost territories if Mexico would ally herself with Germany. Though Carranza had earlier suggested Mexican-German cooperation, the Zimmermann proposal came at a time when the worst crisis in his relations with the United States was being liquidated. He made no response to Zimmermann and rejected a similar approach made four months later by an agent of the German general staff. Carranza's attitude to the United States, however, remained cool throughout the war. His threats to nationalize the property of foreign oil companies and his drastic regulation of their business caused concern north of the border. The oil companies and the Navy, which was largely dependent on Mexican oil for fuel, called for intervention on their behalf. But Wilson, relieved at having recalled Pershing's troops from Mexico, had no notion of sending them back. The oil companies were left to defend their interests as best they could in the Mexican courts.

In 1916 the United States strengthened its control of the Caribbean by purchasing from Denmark the three small islands of St. Thomas, St. John, and St. Croix, situated east and southeast of Puerto Rico. Previous negotiations for the acquisition of these Danish West Indies had been frustrated in 1867 by the United States Senate, and in 1902 by the upper house of the Danish Parliament. Purchased now at a generous price of twenty-five million dollars and known henceforth as the Virgin Islands of the United States, they gave the United States the fine harbor of Charlotte Amalie (useful only for small ships by modern standards) and assurance that no rival power would appropriate their facilities.

One of the powers with which the United States became "associated" in entering the war was Japan. The Japanese, as related elsewhere, had made war upon Germany in pursuit of their own expansionist objectives. They had quickly subdued the Germans at Kiaochow and taken over German holdings in China's Shantung province. With even greater ease they had seized the three groups of German-owned islands in the North Pacific—the Carolines, Marianas, and Marshalls. By secret treaties of 1916 and 1917 the European Allies consented to Japan's retention of these conquests after the war. They were the more ready to do so because of Japan's confidential revelation that Germany was willing to concede title to these possessions to Japan if the Japanese would desert their allies and make a separate peace.

Japan next sought to take advantage of Europe's preoccupation at home by riveting chains on China. Early in 1913, the Wilson administration had unwisely encouraged the American banking group to withdraw from the six-power consortium on the ground that the terms of the proposed loan to China might infringe upon China's sovereignty.[1] The American withdrawal and the outbreak of war in Europe had left China very much at Japan's mercy in her need for funds. These were supplied in small amounts in loans at the price of new concessions. Japan went still further. In a proposal known as the Twenty-one Demands presented to President Yüan Shih-K'ai in January 1915, the Japanese asked for a variety of economic privileges in Manchuria, Inner Mongolia, and elsewhere in China, and for military and policing rights that would have reduced China to the status of a protectorate.

These demands, though presented secretly to the Chinese,

[1] See pp. 84–85.

were leaked by them to the United States, the only power from which any support might be hoped for. The United States responded in two notes from Secretary of State Bryan. In the first (March 13, 1915) the Secretary acknowledged "that territorial contiguity creates special relations between Japan" and neighboring areas on the Chinese mainland. Two months later, alarmed by further evidence of Japan's aggressive purposes and their threat to American policy and American interests in China, Bryan dispatched identical notes (May 11, 1915) to the two antagonists, serving notice on both that the United States would not recognize any agreement between the two which impaired American rights in China, the political or territorial integrity of China, or the principle of the open door. Public exposure of her aggressive designs, Chinese resistance, and American opposition induced Japan to abandon—temporarily, she indicated—the most obnoxious (Group V) of her demands, while China bowed to most of the remainder.

After the United States entered the war, the Japanese government sent Viscount Kikujiro Ishii on a special mission to Washington to seek an understanding with regard to China. By an exchange of notes with Secretary Lansing—the Lansing-Ishii agreement, November 2, 1917—Ishii secured acknowledgment by the United States that Japan had "special interests" in China, based upon "territorial propinquity," while Ishii paid lip service to the territorial integrity of China and the principle of the open door. By a secret protocol the two governments agreed not to take advantage of war conditions "to seek special rights or privileges in China which would abridge the right of the subjects or citizens of other friendly states." It seems clear that the United States had been persuaded to weaken its pro-China policy by discreet hints from Ishii that continuation of Japan's commitment to the Allies in the war might be dependent upon her realizing her ambitions in the Far East. Japan had played a shrewd diplomatic game, using hints of a deal with Germany to exact recognition of her claims from the Allies and of her "special interests" in China from the United States.[2]

One who compares American diplomacy in the two world wars notes at once a striking difference in the relations of the United States with its European associates in the two conflicts. With no European leader in the earlier war did Wilson enter into the camaraderie that was to distinguish the relationship of Franklin Roosevelt and Winston Churchill. Wilson the introvert was temperamentally the opposite of Roosevelt, and even had he been a more outgoing type, he would have found little congeniality in Lloyd George, the supreme opportunist. Wilson attended no summit meetings (until the peace conference). The day of handy trans-Atlantic telephones was not yet; nor was there between Wilson and his contemporaries anything resembling the intimate correspondence that F.D.R. conducted with a "former naval person."

Nor were the regular diplomatic channels conducive to sympathetic Anglo-American understanding. Walter Hines Page, American ambassador in London, had forfeited Wilson's confidence by his extreme Anglophilism. Sir Cecil Spring Rice, once the intimate of Theodore Roosevelt and now British ambassador in Washington, still found his friends and his ideas in Roosevelt's circle and was far from being *en rapport* with a Democratic administration. Both governments were aware of this flaw in their communica-

[2] Wilson, like Theodore Roosevelt before him (see pp. 62–64), found an obstacle to cordial relations with Japan in racial prejudice in the states of the West Coast. Roosevelt had been able to appease Japan in the San Francisco school crisis and had later dissuaded the California legislature from discriminating against Japanese in the ownership of land. Wilson was less successful. Despite his efforts, and those of secretary Bryan, the California legislature in 1913 prohibited ownership of land by "aliens ineligible for citizenship," that is, Japanese and other Asiatics. The Japanese ambassador's protest was so vigorous that Wilson alerted the Army and Navy against possible armed retaliation.

tions. To fill the gap, the British, at Wilson's suggestion, delegated responsibility to a friendly and informal young intelligence officer, Sir William Wiseman, who took an apartment near that of Colonel House in New York. Wiseman was in close touch with the Foreign Office, House had a direct telephone line to the White House, and as the two saw each other daily, they were able to iron out many points of friction without benefit of the State Department or either embassy.

But at best there was mutual suspicion between Wilson and the Allied leaders. Britons especially had long resented what they thought Wilson's blindness to the moral superiority of their case against Germany. Now that he had joined them, they distrusted what seemed to them his vague idealism. Wilson, on his part, was informed by Foreign Secretary Arthur Balfour himself of the secret treaties by which the Allies had agreed to the sharing among themselves of strategic parcels of enemy territory, once the war should have been won. Both the President and Secretary of State Lansing were suspicious of Allied motives as "imperialistic" and were anxious to counter them as far as might be possible.

Such suspicion may have fortified the traditional American prejudice against "entangling alliances." Whatever the reason, Wilson repeatedly made it plain that the United States was not an *ally* of the other powers at war with Germany. It was an associate only. "The principal allied and associated powers" was the awkward phrase used to denote the grouping of the United States and its major European partners and Japan. In World War I there was no counterpart of the Declaration by United Nations of 1942.

In such cooperative machinery as was created to direct the conduct of the war in Europe, the United States participated willingly in military matters, reluctantly and irregularly at the political level. Meeting at Rapallo, Italy, on November 7, 1917, the British, French, and Italian Premiers agreed to set up a Supreme War Council to meet regularly in Versailles. The body would consist of the Premiers, together with one additional member of each government, and there would be military and other technical advisers. This attempt to coordinate the war effort in Europe was the Allied response to the crushing Italian defeat at Caporetto late in October. It coincided with another disaster to the Allies. On November 7, the day of the agreement at Rapallo, the Russian Bolsheviki seized power in Petrograd, portending the complete withdrawal of Russia from the war. It was high time for the Allies, and the United States, to pool their resources and coordinate their military undertakings.

The creation of the Supreme War Council initially had the wholehearted approval of President Wilson and his advisers. The United States was already making available its material resources and its credit for the common military effort and was in process of building an army of four million men for service in France. Wilson not only favored the establishment of the Supreme War Council; he advocated the creation of a unified command of the armies on the Western Front—a step finally taken in April and May 1918, following the initial success of the German spring offensive of that year.

There were, however, limits to Wilson's cooperation. General Tasker H. Bliss met regularly with the other military advisers of the council, but on only two occasions was the United States represented in the council itself. The President, as head of government, would have been the proper opposite number to the European Premiers. His own attendance was hardly feasible, but only at the Supreme War Council's first meeting in December 1917 and at its sessions in October and November 1918 (when armistice terms were up for discussion) did he deputize Colonel House to represent him. At the first of these meetings (December 1917) House pleaded with the Premiers for issuance of a liberal joint statement on war aims, hoping that such a statement might appeal to the Bolsheviki and dissuade them from making a separate peace. The Premiers refused. Thereafter, for ten months, Wilson, in effect, boycotted the council. He feared, apparently, that participation in such a political body might imply acceptance of war aims with which he could not agree and over which he preferred not to argue while there was fighting to be done.

General Bliss, tactful and conciliatory, got on well with the other military advisers to the council, even though he had sometimes to disagree with them. Here the principal controversy was over the method of utilizing American military man power. The Allies, desperate for men to face the series of formidable German drives in the spring of 1918, wished to amalgamate the inexperienced American troops with the British and French veterans, thus making their weight count as soon as possible. General Pershing, commander of the AEF (American Expeditionary Force), insisted on holding back his troops until they were ready to be thrown into the conflict as a distinct American army. He had the backing of Secretary of War Baker, of Wilson, and necessarily of General Bliss, though the latter was much more sympathetic to the Allied point of view than was the stubborn AEF commander. With minor exceptions, Pershing had his way, though at the cost of considerable criticism and ill will.

An issue of serious concern to the United States which from time to time came before the Supreme War Council was the proposal for Allied intervention in Soviet Russia. But before that issue arose, many things had happened in the former domain of the Czars.

The well-intentioned provisional government, which the United States had welcomed into a "league of honor" after the Czar's downfall in March 1917, endured barely eight months. The United States had sought to sustain it with sympathy and material aid. In July Wilson sent to Russia a mission headed by Republican statesman Elihu Root, to convey a message of good will from the American people and to ascertain Russia's most urgent needs for continuation of the war against the common enemy. Another mission headed by engineer John F. Stevens undertook to assist in rehabilitating Russia's disintegrating railway system.

The Root mission, spending too much of its time in banquets and oratorical exchanges, failed to sense the desperate war weariness, the seething popular discontent, and the bitter class and partisan antagonisms, which militated against political stability in Russia and especially against continuance of the war. It reported optimistically to Washington and recommended credits to the provisional government, which were granted to the amount of three hundred and twenty-five million dollars. The grant of credit was on the assumption that Russia would continue fighting. Insistence on this course by the United States and the Western Allies, as George F. Kennan has observed, restrained the provisional government from the one course that might have prevented its overthrow—the making of an early peace.

Alexander Kerensky, member of the relatively moderate Socialist Revolutionary party, took over the premiership in the provisional government from Prince Lvov in July. As Minister of War, he had kept faith with the Allies by launching a new offensive against Austria, only to see his armies thrown back after initial successes. Now the armies were disintegrating, and the radical Bolsheviki, led by the returned exiles Lenin and Trotsky, were successfully playing upon popular hunger for peace and bread. On November 7 their well-organized bands seized power in Petrograd. Their control, exercised through councils (soviets) of workers, peasants, and soldiers, was quickly extended over much of European Russia.

The Soviet government (as it now came to be called) at once issued a "Decree of Peace." This document proposed to the people and governments of all the belligerent nations an immediate armistice and the opening of negotiations for a "just and democratic peace," a peace without annexations or indemnities. It declared in favor of universal self-determination of peoples. It repudiated the imperialistic policies of former Russian regimes and promised publication of secret treaties "concluded or confirmed" by the provisional government. In a special appeal to "the class conscious workers" of England, France, and Germany, it suggested that their role was not only "the liberation of humanity from the horrors of war," but also "the liberation of the laboring and exploited" classes from capitalist oppression. The Decree of Peace was followed within a few days by communications to all the belligerent governments formally proposing negotiations for an armistice and a "democratic peace without annexations and indemnities, and on the basis of self-determination of nations." December 2 was later named as the day on which the armistice negotiations should begin.

A "separate peace" was not the chosen objective of the Soviet leaders. They hoped that the workers in the other belligerent states would heed the Russian appeal and would compel their governments to join in the quest for peace. But nothing of the sort happened. The workers did not rise, and only the governments of the Central Powers responded to the proposal for negotiations. These were begun at Brest-Litovsk early in December 1917, and an armistice agreement between Russia, Germany, and Austria-Hungary was signed on December 15.

But an armistice was not a peace, and until peace was actually made, hope lingered in the West that Russia might be induced to remain in the war. Otherwise, as many as a million German troops might be shifted from Russia to bolster the spring offensive in France.

To Americans like House and Wilson, the most promising

means of winning the cooperation of the Soviets seemed to be acceptance of Soviet war aims—a peace without annexation or indemnities. To the United States this meant no sacrifice, but when House proposed it to the Supreme War Council in December, he got a flat no. England might perhaps renounce expansionist aims, but France and Italy would not forego the booty promised them in the secret treaties. Wilson, consequently, resolved to issue a unilateral statement of the war aims of the United States. This he did in the famous Fourteen Points address to Congress of January 8, 1918.[3]

The Fourteen Points address, one of Wilson's most important pronouncements, was prepared without consultation with the State Department but in collaboration with Colonel House and with the benefit of suggestions from the Inquiry, a group of scholars organized under House's direction for the purpose of formulating American objectives in the war. Various features of the address will be touched upon elsewhere. Those relating to Russia included an introductory passage, in which the President praised the Russian objectives then under discussion with the Germans at Brest-Litovsk, and Point VI, dealing specifically with Russia. Point VI called for the evacuation of all occupied Russian territory and a sincere welcome of Russia "into the society of free nations under institutions of her own choosing."

> The treatment accorded Russia by her sister nations in the months to come [the President added] will be the acid test of their good will, of their comprehension of her needs as distinguished from their own interests, and of their intelligent and unselfish sympathy.

[3] See Appendix for excerpts from the Fourteen Points address. The address was really a characteristic Wilsonian appeal to peoples over the heads of their governments—the Russians, the Germans, and a group of prominent "radicals" in England with whom Wilson and House had maintained informal contacts.

Wilson's address had no effect upon the Soviet-German peace negotiations, which went on with several interruptions from December 1917 until March 3, 1918, when the treaty of Brest-Litovsk was signed. While its ratification by the Congress of Soviets was still pending, Wilson dispatched (March 11, 1918) a message to the Russian people, which some of his advisers thought might strengthen the hands of opponents of the treaty. Regretting the inability of the United States to help the people of Russia in the current crisis with Germany, the President assured them nevertheless that the United States would do everything in its power to bring about Russia's "full restoration to her great rôle in the life of Europe and the modern world." His closing assurance of American sympathy with the people of Russia "in the attempt to free themselves forever from autocratic government and become the masters of their own life," showed a naïve misapprehension of the course the Revolution had taken under the Bolsheviki.

The response of the Congress of Soviets to Wilson's message was, first, to ratify the treaty and thus formally withdraw Russia from the war; second, to thank especially "the laboring and exploited classes of the United States" for the President's expression of sympathy and to assure them "that the happy time is not far distant when the laboring masses of all countries will throw off the yoke of capitalism and will establish a socialistic state of society. . . ." "We slapped the President of the United States in the face," boasted one of the Soviet leaders.[4]

---

[4] A few days before ratification of the treaty by the Congress of Soviets, Leon Trotsky, Commissar for Foreign Affairs, inquired of British and American agents in Moscow what aid Russia might expect from the West if she resumed the war with Germany. Transmission of the inquiry to Washington was bungled, and it was not received until after the treaty was ratified. Raymond Robins of the American Red Cross, who enjoyed friendly relations with Lenin and Trotsky, believed that a prompt and affirmative reply to the inquiry might have kept Russia in the war. George

Neither the United States nor any of its European associates had recognized the Soviet government. That much had been agreed upon at the Supreme War Council meeting, which House attended, in December 1917. But the American ambassador, David R. Francis, did not at once leave Russia. First at Petrograd and later at Vologda, when the Soviet government moved to Moscow, he chose to remain as a symbol of American good will to the Russian people. He had, of course, no official relations with the Soviet leaders; yet, eventually with the approval of the State Department, he kept in touch with those leaders through unofficial agents, of whom the most important was Colonel Raymond Robins, head of an American Red Cross unit in Russia. Robins, who developed friendly relations with Lenin and Trotsky, continued to urge some measure of cooperation with them until he was called home in May 1918. His views were shared by similar informal agents of the British and French. The landing of American troops at Vladivostok and Archangel in August and September 1918 ended even such informal relations between Moscow and Washington. The infuriated Russians incarcerated some of the Allied personnel remaining in Moscow and eventually expelled all. Ambassador Francis had withdrawn in July.

Wilson had sanctioned the landing of American troops on Russian soil only after prolonged argument with the British and French governments. From December 1917 to July 1918 he was repeatedly importuned to consent to the dispatching of Japanese troops into eastern Siberia through Vladivostok. The plan was initially related to a suspicion in Paris and London that the Bolshevik leaders were actually German

---

Kennan shows that this thesis is not tenable. Lenin, who was in control of the situation, never wavered in his insistence that the treaty must be ratified. George F. Kennan, *Russia Leaves the War (Soviet-American Relations, 1917–1920,* Vol. I, Princeton: Princeton University Press, 1956), pp. 497–516.

agents and might make available to the Germans the material resources of all Russia, as well as great quantities of
war material that had accumulated at Vladivostok and at
Archangel on the White Sea. It was feared, too, that large
numbers of German and Austro-Hungarian prisoners of war,
held in Russia and liberated after the signing of the Brest-
Litovsk treaty, would assist in taking over the country for
the Central Powers. (Actually only about ten per cent of
the prisoners were German, and neither they nor those from
the Dual Monarchy were made instruments of any aggressive design.)

With these defensive motives there merged the hope of
reestablishing an Eastern military front against the Germans
and thus easing the pressure on the front in France. It was
even hoped for a while, at least by such agents as Raymond
Robins, that the Soviets might consent to renew the war with
aid from the Western Allies and the Japanese. This latter
hope disappeared after the Congress of Soviets ratified the
treaty with the Central Powers, but in its place there grew
the dream of joining with anti-Bolshevik ("White" vs.
"Red") Russian elements to overthrow the Soviet regime and
replace it with one that would renew the war.

As early as December 1917, Paris and London had agreed
secretly to subsidize anti-Bolshevik groups in southern
Russia. Those plans had failed, but in the spring prospects
seemed better in eastern Siberia, where certain Cossack generals were fighting the Soviets. Hopes were further bolstered
when some sixty thousand Czechoslovak troops, seeking to
leave Russia by way of the Trans-Siberian Railway and
Vladivostok, drifted into hostilities with the Soviets. The
"Czechoslovak legion," made up of former war prisoners
from Austria-Hungary plus some Czechs or Slovaks who
were Russian subjects, remained intact when the Russian
armies disintegrated. It was the original desire of the French
government and of the Czechoslovak National Council (a

would-be government-in-exile in Paris) that the legion
should be conveyed via Vladivostok to Europe to join the
battle on the Western Front. The Soviets had consented, but
the agreement had broken down over the question of dis-
arming the troops in transit. A portion of the Czechoslovaks
then seized the Trans-Siberian Railway from the Urals to
Irkutsk. Here their progress was blocked, and they were cut
off from some fifteen thousand of their comrades who had
already reached Vladivostok.

It was now proposed by the Supreme War Council that
the beleaguered Czechs west of Irkutsk, instead of fighting
their way to Vladivostok, should join with Russian White
elements and link up with Allied troops to be landed at
Archangel, forming an anti-Bolshevik front from the White
Sea to the Black, and that this front be supported by Japanese troops who would land at Vladivostok and push west
along the railway. A few British troops had already landed
at Murmansk, on the Arctic coast northwest of Archangel.
The landing had been made at the request of the local soviet
when Murmansk appeared to be threatened with invasion by
Germans and pro-German Finns, engaged in an ideological
civil war in Finland. This arrangement originally had the
assent of Soviet Foreign Commissar Trotsky, but by May
1918 the Moscow government was demanding the expulsion
of the British and on June 30 broke completely with the
Murmansk soviet, which continued to cooperate with the
invaders. With a beachhead thus established at Murmansk,
the next step in the program was to seize Archangel and
thence to form a junction with the Czechoslovaks and Russian Whites.

The entire plan, however, depended upon the cooperation
of the United States. The British and French had no troops
to spare for the Archangel operation. They urged Wilson to
supply the necessary man power. The Japanese, while anxious for reasons of their own to enter Siberia, hesitated to

embark upon a difficult and costly enterprise without American approval. This Wilson repeatedly refused to give. Both he and his military advisers considered the restoration of an Eastern Front militarily impracticable, and he was unwilling to take part in or to approve a plan to interfere in the internal politics of Russia. He also distrusted the intentions of the Japanese.

But Wilson's resistance finally yielded to a combination of Allied persistence and his aroused desire to succor the Czechoslovak legion. Weary of repeatedly saying no to his associates in the war, he gave his consent (July 17, 1918) to the sending of American troops to the Murmansk area, when assured by Marshal Foch, supreme commander on the Western Front, that the soldiers would be more valuable there than in France. When the Supreme War Council on July 2, 1918, called upon him with the utmost urgency to consent to intervention at Vladivostok, he gave in, but only in part. He proposed that the intervention be undertaken jointly by the United States and Japan instead of by Japan alone (as the Japanese had wished), and that each government limit its expeditionary force to seven thousand men. Wilson stipulated, furthermore, that the action of the American troops would be limited to aiding the Czechoslovaks (who Wilson mistakenly assumed were being attacked by the released German and Austrian prisoners), guarding military supplies, and giving "such aid as may be acceptable to the Russians in the organization of their own self-defense." These last stipulations he made applicable to both the Vladivostok and the Murmansk areas. In neither region was there to be interference in Russia's internal affairs, or any impairment of her territorial integrity. Both the revived Eastern Front and the overthrow of Bolshevism were repudiated as objects of American intervention.

Wilson had defined American policy without consulting the European Allies or the Japanese. The definition was pleasing to neither. He had discussed the problem with Lansing, with Secretary of War Baker, and with General Peyton C. March, Army chief of staff. His decision, however, was wholly his own. The *aide-mémoire* of July 17 which embodied it, and which was the sole official statement of American policy in the intervention, he had drafted on his own typewriter.

The first American troops were landed at Vladivostok in August and at Archangel (not at Murmansk as Wilson had specified) early in September 1918. Two months later the fighting elsewhere ended with the signing of the armistice on November 11. Yet the forty-five hundred American troops at Archangel, mostly Polish-American draftees from Wisconsin and Michigan, remained in the area through the Arctic winter and until May and June 1919. Under British command, they were engaged, contrary to Wilson's directive and quite possibly without his knowledge, in desultory fighting with Soviet forces. They were but a handful, the proposed junction with the Czechoslovaks never materialized, and before the end of the summer of 1919 the whole Archangel-Murmansk area had fallen to the Soviets.

The American forces at and near Vladivostok soon found themselves outnumbered ten to one by Japanese, whose government had cavalierly disregarded Wilson's proposed numerical limit. After helping to guard Vladivostok and certain sections of railway for a year and a half, they were withdrawn in the spring of 1920. Their commander, General William S. Graves, ever mindful of Wilson's directive, had refused to lend them to Allied and Japanese schemes (partly supported, it must be added, by the State Department) for destroying the Bolsheviki. The Japanese troops remained in Siberia, to pose problems for Wilson's successor in the White House.

When Wilson gave his consent to the use of United States troops in Siberia and north Russia, the menace of German might still hung heavily over the Allies in France. It was, in fact, the pressure of the series of formidable German offensives from March to June 1918 that gave urgency to the French and British demand for initiatives on other fronts, which might divert German energies away from France. But weeks before the American landings at Archangel and Vladivostok, the tide of war had turned. The last German drive had been halted in its tracks. The Allied and American armies in France had taken the offensive. Allied arms were meanwhile successful in other theaters. In September and October Germany's minor allies, Bulgaria and Turkey, surrendered. On September 14 Austria-Hungary proposed a general peace conference. When that appeal was rejected, the same government on October 7 followed Germany, which on the preceding day had offered to make peace on the basis of President Wilson's Fourteen Points speech and subsequent addresses.

The Fourteen Points address, previously noted in connection with Russia, had set forth Wilson's idea of the essential features of a lasting peace.[5] These included "open covenants of peace, openly arrived at," freedom of the seas, removal of economic barriers, limitation of armaments, recognition of the interests of native populations in the adjustment of colonial claims, evacuation and restoration of Allied territory invaded by the Central Powers, readjustment of the boundaries of Italy, the Balkan States, and Turkey on lines of nationality, an independent Poland, and the creation of "a general association of nations." "The peoples of Austria-Hungary," stated the tenth point, ". . . should be accorded the freest opportunity of autonomous development."

It was this last point, now outdistanced by events, that presented an obstacle to acceptance of the Fourteen Points as a basis for peace with Austria-Hungary. Until the spring of 1918, Wilson, as mentioned before, had hoped to detach

[5] See Appendix for text of Fourteen Points.

Austria-Hungary from her German partner. With that end in view he had carefully avoided calling for a breakup of the Dual Monarchy and had persuaded the French and British to do the same. "Autonomous development" of the subject peoples within the Empire was all that was asked. With this understood, secret and unofficial negotiations for peace had taken place intermittently through Switzerland. But in April 1918 Premier Clemenceau of France, to clear himself of charges of appeasement, revealed the fact that Austrian Emperor Karl had initiated the peace feelers. The revelation put an end to any such negotiations on Austria's part and thus removed any motive for being kind to Austria.

The United States, consequently, declared itself in favor of the complete independence rather than the "autonomous development" of the national minorities under Austrian and Hungarian rule. The Secretary of State announced on May 29 "that the nationalistic aspirations of the Czecho-Slovaks and Jugo-Slavs for freedom have the earnest sympathy of this government." Following the example of the French and British, the United States on September 3 recognized the Czechoslovak National Council in Paris "as a *de facto* belligerent government." Accordingly, Wilson informed the Austrian government that Point X of the Fourteen was no longer valid. Because of the recognition by the United States of the Czechoslovak National Council and its recognition also of "the justice of the nationalistic aspirations of the Jugo-Slavs for freedom," those nationalities and not the President must decide what actions on the part of the Austro-Hungarian government would satisfy their aspirations. Austria-Hungary, now reeling under the blows of a new Italian offensive, signed a strictly military armistice agreement with Italy on November 3.

To Germany's peace offer the President's reply was more forthright. He insisted on four things: full acceptance of the terms stated in his addresses; evacuation of Allied territory;

abandonment of illegal practices on land and sea; and an assurance that the government with which terms might be made should represent the German people and not "the military masters and monarchical autocrats of Germany." This last demand was construed in Germany, as was presumably intended, as requiring the abdication of the Kaiser. This took place on November 9, and on the same day a German People's Government was formed, headed by the Socialist Deputy Friedrich Ebert. Germany had meanwhile accepted Wilson's other conditions, and the correspondence had been submitted to the Allied governments for their approval.

Here the negotiations struck a snag. The Allies had not authorized Wilson to act as their spokesman and had resented his presuming to prescribe peace terms without consulting them. Now they found his prescription too vague on some points and on others too idealistic. Only when Colonel House, speaking for Wilson in the Supreme War Council, threatened to make a separate peace with Germany, did the Allies accept the Fourteen Points, and then only with two reservations. The first reserved to the Allies complete freedom with regard to the stipulation as to the freedom of the seas. In the second, the Allied leaders declared it to be their understanding that the word "restore" with reference to invaded territory signified that Germany would make compensation "for all damage done to the civilian population of the Allies and their property by the aggression of Germany by land, by sea and from the air."

The reply of the Allies, including the reservations, was made known to the Germans by President Wilson on November 5, and they were informed that Marshal Foch would communicate the military terms of an armistice. These terms, also hammered out in the Supreme War Council, included the evacuation of all Allied territory and of the German lands west of the Rhine, and the virtual disarmament of Germany on land and sea. They were accepted by the

German delegation, and the armistice agreement was signed at Foch's headquarters in a railway car near Compiègne at 5 A.M., November 11, 1918, to become effective six hours later. The signing of this armistice virtually ended World War I.

CHAPTER XII

The Peace Conference in Paris

President Wilson had conducted the negotiations leading to the armistice with great firmness and skill. He had brought the fighting and bloodshed to an end on gratifying terms at a time when vindictive voices in the United States and the Allied countries were shouting "Unconditional Surrender!" and "On to Berlin!" Unfortunately, before those negotiations were ended, he had committed the first in a series of errors that were to contribute substantially to the frustration of his hopes for a peace made permanent by American participation in a league of nations.

Wilson's initial error was his appeal to the country, on the eve of the congressional elections, to give him Democratic majorities in House and Senate. "This is no time," he warned, "either for divided counsels or for divided leadership"; and he went on to make what in the sequel was the damaging admission that the election of a Republican majority to either house of Congress would "be interpreted on the other side of the water as a repudiation of my leadership." What Wilson was saying, in effect, was that though the Republicans, whose patriotism he explicitly recognized, could be trusted to make war, their control of either house would complicate his handling of "the difficulties and delicacies of our present task," the making of peace.

Wilson issued this appeal apparently on his own initiative, though urged on by certain Democratic Congressmen or Senators who feared losing their seats. He did not consult his cabinet. Both Joseph Tumulty, his secretary, and Colonel House thought it a mistake, as did his wife, to whom he read it on the evening before it was published. Whether it gained or lost Democratic votes is unknown. It is certain that it infuriated Republicans everywhere and that when the election of November 5, 1918, did in fact return Republican majorities to both House and Senate, partisanship would play an important role in their attitude to Wilson's policies. And Wilson, having advertised in advance that a Republican victory would mean repudiation of his leadership in international matters, could not ascribe his defeat to the normal mid-term anti-administration reaction or to pique at his domestic policies. No wonder that Theodore Roosevelt triumphantly proclaimed: "Our allies and our enemies and Mr. Wilson himself should all understand that Mr. Wilson has no authority whatever to speak for the American people at this time. His leadership has just been emphatically repudiated by them."

Had Wilson headed a parliamentary government like those of the Premiers he would meet in Paris, he would of course have had to resign after his electoral defeat. But facing no such necessity, Wilson was undaunted and unchastened. "You may be sure," he wrote, "that the stubborn Scotch-Irish in me will be rendered no less stubborn and aggressive . . ."

That "stubborn and aggressive," not to say defiant, streak—either that or a surprising blindness to political realities—was apparent in Wilson's choice of the delegation to represent the United States at the Peace Conference. Opinions will forever differ on whether Wilson erred in going in person as head of the delegation, but that he blundered in choosing his colleagues is beyond dispute. The Senate that would act on any treaty he might make would be controlled by Republicans. The chairman of the Senate Foreign Relations Committee would be his archenemy, Henry Cabot Lodge. It was obvious that diplomacy called for a conciliatory gesture to what was now the majority party. Taking Lodge to Paris was out of the question, but there were prominent Republicans who shared Wilson's hope for a league of nations and who could have worked with him in harmony on the main issues. Notable among them were former President Taft and former Senator and Secretary of State Elihu Root. The presence of either on the American delegation would have given it a bipartisan coloring and have shielded the resulting treaty against purely partisan attack in the Senate.

But for whatever reason—partly perhaps an ingrained distrust of lawyers—Wilson refused to heed those who advised that he include Root or Taft. The only Republican in the delegation was the aging career diplomat Henry White. White's Republicanism was nominal. He had lived abroad most of his life and had no influence in the party. He was useful to Wilson in Paris through his knowledge of Europe and his acquaintance with diplomatic protocol. Though a friend of Lodge and Roosevelt, he was entirely loyal to his chief and even sang Wilson's praises to an unreceptive Lodge, but he could really give Wilson no help where he would need it most—in the Senate.

Two of Wilson's appointees were almost inevitable—Secretary Lansing and Colonel House. The Secretary of State, though lukewarm to the President's idealistic aims, could hardly be left at home; and House was already in Europe, where he had represented the President on the Supreme War Council. The fifth delegate was General Tasker H. Bliss, a high-minded and capable officer, who had served for a year as one of the military advisers to the council. Unlike most West Pointers, Bliss was a devotee of the Greek and Latin classics and a sincere advocate of disarmament. Wilson needed his knowledge and advice in Paris, but it has been suggested that the general might have served as an adviser rather than as a member of the delegation, thereby perhaps making room for yet another Republican on the five-man commission.

Wilson, Lansing, House, White, and Bliss, then, were the official representatives, the commissioners, of the United States at the peace conference. Supporting them were several scores of advisers—twenty-three of the experts from the Inquiry, and spokesmen for the State Department, the Treasury, the Army, the Navy, and other Executive agencies. Through its corps of experts, especially those on the political and territorial problems of Europe, the United States was perhaps as well equipped as any power at the conference to tackle the problems of peacemaking.

Wilson himself, beyond the generalities of the Fourteen Points, had not thought out a peace program or an agenda for the conference. On the steamer *George Washington*, which carried the President and his entourage to France early in December, he held only one rather perfunctory colloquy with the experts of the Inquiry as a group. Though somewhat cheered by his injunction and promise—"Tell me what's right and I'll fight for it; give me a guaranteed position"—they were disturbed at the vagueness of his plans. As for an agenda for the conference, Wilson rejected a plan of work proposed by France—which incidentally would have set aside all secret treaties—and when Lansing reported that he had set two of his legal experts to work on a draft of a skeleton treaty, the President responded with annoyance "that he did not propose to have lawyers drafting the treaty."

The very vagueness of Wilson's program, which left doubt in the minds of his subordinates and aroused suspicions in Europe's statesmen, contributed to the welcome accorded him by the populace of the Allied countries. To war-weary people here was a hero who came to bring not only peace but justice, and since everyone inclined to equate justice with his own desires, the American President was acclaimed with wild joy on his journeys—in France, in Italy, even in England. In faraway lands where he never set foot—in Vienna, in the Balkans, in Egypt, in the wastes of northern Russia—Wilson's name and often Wilson's picture became symbols of hope.

A month's delay in the opening of the conference had given the President time for his visits to England and Italy. His first formal meeting with the leaders of the principal Allied powers took place on January 12, 1919. By this time the American Commission to Negotiate Peace—to give the delegation its official name—had become organized. Below the five commissioners, Joseph C. Grew, a young career diplomat who had spent several pre-war years in Berlin, served as secretary-general of the American commission and as a member of the Secretariat of the conference. Members of the Inquiry, now reconstituted as the Division of Territorial, Economic, and Political Intelligence, were accepted as front-rank advisers to the commissioners, especially on territorial matters, somewhat to the chagrin of State Department and Military Intelligence personnel. In addition there were numerous technical advisers on a variety of legal, financial, economic, and military aspects of the peace settlement.

Beginning with their meeting on January 12 the commissioners of the five Great Powers—the United States, Great Britain, France, Italy, and Japan—assumed authority to direct the work of the conference and make the decisions. When spokesmen of the small belligerents, such as Belgium and Serbia, protested, they were met with the response, "We won the war!" The real governing body of the conference in its first two months was the Council of Ten, composed of the Premiers and Foreign Ministers of France, Britain, and Italy, President Wilson (or in his absence, Colonel

House) and Secretary Lansing, and two of the Japanese delegates. This body proceeded to determine what governments should be represented at the conference and to fix the size of the official delegations—five members for each of the Great Powers, three, two, or one each for the remaining twenty-seven. Between Lloyd George and Wilson a lively argument took place over admission to the conference of delegations from the British Dominions and India. Lloyd George contended that they were entitled to representation as autonomous entities which had made substantial contributions to the war effort, while Wilson objected to the resulting multiple voice for the British Empire. The President eventually yielded, stipulating only that one of the two delegates assigned to India should represent the native princes.

Russia, still in the throes of civil war, was not represented at the Peace Conference. None of the powers had as yet recognized the Soviet government, and France in particular held that in making peace with Germany that government had betrayed its allies and was entitled to no voice at the conference. Wilson and Lloyd George felt that the Russian people should be represented, but while the civil war lasted, what government could speak for the Russian people? On Wilson's initiative the contending factions were invited to agree to a cease-fire and to send representatives to the island of Prinkipo in the Sea of Marmora, there to confer with one another and with spokesmen of the Allies and the United States. It was hoped that the civil war could thus be brought to an end and that a delegation representing all Russian factions could be sent to Paris. The plan collapsed despite Soviet acceptance when the chief "White" leaders refused to take part. Later an American secret mission to Russia by William C. Bullitt brought back a Soviet proposal which the conference leaders, including Wilson, chose to ignore.

In addition to deciding what governments should be represented at the conference, the Council of Ten also determined the makeup of the numerous commissions and committees to which most of the technical work of the conference was assigned. On these bodies again the Big Five (or the Big Four in matters of no concern to Japan) retained control with two delegates each, while the small powers were given an aggregate of five, though this number was increased in special cases. The territorial commissions that fixed the boundaries of new or reconstituted states—Poland, Czechoslovakia, Rumania, Austria, Hungary—were made up of representatives of the Big Four alone. The little states whose fate was being sealed could present their cases but could not vote on them.

With all authority thus monopolized by the Great Powers and exercised through the Council of Ten and the commissions, the plenary sessions of the conference became rubber-stamp affairs, giving formal approval to decisions already taken. The first plenary session was held on January 18, the tenth on June 28 for the formal signing of the treaty with Germany.

The work of the Peace Conference falls into two clearly distinguishable periods, before and after Wilson's visit to the United States in February and March 1919. The first of these, ending with his sailing for America on February 14, was marked by two notable victories for the American President. He succeeded in blocking outright annexation of Germany's former colonies by the victorious powers. He persuaded his colleagues on the Council of Ten that provision for a league of nations should be made an integral part of the treaty of peace, and he saw the Covenant of the League completed by a commission which he headed, and presented to a plenary session of the conference. It was then deposited with the bureau of the conference for examination and discussion preparatory to final acceptance.

German colonies in Africa and the Pacific had been over-run and conquered during the war, chiefly through the exertions of Japan and of the British Dominions, South Africa, Australia, and New Zealand. The Dominions and Japan wished to retain them after the time-honored manner of conquerors. Prime Minister William M. Hughes of Australia was particularly bellicose in insisting that Australia keep possession of former German New Guinea and other spoils of war. All agreed that Germany, which the Allies somewhat self-righteously charged with misgoverning colonial peoples, should not get her colonies back, but to permit them to be simply annexed by the conquerors would violate Wilson's precept of "no annexations" and also the fifth of his Fourteen Points, which pledged regard for the interests of native populations in settling the future of enemy colonies. The threatened impasse was solved by acceptance of the mandate system as conceived by Inquiry member Professor G. L. Beer and promoted by Prime Minister Jan Christiaan Smuts of South Africa. Under this plan the former German colonies, and also certain non-Turkish portions of the Ottoman Empire, were "mandated" for administration to different members of the Allied coalition, which became responsible to the League of Nations for the proper administration of the "mandates" and for preparing the native populations for self-government whenever feasible.

Wilson initially thought of assigning the mandates to small neutral nations such as Switzerland and the Scandinavian countries; in practice they went principally to the Allied countries which had seized them—Australia and New Zealand in the South Pacific, Japan in the North Pacific, the Union of South Africa in German Southwest Africa, France and Great Britain in the Middle East and, with Belgium, in East and West Africa. In some degree, therefore, the mandate system was camouflage for old-fashioned colonialism; to the quite notable extent to which the mandatory governments took their responsibilities seriously, it approximated Wilson's ideal.

If adoption of the mandate system was an ambiguous victory for the American President, acceptance of his plan for a league of nations was, or seemed at the time, realization of his highest hopes. From the time in May 1916, when he had spoken under the auspices of the League to Enforce Peace, the idea of such an international body had more and more dominated Wilson's conception of a peace settlement that might endure. It was included in his "peace without victory" speech of January 1917 and occupied the climactic position in his Fourteen Points of a year later. By the time the Peace Conference opened it seemed to him so important that he would sacrifice other objectives to attain it. He was, therefore, immensely gratified when the plenary session of January 25 resolved that provision for a league of nations should be part of the treaty of peace and made him a member—he was promptly elected chairman—of a commission to draft the Covenant.

Taking as a basis a draft already prepared by the joint efforts of British and American advocates (including Wilson himself), the League of Nations Commission completed its work in ten meetings from February 3 to 13. The meetings were all held in the evening in order not to interfere with the other work of the conference. Finally, on February 14, Wilson presented the Covenant to a plenary session of the Conference, which made it available for study by the members. Wilson then departed for Washington, where his presence would be necessary at the adjournment of Congress on March 4.

Briefly described, the Covenant provided for a League of Nations comprising the nations then participating in the conference (Germany was not as yet participating and was excluded from immediate membership) and others enumerated which would accept the obligations of membership.

The League itself could thereafter admit additional members. Organs of the League (including a future World Court) would be available for the peaceful settlement of disputes and for dealing with violations of the Covenant. The members would pledge themselves, with certain qualifications, not to resort to war and to impose sanctions—diplomatic, economic, and even military—upon nations that did so. The most controversial feature of the Covenant, in American eyes, was Article Ten, by which each member of the League undertook to "respect and preserve as against external aggression the territorial integrity and existing political independence" of all other members. To Wilson this was "the heart of the Covenant"; to many of his fellow countrymen, as the future would show, it meant acceptance of intolerable responsibility.

Aware of growing criticism at home of his plans for a League of Nations, Wilson, upon his return to the United States, invited the members of the appropriate Senate and House committees to dine with him at the White House and there explained and defended the Covenant and answered the questions of his visitors. Appraisals of his performance differed sharply, mainly along party lines; but it is certain that he made no converts among the opposing Senators. Indeed, a few days later Senator Lodge obtained the signatures of thirty-nine Senators to a declaration (the "Round Robin") that the Covenant in its existing form was not acceptable to the United States, and that the Peace Conference should hasten to make peace with Germany and leave the question of a league "for careful and serious consideration" at some future time.

In response to this challenge—signed by six more Senators than required to defeat a treaty—Wilson made what must be considered his third error in political tactics. He chose defiance where conciliation was imperative. In a speech at the Metropolitan Opera House in New York, on the eve of his return to Paris—at a meeting where he shared the platform with ex-President Taft, who had been campaigning valiantly in behalf of the League—Wilson laid down the law to his opponents. When his work was done in Paris, he warned them, the treaty of peace would be tied with so many threads to the League Covenant that Senators would find they could not separate the League from the treaty. It did not occur to Wilson, apparently, that such organic union might result not in acceptance of the Covenant but in rejection of the treaty.

From the opera house the President went at once to the pier where the *George Washington* waited to convey him again to France. In Paris some dark and difficult days lay ahead of him.

It was perhaps at this time that an estrangement began between Wilson and his friend and confidant, Colonel House. There were rumors that House, who had been left in charge during Wilson's absence, had shown a disposition to compromise on matters that the President considered vital; specifically, that he had intimated that the League Covenant might be divorced from the treaty of peace, and that he had encouraged a French desire to carve an independent Rhenish republic out of the German Rhineland. It is difficult to know how much basis there was for these rumors or how much credence Wilson gave them. At any rate, he thought it necessary, upon arriving in Paris, to issue an emphatic statement of his continued determination to make the League Covenant part of the treaty; and it is possible that his hard fight to save the Rhineland for Germany may have been made more difficult by the colonel's sympathetic listening to the French case.[1] It may be, too, as some have suggested,

---

[1] There is a good summary of this controversial matter in Arthur Walworth, *Woodrow Wilson* (2nd edition, revised, two volumes in one, Boston: Houghton Mifflin Co., 1965), II, 279–281. Two contrasting explanations of the House-Wilson break by House and by Dr. Grayson, Wilson's

that Wilson took umbrage at a new tendency to self-assertion on House's part and at news dispatches emanating from indiscreet members of House's entourage which acclaimed the colonel's diplomatic achievements to the apparent disparagement of the President's.

The President continued, of course, to work with House, and when he fell ill early in April, House again took his place in the negotiations; but the intimate and confidential relations between the two men were never restored.

Wilson, in fact, now secluded himself more than formerly from all four of his fellow commissioners. Late in March the Council of Ten, in which he and Lansing had sat together, was superseded by the Council of Four, consisting of the President and the three Premiers, Lloyd George, Clemenceau, and Orlando. The four men sometimes had advisers with them, but Wilson ordinarily sat unattended. Thus he had no one to advise or prompt him and no record of his own that he could appeal to in case of need. The only consistent record of the sessions was kept by a British secretary, Sir Maurice Hankey, and of some meetings no minutes at all were kept. The other American commissioners heard little of what went on among the Four. "Our only link with the President," complained Joseph C. Grew, "is Arthur Hugh Frazier [member of the Secretariat] and he has become more sphinxlike than the Sphinx." Furthermore, Grew remarked in the same letter, "Colonel House never attends the daily meetings of the other Commissioners and his office frequently takes action unknown to them and often disap-

---

physician, both published posthumously, are found in Charles Seymour, "End of a Friendship," *American Heritage*, August 1963, and Cary T. Grayson, "The Colonel's Folly and the President's Distress," *ibid.*, October 1964. Probably one should not take too literally Mrs. Wilson's dramatic account, published twenty years after the event in Edith Bolling Wilson, *My Memoir* (Indianapolis & New York: The Bobbs-Merrill Co., 1939), pp. 245–246.

proved by them when they finally learn of it." [2] Lansing, Bliss, and White were left with practically nothing to do.

It was under this frustrating state of disorganization in the American commission that the final phase of peace-making took place. All the crucial questions before the conference were decided by the Council of Four (which became temporarily a Council of Three during Orlando's absence in April and May). Not that the Four did all the work by any means. The territorial and other technical commissions had been extremely busy and the reports that they brought up to the Four were generally approved for incorporation in the treaties. Notable among others for their work on these commissions were the Americans, former members of the Inquiry, Charles Seymour (for Austria-Hungary), Robert H. Lord (for Poland), G. L. Beer (for the German colonies), and William L. Westermann (for the Near East).

But on such touchy problems as Italy's boundary claims, French demands with reference to the Rhineland and the Saar Basin, Japan's claim to German rights in China's Shantung province, and the amount of reparations to be demanded from Germany, decisions could be reached only at the highest level, in the Council of Four.

On all these issues Wilson found it necessary to make concessions, too often at the cost of violating principles inherent in the Fourteen Points or other declarations agreed to by all parties in signing the armistice. The President's bargaining position had been weakened by the necessity of reconvoking the League of Nations Commission and asking that the Covenant be amended to meet criticism in the United States. Despite the defiant tone of his Metropolitan Opera House address, he had yielded to sound advice from ex-President Taft and other friends of the League proposal, who believed

[2] Joseph C. Grew, *Turbulent Era: A Diplomatic Record of Forty Years, 1904–1945.* Edited by Walter Johnson (2 vols. Boston: Houghton Mifflin Co., 1952), I, 384.

that a few simple amendments would make the Covenant acceptable to the Senate. At considerable embarrassment, therefore, the President reconvened the League Commission and asked his European colleagues to agree to four amendments. These stated explicitly (1) that members would have the right to withdraw from the League; (2) that domestic questions were exempt from League jurisdiction; (3) that no member could be required against its will to accept a mandate; and (4) that nothing in the League Covenant contravened "regional understandings like the Monroe Doctrine."

With some reluctance the spokesmen for the other members of the Big Five accepted these changes, but they thereupon stepped up their insistence on objectives of their own to which Wilson could not willingly agree. The French, in the interest of security, wished the Rhineland detached from Germany and made into an independent and demilitarized republic. To compensate for French coal mines wrecked by the German invaders they asked annexation of the rich coal-bearing Saar Basin. In support of these demands they cited, among other things, a secret agreement with Russia in 1917. Clemenceau also asked for an international general staff to direct action against future, presumably German, aggression.

Italy claimed the frontiers promised her in the secret Treaty of London of 1915 as a condition of her joining the Allies. Early in the conference Wilson had agreed to these frontiers, though in the South Tyrol they brought more than two hundred thousand Austrian Germans under Italian rule. Wilson later admitted that this was an error, a flagrant violation of self-determination. Apparently he had spoken impulsively, moved by Orlando's warm support of Wilson's League proposal. Now, however, the Italians were demanding accessions not granted in the Treaty of London: the city of Fiume near the head of the Adriatic and portions of the Dalmatian coast, which would give Italy complete control of the Adriatic at the expense of the new state of Yugoslavia and in direct violation of self-determination.

Japan, for her part, brought forward for a second time a proposal that the League Covenant endorse the principle of the equality of all sovereign states—actually a plea for recognition of racial equality. The Japanese delegation did not insist upon this proposal, but they did insist upon cession to Japan of former German rights in Shantung. In support of their claim they cited secret agreements with Great Britain, France, and Russia and treaties of somewhat doubtful validity with China. The Chinese asserted that their treaties had been signed under duress and were not binding. They contended, as did Wilson, that German holdings in Shantung, fruits of a supposedly repudiated imperialism, should be returned to China, not transferred to Japan.

In his resistance to these acquisitive ambitions of the Allies Wilson had the support of most of the American experts and of the other commissioners, with the partial exception of House. But it was he, in the Council of Four, who had to meet the arguments of the persuasive Allied statesmen and to give the final yes or no to their demands. With Clemenceau he reached a compromise. The Rhenish Republic project was given up; the coal mines of the Saar Basin were ceded to France and the government of the Saar was placed under League of Nations control for fifteen years, after which its people might choose between France, Germany, and continued League administration.[3] The Rhineland was demilitarized, and for fifteen years the Allies might hold bridgeheads east of the river.

Wilson and Lloyd George went a step further to satisfy the French craving for security. They signed treaties promising joint American and British military aid to France should she again be attacked by Germany. Wilson was apparently

[3] In 1935, after a vigorous campaign of Nazi propaganda, the people of the Saar voted overwhelmingly for reannexation to Germany.

little concerned over the plain contradiction between this new triple alliance and the principles of the League of Nations, or over the practical certainty that the Senate of the United States would never approve such a treaty.

Against the Italian claim to Fiume and the Dalmatian coast Wilson held out to the end, his resistance perhaps bolstered by an unsolicited letter from six of the American experts who feared that he was weakening. He even took the unconventional step of addressing an appeal to the Italian people over the heads of their delegation. Orlando and Sonnino, the Italian Foreign Minister, thereupon left the conference in a huff and returned to Italy, where they received popular acclaim and a vote of confidence from the Italian Parliament. But since Lloyd George and Clemenceau stood with Wilson on this issue, though without publicizing their position as he had done, the Italians failed to get their way, and the fate of Fiume was left to be settled between Italy and Yugoslavia.

The Japanese fared better. Unlike the Italian claim to Fiume, theirs to Shantung had British and French support based upon the wartime agreements. Though Lansing and Bliss would have called what they thought a Japanese bluff to boycott the League, Wilson yielded to the Nipponese demands, salving his conscience with a promise by the Japanese delegation that Japan would retain only economic rights and privileges, returning political control of Shantung to China.

Of the many compromises that Wilson thought it necessary to make in Paris, perhaps the least justified, and the most unfortunate in its consequences, was that on reparations. In a speech on February 11, 1918, he had declared that there should be "no contributions, no punitive damages." This speech was one of the "subsequent addresses" which, with the Fourteen Points, had been accepted as the basis of Germany's surrender. This particular stipulation had been qualified by the Allied reservation that Germany's obligation to "restore" occupied territory was to embrace payment "for all damages done to the civilian population of the Allies and their property by the aggression of Germany by land, by sea and from the air." This phrasing seemed to preclude any attempt to impose an indemnity or to levy the cost of the war upon Germany, but Allied statesmen had promised to do just that, particularly the British in the parliamentary election campaign of December 1918.

When Wilson rejected "war costs" as contrary to the terms of the armistice, Lloyd George brought forward the specious contention that pensions and separation allowances paid to Allied soldiers and their dependents could properly be classified as "damage done to the civilian population." In British eyes this thesis had the merit not only of doubling the aggregate reparations bill but of substantially increasing Britain's share, since actual damage to British civilian property had been comparatively slight. Wilson allowed himself to be convinced by the British argument, apparently under the impression that inclusion of pensions would merely increase the British share of a fixed sum based on calculations of Germany's capacity to pay. When one of his economic advisers questioned the logic of the position, he responded: "Logic? Logic? I don't give a damn for logic! I am going to include pensions."

The claim based on pensions and separation allowances was in fact added to claims for other losses. It brought the total reparations bill to a sum far surpassing Germany's reasonable capacity to pay, particularly when other features of the treaty deprived her of resources that could have facilitated payment. These included her colonies, most of her merchant marine, German-owned property in Allied countries, the coal of the Saar, the iron ore of Lorraine (which with Alsace was ceded to France), and a substantial fraction of both her industrial and her agricultural capacity. Wilson and his American advisers would have preferred to fix the sum to be paid then and there. The Allies, unable to agree on a figure, left it to be determined after the conference by a Reparations Commission. It was eventually set at thirty-three billion dollars—thirty-three times the indemnity that Germany had imposed on France in 1871. Though only a small part of it was ever actually paid, the enormous bill left Germany with a justified sense of having been double-crossed. This feeling was aggravated by the imposition of the "war guilt" clause (Article 231) of the treaty, by which Germany was required to accept for herself and her allies responsibility "for causing all the loss and damage" which the Allies and their nationals had suffered "as a consequence of the war imposed upon them by the aggression of Germany and her allies." This thesis of the exclusive responsibility of the Central Powers for the war may have been genuinely believed by the men who wrote the treaty. Accepted by the Germans under duress, it was not believed by them and is not sustained by history.

The Germans had so far had no voice in making the treaty. They were now invited to send representatives to Paris, not to negotiate but to receive, and presumably to sign, the treaty drawn by the victors. The German delegation, headed by Foreign Minister Count Brockdorff-Rantzau, arrived in Paris on April 30. They were kept secluded for a week while the treaty received some last-moment tinkering. Then at a plenary session on May 7 they were handed the bulky four hundred page document after some brief and acid remarks by Clemenceau. Brockdorff-Rantzau made his reply without rising from his seat. What seemed to most of the gathering a studied discourtesy was perhaps, as General Bliss believed, the consequence of the German's being in such a "broken, nervous physical condition" that he dared not try to stand.

The German government presented its reply on May 29,

taking issue with the treaty on nearly all points and presenting a list of counterproposals. These asked, among other things, that Germany be admitted at once to a League of Nations differing in some respects from Wilson's League; that she be given the mandate for her former colonies; that the proposed boundaries with Poland and Denmark be modified in Germany's favor to conform more nearly to ethnographic frontiers; that the amount of reparations be fixed at a reasonable figure; that the question of war guilt (Article 231) be determined by a neutral inquiry.

The German reply came near to producing a division among the Big Four. There was, as a matter of fact, serious dissatisfaction with the treaty, especially among the American and British experts who had helped to write it. The various commissions had worked without adequate coordination, and many of them under the impression that they were proposing terms for negotiation and probable compromise. When they saw the treaty as a whole and realized that it was meant to be final, many of them were deeply disturbed at its severity. And not only the experts. Lloyd George, in particular, feared that the Germans would not sign and that the war would have to be renewed, with the prospect of a prolonged occupation of Germany. Had he had his way, much of the treaty would have been rewritten.

Clemenceau, however, refused to concede that the treaty was unduly harsh, and Wilson stood with Clemenceau. "Personally," he remarked to the American delegation, "I do not want to soften the terms for Germany. . . . If the Germans won't sign the treaty as we have written it then we must renew the war; at all events we must not allow ourselves to flop and wobble trying to find something they will sign."[4]

[4] Charles Seymour, *Letters from the Paris Peace Conference*, edited by Harold B. Whiteman, Jr. (New Haven: Yale University Press, 1965), pp. 255–256.

In the upshot a few minor concessions were made. The boundaries with Poland and Denmark were modified slightly in Germany's favor; Germany was given better representation on the international commissions that were to control her navigable rivers and was assured that the drastic limitation of her armament imposed by the treaty was merely the first step toward a general reduction and limitation of armaments.

Refused further concessions, the German ministry resigned. Their successors accepted the treaty a bare hour and a half before the deadline on June 23. Five days later, in the Hall of Mirrors at Versailles—where Wilhelm I and Bismarck had proclaimed the German Empire in 1871—the Treaty of Versailles was signed by a new German delegation and by the delegates of all but one of the Allied and Associated Powers. China alone, unwilling to subscribe to the Shantung article, withheld its signature.[5]

In later years, particularly in the isolationist 1930s, it became fashionable to regard the Treaty of Versailles as a colossal failure and to hold Wilson responsible for its shortcomings. There is no doubt that in the Draconian terms imposed upon Germany the treaty supplied ammunition for Hitler and the Nazis. Wilson had compromised or abandoned a number of the Fourteen Points. Freedom of the seas had been forgotten, disarmament in practice applied only to the enemy, self-determination followed where it suited the victors. But to condemn Wilson for all these surrenders and compromises is to overlook the powerful forces that he had to contend with and the inescapable necessity of compromising with the *Realpolitik* of the European and Japanese leaders.

[5] The Treaty of Versailles made peace with Germany alone. Treaties were subsequently signed with Austria, Hungary, Bulgaria, and Turkey. The United States ratified none of these. It made separate treaties with Germany, Austria, and Hungary and reestablished diplomatic relations with Turkey by executive agreement. With Bulgaria it had not been at war nor broken diplomatic relations.

Under the circumstances, his successes are quite as surprising as his failures. He had prevented flagrant violations of self-determination by powerful French and Italian drives. He had secured the liberation of Poles, Czechoslovaks, South Slavs, and Rumanians from alien rule. In the mandate system he had introduced a new concept of responsibility into colonial administration. Above all, he had induced a skeptical world to accept the League of Nations, which, had his own nation not rejected it, might have supplied the cure for many of the defects in the peace settlement.

The contemporary opinion of some of the younger men who worked under Wilson in Paris is worth noting. Charles Seymour, one of the Inquiry, though far from oblivious to Wilson's faults, recorded that the members of the Inquiry who had served in the peacemaking, most of them like himself Republicans, were unanimous in the belief "that no one living in America could have secured what Wilson has secured at the Conference," though some of the group, he conceded, "feel that Roosevelt in his prime would have done better." (Theodore Roosevelt had died in the preceding January.) Joseph C. Grew, secretary-general of the American commission, acknowledged that the treaties with Germany and Austria contained "the seeds for future wars. But," he continued, "no one will ever know all the difficulties the President and the Commission have had to contend with. . . . On the whole the President has fought a great fight and the Peace Conference has been as great a fight as was the war that led to it. All we can do now is to put our trust in the League of Nations; it is the only solution for the future; the cornerstone has been laid and the name of the President will always be great for laying it; the structure has yet to be built. . . ."

What part, if any, the United States would play in completing the structure remained to be determined.

CHAPTER XIII

The Renunciation of World Leadership

Home again after his six months' mission in Paris, President Wilson formally submitted the peace treaty in a personal appearance before the Senate on July 10, 1919. The treaty, he confessed to the Senators, exhibited many compromises, many imperfections. Its most important feature, he asserted, was the Covenant of the League of Nations. "Dare we reject it and break the heart of the world?" he asked. He closed his address with a rhetorical flourish that can have had little appeal to the hardheaded Senators in his audience. The moral leadership of the world, he declared, had fallen to the United States "by no plan of our own conceiving, but by the hand of God who led us into this way. We cannot turn back. We can only go forward, with lifted eyes and freshened spirit, to follow the vision. It was this that we dreamed at our birth. America shall in truth show the way. The light streams upon the path ahead, and nowhere else."

If Wilson saw only one path ahead, members of the Senate saw many paths. The terms of the treaty were no surprise to them, for though they now gazed for the first time upon an official copy of the document, an unofficial copy had been obtained many weeks before and printed in the *Con-*

gressional Record. Since June 9 it had occupied much of the Senate's time and had been subjected to vigorous attack by Senate Republicans. Senator Knox of Pennsylvania (former Secretary of State) had proposed to divorce the League Covenant entirely from other parts of the treaty, thus making peace with Germany but leaving the question of joining the League for later decision. This was going too far for most of Knox's Republican colleagues. Though fourteen Republican isolationists, joined by three Democrats—a group that became known as the "irreconcilables"—rejected all thought of American participation in the League, the majority of the Republican Senators were willing to take the treaty, League and all, subject to either amendments or reservations which would make it clear that the United States was not surrendering its sovereignty to an alleged "superstate."

The chief sticking point for nearly all Republican Senators was Article Ten of the Covenant, the mutual guarantee by members of the League of one another's independence and territorial integrity against external aggression. This guarantee, and the assignment to the League Council of responsibility for advising "upon the means by which this obligation shall be fulfilled," raised the specter of American troops being sent to remote regions of the globe to defend the independence of such unfamiliar entities as the Hedjaz or Siam. Elihu Root, Republican elder statesman, who though not now in the Senate was glad to counsel those who were, suggested outright elimination of Article Ten; others would be satisfied with making it plain that only by consent of Congress could United States troops be sent to fight abroad.

In addition to their dislike of Article Ten, Republican Senators were of the opinion that the amendments to the Covenant that Wilson had secured in Paris were not sufficiently explicit in regard to right of withdrawal from the League and the exclusion from League jurisdiction of domestic questions and questions involving the Monroe Doctrine. Other features of the treaty which many found objectionable were the turning over to Japan of former German rights in Shantung and the multiple votes of the British Empire (the United Kingdom, India, and the four Dominions) in the League Assembly.

All of these points of view on the Republican side, as well as the disposition of nearly all the Senate Democrats to defend the work of their Democratic President, were apparent before the Senate officially received the treaty. Since the Republicans controlled the Senate by a slender margin, it was apparent that unless Wilson would consent to compromise, his treaty was in for trouble.

It was unfortunate for Wilson in this situation that the chairman of the Senate Foreign Relations Committee, to which the treaty was at once referred, was Henry Cabot Lodge; for the Massachusetts Senator was not only a political antagonist of the President but also harbored a personal animus against him. There was no doubt that he would find satisfaction in defeating and humiliating Wilson if that were possible. There *is* doubt as to whether he hoped to see the treaty defeated altogether or merely so modified as to remove what he considered dangers to the independence and vital interests of the United States.

Whatever Lodge's exact purpose, he saw to it that the Committee on Foreign Relations was "packed" with irreconcilables. Of ten Republican Senators on the committee, six were of that group, among them such outspoken foes of the League as Borah of Idaho, Brandegee of Connecticut, and Hiram Johnson of California. Having organized the committee to suit his purposes, Lodge next resorted to a strategy of delay. If action were postponed, initial popular (and congressional) enthusiasm for the League might cool, yielding to the force of isolationist tradition, the prejudices of dissatisfied racial minorities, and the criticism of liberal groups and periodicals (e.g. *The Nation* and *The New Republic*), former supporters of Wilson who damned him for surrendering (as they charged) to Old World reactionaries at the peace conference. To give these negative forces time to assert themselves, Lodge postponed public hearings on the treaty until July 31, meanwhile killing two weeks of valuable time by reading the 268-page treaty verbatim into the committee's minutes.

By this time it was clear that the Republicans in the Senate fell into three groups. First there were the fourteen or fifteen irreconcilables, who would not have the League on any terms. At the other end of the spectrum were about twelve "mild reservationists," men who would vote for the treaty with a few simple reservations clarifying the obligations of the United States to the League. Between these two groups were some twenty-three or twenty-four "strong reservationists," led by Lodge, who thought it necessary to define strictly, by either amendment or drastic reservations, American responsibilities to the League and the attitude of the United States to certain other articles of the treaty, such as the section on Shantung.

It was Lodge's cue, as Republican leader, to hold together the three groups of Republican Senators, at least on a program of reservations which they, with their slim majority, could attach to the treaty. (It was foreseen that the irreconcilables would in the end vote against the treaty, even with Republican reservations.) It was, or should have been, equally Wilson's cue to seek to divide the Republicans by reaching agreement with the mild reservationists. Senators of this group obviously held the balance of power. With the other Republicans, or with the Democrats, they constituted a majority of the Senate. If they and the Democrats could put through a set of relatively innocuous reservations by majority vote, then it could be hoped that enough of the strong reservationists could be won over to provide the two-thirds necessary to approve the treaty. How far apart, then, were Wilson and the mild reservationists?

The principal issue that divided them during July and August was apparently one of form rather than of substance. Wilson was willing to accept interpretative reservations provided they were set forth in a separate instrument, not in the resolution of advice and consent. Even on Article Ten, which he considered "the heart of the Covenant," he told the Foreign Relations Committee when he met with them on August 19 that he would not object to the substance of a reservation making it plain that Congress might use its own judgment in responding to decisions of the League Council. But "it would be a very serious practical mistake," he added, "to put it in the resolution of ratification." If that were done, he believed, it would be necessary to secure the consent of all the other signatories to the reservation. Then other governments might choose to attach reservations of their own, and "the floodgates would be open." Actually, although any amendment of the text of a treaty of course required the consent of all parties, an interpretative reservation did not require such consent unless the reservation itself so stipulated.

A month prior to this statement, Wilson had begun a series of individual conferences with the mild reservationists and some other Republican Senators. He was not, it would appear, trying to understand their views but seeking to win them to his own. His chances were not improved by the publicity attending the conferences. A Senator emerging from the White House was not likely to tell the press: "Yes, the President has convinced me." All the visitors, in fact, assured reporters that their opinions were unchanged. Most of them had taken occasion to warn Wilson that unless he would agree to reservations in the resolution of ratification the treaty would never command the votes of two-thirds of the Senators.

On July 31 seven mild reservationists met at the Capitol in an effort to agree on a program. They were Senators Colt (Rhode Island), Cummins (Iowa), Kellogg (Minnesota), Lenroot (Wisconsin), McCumber (North Dakota), McNary (Oregon), and Spencer (Missouri). According to press reports, the seven agreed on the need for reservations on the Monroe Doctrine, domestic questions, and the right to withdraw from the League. On Article Ten, five of the seven were said to favor an explicit statement that Congress alone had authority to send American troops into action in foreign lands. The other two Senators thought the exclusive right of Congress to make war so clear that such a reservation was unnecessary.

An AP dispatch represented the seven Senators as hoping that their middle-ground program would attract enough members of both parties to ensure acceptance of the League by the Senate. If not, Senator Colt was quoted as saying, adoption by the Republicans of such clarifying reservations as the seven proposed would produce a situation "that would put the onus on the Democrats of rejecting the treaty if they saw fit to do so, rather than on the Republicans." It is evident that some of the mild reservationists were thinking in terms of partisan advantage as well as of saving the treaty.

Though the press gained the impression that negotiations looking to a compromise were under way between mild reservationists and Democratic Senators, the public Democratic response to the overture of the seven was a plain rebuff. The acting Democratic leader in the Senate (in the absence of the fatally ill Senator T. S. Martin of Virginia) was Gilbert M. Hitchcock of Nebraska. Hitchcock had never been close to Wilson nor had he enjoyed his full confidence. Though completely loyal to the President throughout the fight over the treaty, he showed little imagination or flexibility in a situation that called for both. Informed of the proposals of the mild reservationists, he remarked sarcastically that they "gave fresh indication of the muddle in the opposition camp," and added that "the fight of the League opponents will come to 'nothing at all,' with the treaty being ratified exactly as submitted to the Senate." This was an attitude—and it must be said that Wilson shared it—calculated to consolidate rather than to divide the Senate Republicans.

Meanwhile the Foreign Relations Committee proceeded in its hearings on the treaty, calling hostile witnesses for the most part and publicizing their criticism of treaty and League. By the end of August it was clear even to Wilson that his treaty was in serious trouble; that the Senate in its existing mood would never approve it without reservations that to him would be more or less objectionable. Two courses lay open to him. He could seek a compromise with the mild reservationists in the form of reservations that would be relatively harmless; or he could, through some extraordinary exertion, seek to alter the mood of the Senate and push the treaty through without reservations.

Most students of the period today believe that Wilson should have chosen the road of compromise and conciliation; that in this way he could have secured virtually all that was valuable and workable in the treaty and the League Covenant. But Wilson chose otherwise. His combination of faith in himself (perhaps in his God-given mission) and faith in the people convinced him that an appeal to the American people over the heads of the Senate would produce such a surge of popular support for the League of Nations that Senators would see the handwriting on the wall and give him a two-thirds vote for the treaty without crippling reservations. The decision on a nationwide speaking tour, a "swing around the circle," was not, however, the result of a sudden impulse, born of desperation. The idea had been in Wilson's mind for months. He had thought of going through with it immediately after his return from France in July, but had delayed because of pressing duties in Washington. The precarious situation of the treaty in a committee dominated by its foes now convinced him that such an effort was imperative.

Wilson's proposal alarmed Dr. Grayson, the White House physician. The President had been seriously ill in Paris early in April and had had no chance for rest or relaxation for many months. The strenuous exertion of a month-long, countrywide speaking campaign, the doctor cautioned, might be more than his impaired constitution could stand. It might even be fatal. But Wilson was not to be dissuaded. "Even though, in my condition, it might mean the giving up of my life," he told the doctor, "I will gladly make the sacrifice to save the Treaty."

But Wilson was not spurning all compromise. Before leaving on his trip he typed out and handed to Hitchcock four interpretative reservations which he would be willing to accept and which he authorized the Senator to use at his discretion, though without revealing their source. They pertained to the right of withdrawal, Article Ten, domestic questions, and the Monroe Doctrine. Presumably, though this is not clear, he intended that they should be embodied in a separate resolution, not in the resolution of ratification. If he did not mean to insist on this—and Hitchcock did not so insist when he tardily introduced the reservations—it is difficult to see any essential difference at this point between Wilson's position and that of the mild reservationists. And if the difference was one of form, it still, to the eye of today, seems nonessential. It is difficult to disagree with Professor T. A. Bailey, who holds that Wilson's better course would have been to stay in Washington and seek common ground with the Republican moderates.

Leaving Washington on September 3, 1919, Wilson carried his appeal for the treaty into seventeen states from the Ohio Valley to the Pacific Coast. He made thirty-six formal speeches averaging an hour in length and spoke to waiting crowds from the rear platform of his train at dozens of railway stations. There were parades and conferences in September heat without benefit of air conditioning. How different was his ordeal from the experience of later Presidents, sitting in air-conditioned studios and reaching millions of their constituents via radio or TV!

The gist of Wilson's argument was that unless America assumed her due share in making the League of Nations effective, the tragedy of the war just ended would be repeated, and America would inevitably be drawn in again, as she had been in 1917. In words that sound like a prophecy of Hitler and Hitlerism, he warned an Indianapolis audience that without the restraint of an effective League, Germany, led by "masters of the very things that we hate and mean always to fight," might again seek to dominate Europe by force; and then, he declared, "whether we are in the League of Nations or not, we will join to prevent it. We do not stand off and see murder done. . . . We are not the friends and advocates of free government and then willing to stand by and see free government die before our eyes."

To those who feared Article Ten as an "entangling alliance," he retorted: "There is no entangling alliance in a concert of power." Article Ten, in any case, was not a break with traditional American policy, but an extension to the world of the long accepted principles of the Monroe Doctrine. As to the sending of American troops to distant lands, in the application of Article Ten, the President assured his hearers that enforcement would be regional. The military responsibility of the United States might well be limited to the Western Hemisphere, where for the present there were no apparent threats to the peace. Furthermore, said Wilson, not altogether candidly, since decisions in the Council of the League must be by unanimous vote, the United States could not be called upon to act against her will.

Whatever the effect of Wilson's oratory upon his audiences

—and their responses ranged from cool to highly enthusiastic —its effect upon the Senate was, in modern jargon, counter-productive. His denunciation of those opposing his program as "contemptible quitters" offended the Republican moderates and reduced still further the chances of compromise. The irreconcilable Senators sent members of their group to trail Wilson and refute his arguments. The surge of public opinion that he had hoped to raise against his opponents did not materialize.

Then came tragedy. As Wilson's physician had warned, the intense exertion, coupled with the heat and the discomfort of prolonged train travel, proved too much for his already overworked body. After an especially effective speech at Pueblo, Colorado, on September 25, the President collapsed. All further speeches were cancelled, and the special train was rushed back to Washington. A few days later came the cerebral thrombosis which incapacitated him for many months and left him a permanent invalid during the four years of life that remained.

Meanwhile the Committee on Foreign Relations had completed its hearings, and on September 10 Senator Lodge introduced the majority report, proposing forty-five amendments and four reservations. The mild reservationists had consistently opposed amendments, and they now joined the Democrats in rejecting them all. Thereupon Lodge and his committee proceeded to translate the substance of most of the amendments into reservations, fourteen in all, with a preamble making them a part of the resolution of ratification and requiring that three of the four "principal allied and associated powers," Great Britain, France, Italy, and Japan, agree to them by an exchange of notes before ratification should take effect.

This was the form of stating reservations which Wilson had pronounced objectionable if not wholly unacceptable. Still more objectionable in his eyes was the reservation (eventually Number Two) on Article Ten. This refused for the United States any obligation to carry out the guarantees of Article Ten, to interfere in controversies between nations, or to employ the armed forces of the United States under any article of the treaty, unless Congress should so provide in any particular case. Though this reservation differed chiefly in tone and emphasis from the one that Wilson himself had drafted, it now seemed to him nothing short of nullification of Article Ten, and he informed Hitchcock that if the Senate approved the treaty with this reservation, he would not ratify it; in other words, that he would "pocket" the treaty.

Of the other reservations, most were quite harmless, simply making explicit the retention by the United States or by Congress of powers which under the Covenant could hardly have been denied them. But there were three that were likely to make trouble. The fifth excluded entirely from League jurisdiction any question involving the Monroe Doctrine, which, it was stated, was "to be interpreted by the United States alone." The sixth withheld the assent of the United States from the Shantung settlement. The fourteenth, alluding to the fact that the four British Dominions and India were to be members of the League, announced that the United States assumed no obligation to be bound by any decision of the Council or the Assembly in which "any member of the league and its self-governing dominions, colonies, or parts of empire, in the aggregate have cast more than one vote." These three reservations were certain to be viewed askance by other governments. It was, however, the reservation on Article Ten which Wilson held wholly unacceptable.

Now was the time when agreement with the mild reservationists would have paid off. They had helped to defeat the amendments. Had they continued to cooperate with the Democrats, they could have substituted relatively mild reservations for those proposed by Lodge. They did not do so.

Senator McCumber, the most strongly pro-treaty of the group, did make two proposals, as he said, to save the treaty. He moved to strike out of the preamble the requirement that three of the four major powers accept the reservations. His motion was rejected, receiving no Republican vote except his own. His later attempt to amend the reservation on Shantung with a view to making it less objectionable to Japan met the same fate.

The mild reservationists did join with the Democrats to defeat a reservation proposed by Senator Knox, which would in effect have made peace with Germany while leaving the United States wholly uncommitted as to its relations with the League of Nations. The fact that Lodge joined the irreconcilables and a few others in voting for this proposal supports the belief that he was really against the League rather than, as he officially maintained, for the League with strong reservations.

But when Hitchcock or other Democrats offered substitute reservations on Article Ten, the Monroe Doctrine, and domestic questions—reservations similar to those that Wilson had drafted (and similar also to the earlier proposals of the mild reservationists)—the mild reservationists joined with other Republicans to reject them. In defense of his position McCumber explained that he and other moderate Republicans had received no encouragement from the Democratic side and that after trying in vain for two months to change the views of Republicans on the committee, they had agreed to go along with the committee's reservations and were now honor-bound to do so. Perhaps their motives were, as one Democrat charged, "purely political," but it must be admitted that the Democrats had been fatally slow in seeking compromise.

With minor changes and substitutions the Lodge reservations (as they came to be called) were adopted by majorities composed of all the Republicans and a few Democrats, and the time came for the Senate to grant or withhold its advice and consent to the treaty with the reservations. All now depended on the Democrats. The irreconcilables, it was known, would vote against the treaty, even with the reservations which they had supported. The other Republicans presumably would support it. The addition of about thirty Democrats would make up the needed two-thirds of the Senate.

The Democrats, without strong leadership in the Senate, looked to the ill statesman in the White House for advice or, as the Republicans charged, for orders. Wilson, confined to his bed and shielded by his solicitous wife from all contacts, especially all unpalatable advice that might upset him emotionally, had grown if anything harder and more inflexible in his insistence that the treaty be approved without material change. After a talk with Hitchcock he addressed a letter to the latter, dated November 18, 1919. Declaring his opinion that the Lodge reservations meant *nullification,* not ratification, of the treaty, he said flatly: "I sincerely hope that the friends and supporters of the treaty will vote against the Lodge resolution of ratification."

All but a handful of the Democrats obeyed their stricken leader's "orders." The vote on the treaty, November 19, stood thirty-nine for, fifty-five against approval. The Democrats had joined the irreconcilable Republicans to defeat the treaty. A second vote showed forty-one to fifty-one. An attempt by Hitchcock to have the treaty reconsidered with his (and Wilson's) reservations was defeated, and a final motion to approve the treaty without any reservations was lost, thirty-eight to fifty-three. Neither with nor without the Lodge reservations could the Senate approve the treaty. The Democrats blocked the first road, the Republicans the second. But had the Democrats voted with the Republicans to approve the treaty with the Lodge resolution, it seems certain that the President would have refused to ratify it.

Wilson and Hitchcock appear to have relied upon what

Professor Bailey terms a "strategy of deadlock." Let the Democrats show that Lodge's program could not win, and public opinion would come to the support of the President's program so strongly that Lodge and his following would be forced to yield. The hope proved fallacious. While there was widespread clamor for compromise, the pressure appears to have been directed more at Wilson than at Lodge. The public saw that the treaty had been defeated by Democratic votes, and to the man in the street the difference between the treaty with and without the Lodge reservations was too subtle to get excited over. And not only to the man in the street. To many Democratic Senators, to William Jennings Bryan, to Colonel House, to William H. Taft and the executive committee of the League to Enforce Peace, acceptance of the Lodge reservations seemed a small price to pay for American entry into the League of Nations. Likewise the British government, which sent Viscount Grey (who as Sir Edward Grey had presided over the Foreign Office) to Washington as a special ambassador to urge Wilson to yield to the Senate majority.

All such efforts failed. Few of them actually reached the President, still chaperoned in the sickroom by his anxious and officious wife. The break with House was complete. Wilson would not see him, and it is probable that he never saw his letters. He refused to see Lord Grey, and the former Foreign Secretary, unable to present his credentials, went home frustrated. Instead of taking what the Senate would give, the President thought up the fantastic notion of challenging the opposing Senators to resign their seats and stand for reelection on the issue of the treaty without reservations. If a majority of them won, he would name a man of their choice to be Secretary of State; then he and Vice-President Marshall would resign, and the new Secretary of State would become President. The plan was in keeping with Wilson's fondness for the British parliamentary system, but that he could suppose that the Republican Senators would accept it suggests that his illness had done strange things to his thinking.

There was no inkling of this proposal at the time. It lay hidden in Wilson's papers till long afterward. Whether he himself saw its fatuity, or was dissuaded by others from trying it, is not known. But he found a substitute. To the Democrats gathered for the Jackson Day dinner in Washington, January 8, 1920, he sent a letter addressed to the chairman of the Democratic National Committee. Asserting that the Senate must take the treaty as it was or *"leave* it," he repeated his conviction that the great majority of the American people wished the treaty ratified. If there was any doubt of this, the next election should be given the form of *"a great and solemn referendum"* on that issue.

Republicans, confident that the tide of public opinion was turning their way, professed to welcome the idea of making the 1920 election a referendum on the treaty. William Jennings Bryan, on the other hand, deplored the proposal to prolong the fight over the treaty. At the same Jackson Day dinner at which Wilson's letter was read, he proclaimed that under the principles of democracy the President should accept the verdict of the majority of the Senate and take the treaty as that body chose to interpret it.

The treaty, in fact, was not yet dead. Both Republicans and Democrats, in the new session of Congress that met in December, were willing to revive it and make a new effort at agreement. They were under heavy pressure to do so. Prominent public men like Taft, Herbert Hoover, and President Lowell of Harvard; organizations representing many millions of people and including the League to Enforce Peace and the League of Free Nations Association; leaders in the worlds of business, journalism, education, and religion put pressure on the Senate and the White House, on Lodge and Hitchcock, to compose their differences and get the treaty ratified.

Yielding to such pressure, Lodge consented to the setting
up of a bipartisan committee of Senators, which in the last
half of January 1920 attempted to agree on a compromise
set of reservations. If the committee kept any records, they
have never been made public, and all that is certainly known
about its proceedings is that rumors of an approach to agreement on Article Ten so alarmed Borah and other irreconcilables that they threatened Lodge with political reprisals
if he made any material concessions. Lodge, whose heart
was probably not in the enterprise anyway, assured Borah
that he would stand firm, and the committee ended its sessions with little to show for them.

Nevertheless, on February 9, the Senate voted to recon-
sider the treaty and for the next five weeks spent much of
its time going over the same ground traversed in the preceding fall. The reservations were again taken up and debated
one by one. Lodge made some concessions. In response to a
suggestion from Lloyd George, the preamble was altered to
make silence on the part of the allies equivalent to acceptance of the reservations. However, instead of confining the
required acceptance to three of the four principal powers,
the new preamble required the tacit assent of all thirty-one
allies; in other words, it gave to each of the thirty-one the
right of veto. The reservation on Shantung was made more
discreet by omitting reference to China and Japan as parties
to some possible future controversy. The reservation regard-
ing the six votes of the British Empire was qualified with a
suggestion that the enjoyment of an equal number of votes
by the United States would remove all objection. However,
the reservation on Article Ten was made even more sweeping than before; and Senator Gerry of Rhode Island, with
Democratic support and over Lodge's opposition, injected a
fifteenth reservation endorsing Irish independence.

Any hope that agreement might be reached vanished with
publication of a letter from Wilson to Hitchcock of March 8.

Without waiting for completion of the Senate's action on the reservations, without knowing what position it would take on Article Ten, the President denounced the reservations as a whole as "rather sweeping nullification" of the terms of the treaty. He asked Hitchcock to make known his views to the Senate Democrats. He had already repeated his warning that he would pocket the treaty if it came to him encumbered with the Lodge reservations.

In view of the President's uncompromising attitude there was little point in prolonging the agony in the Senate. The final vote was taken on March 19, 1920. The President's grip on his fellow-Democrats had slipped. This time twenty-one Democratic Senators voted with twenty-eight Republicans for approval of the treaty with the Lodge reservations. Twenty-three Democrats voted against approval. Two of them had voted consistently with the Republican irreconcilables as they did now. The other twenty-one voted nay out of loyalty to their President. The tally showed forty-nine ayes to thirty-five nays—a majority, but short of two-thirds, in favor of the treaty. A shift of seven Democratic votes from nay to aye would have sent the treaty to the President with the Senate's advice and consent. Without doubt he would have pocketed it.

One man, Woodrow Wilson, could have saved the treaty and have paved the way for the entry of the United States into the League of Nations. America's participation would, of course, have been qualified by the Lodge reservations, but experience was to show that such independence of action as the Senate had insisted on retaining in reference to Article Ten, for example, was in practice exercised by the members of the League anyway. It should have been evident to Wilson, first, that there was no possibility of the Senate's ever approving the treaty without meaningful reservations, and, second, that the League would gain far more from American membership than it would lose because of the reservations.

That Wilson failed to see these truths that are so evident today must be attributed in part to his illness and the attendant insulation from sound advice, but probably quite as much to a peculiarly stubborn streak in his character and a religious faith in his mission which sometimes approached the quality of a messianic complex.

There is, of course, no certainty that the other governments concerned would have given the necessary tacit consent to the reservations. Several of the reservations—notably those on the Monroe Doctrine, Shantung, the multiple votes of the British Empire, and the last minute obeisance to Irish independence—would have been resented and might have resulted in formal rejection by one or more of the foreign governments. Yet so vital to the success of the League was the inclusion of the power, the wealth, and the moral support of the United States that other governments might well have refrained from voicing their objections to unpalatable items in the reservations. Most likely to make trouble was that on the six votes of the British Empire. Quite probably Britain would have rejected this as it stood, but there would have remained the possibility of agreement by negotiation. In the opinion of Professor Thomas A. Bailey, one of the most careful analysts of the problem, the other governments would have ended by reconciling themselves to the American reservations, perhaps with some adjustments. If not, the responsibility for America's nonparticipation in the League would have rested clearly with them and with the Senate. Wilson would have done his utmost.

By the time of the final vote on the treaty, Wilson had made a partial recovery from his illness and was displaying an erratic and sometimes startling vigor. Early in February he abruptly dismissed Lansing as Secretary of State. He and Lansing had disagreed on many points, but the President's publicly announced reason for demanding the Secretary's resignation was that Lansing had had the temer-

ity to call the cabinet together several times while Wilson
lay incapacitated. The flimsiness of the excuse and the vitri-
olic tone of the President's language aroused popular sympathy for the displaced official.

A few days later, the press published a diatribe which
Wilson, speaking through the State Department, had aimed
at the governments of Great Britain, France, and Italy.
Charging them with scheming to bring about a settlement
of the Fiume question contrary to the moral principle that,
as he claimed, the British and French had subscribed to in
Paris, he threatened to withdraw the treaty from the Senate
and leave Europe on its own (where it was about to be left
anyway), if they went through with the alleged steal.

More like the old Wilson was a dignified veto message
that he sent to Congress on May 27, 1920. Defeat of the
treaty had left the United States technically at war with
Germany. To put the *de facto* peace on a *de jure* basis, Congress passed a joint resolution on May 21, declaring the war
at an end and claiming for the United States all the rights
(while assuming none of the responsibilities) that would
have accrued to it under the Treaty of Versailles. In returning the resolution to the House without his signature, the
President denounced it as "an action which would place in-
effaceable stain upon the gallantry and honor of the United
States."

To replace Lansing as Secretary of State, Wilson had
named Bainbridge Colby, a New York lawyer. Colby, a liberal, had left the Republican party to follow Roosevelt in
1912 and switched to support Wilson in 1916 when Roosevelt returned to the Republican fold. Wilson had made him
a member of the wartime United States Shipping Board,
and as such he had represented the United States in international conferences in London and Paris. He sympathized
fully with Wilson in his fight for the League, but as Secre-

tary of State his most important contributions to American foreign policy were in relations with Latin America and the Soviet Union. He and other new appointees to the State Department (notably Sumner Welles and Leo S. Rowe) initiated the reversal of American policy in the Caribbean which led in the 1930s to the acceptance of the principle of nonintervention, long advocated by the Latin Americans. Colby himself, as a representative of the President, visited Brazil, Uruguay, and Argentina, where he made an excellent impression and, in Buenos Aires, overcame an initial spirit of hostility, characteristic of Argentina's chronic antagonism to the United States.

If toward Latin America Colby's policy was a prelude to that of F.D.R. and Cordell Hull, toward Russia he formulated the policy of nonrecognition which F.D.R. was later to reverse. Replying to an Italian inquiry as to the American attitude toward hostilities between the Soviet Union and Poland, Colby seized the occasion to state (August 10, 1920): "It is not possible for the Government of the United States to recognize the present rulers of Russia as a government with which the relations common to friendly governments can be maintained." The Bolshevik government, he added, was one "which is determined and bound to conspire against our institutions, whose diplomats will be the agitators of dangerous revolt, whose spokesmen say that they sign agreements with no intention of keeping them." Thus Colby—or actually his unofficial adviser, the erstwhile Socialist John Spargo—laid the basis for the Russian policy of three Republican administrations.[1]

[1] See Ronald Radosh, "John Spargo and Wilson's Russian Policy, 1920," *Journal of American History*, LII, 548–565 (December 1965). Spargo, whose authorship of the note was not known till forty-five years later, had an unusual opportunity to praise his own work. In his sketch of Colby in Samuel F. Bemis, ed., *The American Secretaries of State and Their Diplomacy* (10 vols., New York: Alfred A. Knopf, 1927–29), X,

Of all Wilson's advisers, Colby alone (except for Mrs. Wilson) encouraged him in his quixotic desire to lead in person, as candidate for a third term, the fight for the League in the "great and solemn referendum" of 1920. Wilson never actually announced his candidacy, but he failed to heed the urgent and repeated advice of his secretary, Joe Tumulty, to eliminate himself from the race. On the eve of the Democratic National Convention in San Francisco, Wilson granted an interview to reporter Louis Seibold, of the New York *World*, which gave the quite erroneous impression that the President had fully recovered his health and was carrying out his responsibilities in a normal way. The widely publicized interview was generally regarded as a bid for the nomination. The President's son-in-law, William G. McAdoo, a leading candidate, announced his withdrawal from the contest. Wall Street betting now favored Wilson as the Democratic nominee.

Democratic leaders were aghast. Wilson's real friends among them were convinced, upon the word of Dr. Grayson, that the President could not survive the effort of a campaign. And they knew, whether friends or not, that Wilson's popularity had slipped so far that his candidacy would be at best a dubious asset to the party. Colby alone, perhaps out of excessive loyalty, hoped to put the nomination over. Wilson took the unusual step of sending him to the San Francisco convention as a delegate from the District of Columbia. His plan, communicated by wire to Wilson at the White House, was to take advantage of an anticipated deadlock among the announced candidates to call for a suspension of the rules and move for the nomination of Wilson by acclamation. The convention leaders learned of the plan, however, and compelled Colby to abandon it. A word from Wilson at any time

200, Spargo described Colby's note (really his own) as "one of the great outstanding landmarks in the development of American policy."

could have thrown the nomination to McAdoo. But Wilson remained silent, and on the forty-fourth ballot the convention chose Governor James M. Cox of Ohio, a candidate acceptable to the boss-dominated and "wet" Northern wing of the party. Franklin Delano Roosevelt, Assistant Secretary of the Navy through Wilson's two terms, was selected as his running mate.

The Democratic platform called for "the immediate ratification of the treaty without reservations that would impair its essential integrity," but added, over White House objection, that the party did not "oppose reservations which make more clear or specific our obligations to the associated nations." Cox and Roosevelt paid an early call on the President to assure him, in Cox's words, "Mr. President, we are going to be a million per cent for you." Both the Democratic nominees campaigned vigorously in behalf of the treaty and the League of Nations, though Cox toward the end offered to accept a reservation differing little from Lodge's on Article Ten. Wilson issued a single campaign statement, October 3. Overriding Tumulty's objection, he declared that the coming election would be a "genuine national referendum" on the League of Nations.

Meanwhile the Republicans had found their convention (which preceded that of the Democrats) deadlocked between two strong men, General Leonard Wood and Governor Frank O. Lowden of Illinois, and had turned to a respectable mediocrity, the handsome and platitudinous Senator Warren G. Harding of Ohio. The platform damned Wilson's treaty and praised the Senators who had made it safe with reservations. The irreconcilables, however, with Lodge's help, prevented an endorsement of the treaty with those Republican reservations, and held the convention to an innocuous declaration that it favored international agreements to keep the peace.

Harding, who in the Senate had voted for the treaty with

the Lodge reservations, was now, if his words meant what they seemed to mean, against the League altogether—but for contrary reasons on different days. The Senate Republicans, he boasted in his acceptance speech, had "halted the barter of independent America's eminence and influence . . . for an obscure and unequal place in the merged government of the world." But a month later he was proclaiming that this "merged government of the world," this superstate, had shown its futility by failing to halt hostilities between Poland and Soviet Russia, and was practically dead. Some weeks later, however, in an important speech at Des Moines, Iowa, the candidate apparently found that the League had revived. "My position is," he declared, "that the proposed league strikes a deadly blow at our constitutional integrity and surrenders to a dangerous extent our independence of action."

Harding denied that the Republican position was isolationist. "We do not mean to shun a single responsibility of this Republic to world civilization," he said in July; and he assured his hearers of "the Republican committal for an association of nations, cooperating in sublime accord, to attain and preserve peace through justice rather than force . . ." He recurred time after time to this promise of an "association of nations," but he did not elaborate more than to say that the Hague Tribunal should constitute its framework, and that if teeth were needed, they might be taken from the defunct League. But as to the League itself, he said at Des Moines, the issue was clear. "In simple words it is that he [Cox] favors going into the Paris League and I favor staying out."

In view of Harding's repeated anti-League statements, it is difficult to follow the reasoning of thirty-one pro-League Republicans who on October 14 published a statement drafted by Elihu Root. Voters who favored the League, it argued, should vote for Harding. The chief defect in the

League was Article Ten, which was "very objectionable to great numbers of the American people." Should Cox be elected, it was to be expected that he, like Wilson, would insist on keeping Article Ten intact, and the result would be continued deadlock between President and Senate. If Harding were elected, on the other hand, he and the Senate would quickly agree to eliminate Article Ten, and he would then call upon other nations to accept the changes desired by the United States.

A contemporary critic remarked that the thirty-one seemed to be appealing for votes for Harding with the assurance that if elected the candidate would not keep his campaign promises. Nevertheless, the statement probably saved for Harding the votes of many pro-League Republicans who were reluctant to vote the Democratic ticket. It was one of many factors that made it impossible to regard the election as, in Wilson's words, "a genuine national referendum" on the League issue. But when Harding won the election by an unprecedented landslide (sixteen million votes to nine million), that was precisely how he did choose to regard it. Forgetful of the assurances of the thirty-one (who, incidentally, did little to remind Harding of their promises in his behalf), Harding informed Congress, on April 12, 1921, that "there will be no betrayal of the deliberate expression of the American people in the recent election . . . the League Covenant can have no sanction from us."

As the months went by, furthermore, Harding made no move toward the formation of the association of nations that he had promised as a substitute for the League. He even denied that he had made the promise. Whatever the American people had actually voted for in November 1920, the issue of the League of Nations and of collective security in general was dead, not to be revived for twenty years. The irreconcilables, the Borahs, Johnsons, and Brandegees, small though their number, were in key positions to shape foreign policy; and the majority of the American people, weary of Wilsonian idealism, were ready to adopt an attitude of comfortable and prosperous isolationism. They readily acquiesced as the exciting statesmanship of Theodore Roosevelt and Woodrow Wilson gave way to the placidity of Harding, the conservatism of Coolidge, and the qualified pacifism of Herbert Hoover.

The Fourteen Points

Excerpts from President Wilson's address to a joint session of Congress, January 8, 1918. (*Papers Relating to the Foreign Relations of the United States, 1918,* Supplement I, Vol. I, 12–17.)

Beginning with a reference to the negotiations at Brest-Litovsk between representatives of the Bolshevik government of Russia and of the Central Powers, Wilson remarked that the Russian representatives had "presented not only a perfectly definite statement of the principles upon which they would be willing to conclude peace but also an equally definite programme of the concrete application of those principles." The program of the Central Powers, on the other hand, "proposed no concessions at all either to the sovereignty of Russia or to the preferences of the populations with whose fortunes it dealt, but meant, in a word, that the Central Powers were to keep every foot of territory their armed forces had occupied . . . as a permanent addition to their territories and their power."

The Brest-Litovsk negotiations, Wilson remarked, illustrated the need for a clear definition of war aims, and he continued:

"There is, moreover, a voice calling for these definitions of principle and of purpose which is, it seems to me, more thrilling and more compelling than any of the many moving voices with which the troubled air of the world is filled. It is the voice of the Russian people. They are prostrate and all but helpless, it would

seem, before the grim power of Germany, which has hitherto
known no relenting and no pity. Their power, apparently, is shat-
tered. And yet their soul is not subservient. They will not yield
either in principle or in action. Their conception of what is right,
of what it is humane and honorable for them to accept, has been
stated with a frankness, a largeness of view, a generosity of spirit,
and a universal human sympathy which must challenge the admiration of every friend of mankind; and they have refused to
compound their ideals or desert others that they themselves may
be safe. They call to us to say what it is that we desire, in what,
if anything, our purpose and our spirit differ from theirs; and I
believe that the people of the United States would wish me to
respond, with utter simplicity and frankness. Whether their present leaders believe it or not, it is our heartfelt desire and hope
that some way may be opened whereby we may be privileged to
assist the people of Russia to attain their utmost hope of liberty
and ordered peace.

"It will be our wish and purpose that the processes of peace,
when they are begun, shall be absolutely open and that they shall
involve and permit henceforth no secret understandings of any
kind. The day of conquest and aggrandizement is gone by; so is
also the day of secret covenants entered into in the interest of
particular governments and likely at some unlooked-for moment
to upset the peace of the world. It is this happy fact, now clear to
the view of every public man whose thoughts do not still linger
in an age that is dead and gone, which makes it possible for every
nation whose purposes are consistent with justice and the peace
of the world to avow now or at any other time the objects it has
in view.

"We entered this war because violations of right had occurred
which touched us to the quick and made the life of our own people impossible unless they were corrected and the world secured
once for all against their recurrence. What we demand in this
war, therefore, is nothing peculiar to ourselves. It is that the
world be made fit and safe to live in; and particularly that it be
made safe for every peace-loving nation which, like our own,
wishes to live its own life, determine its own institutions, be assured of justice and fair dealing by the other peoples of the world

as against force and selfish aggression. All the peoples of the world are in effect partners in this interest, and for our own part we see very clearly that unless justice be done to others it will not be done to us. The programme of the world's peace, therefore, is our programme; and that programme, the only possible programme, as we see it is this:

"I. Open covenants of peace, openly arrived at, after which there shall be no private international understandings of any kind but diplomacy shall proceed always frankly and in the public view.

"II. Absolute freedom of navigation upon the seas, outside territorial waters, alike in peace and in war, except as the seas may be closed in whole or in part by international action for the enforcement of international covenants.

"III. The removal, so far as possible, of all economic barriers and the establishment of an equality of trade conditions among all the nations consenting to the peace and associating themselves for its maintenance.

"IV. Adequate guarantees given and taken that national armaments will be reduced to the lowest point consistent with domestic safety.

"V. A free, open-minded, and absolutely impartial adjustment of all colonial claims, based upon a strict observance of the principle that in determining all such questions of sovereignty the interests of the populations concerned must have equal weight with the equitable claims of the government whose title is to be determined.

"VI. The evacuation of all Russian territory and such a settlement of all questions affecting Russia as will secure the best and freest cooperation of the other nations of the world in obtaining for her an unhampered and unembarrassed opportunity for the independent determination of her own political development and national policy and assure her of a sincere welcome into the society of free nations under institutions of her own choosing; and, more than a welcome, assistance also of every kind that she may need and may herself desire. The treatment accorded Russia by her sister nations in the months to come will be the acid test of their good will, of their comprehension of her needs as distinguished from their own interests, and of their intelligent and unselfish sympathy.

"VII. Belgium, the whole world will agree, must be evacuated and restored, without any attempt to limit the sovereignty which she enjoys in common with all other free nations. No other single act will serve as this will serve to restore confidence among the nations in the laws which they have themselves set and determined for the government of their relations with one another. Without this healing act the whole structure and validity of international law is forever impaired.

"VIII. All French territory should be freed and the invaded portions restored, and the wrong done to France by Prussia in 1871 in the matter of Alsace-Lorraine, which has unsettled the peace of the world for nearly fifty years, should be righted, in order that peace may once more be made secure in the interest of all.

"IX. A readjustment of the frontiers of Italy should be effected along clearly recognizable lines of nationality.

"X. The peoples of Austria-Hungary, whose place among the nations we wish to see safeguarded and assured, should be accorded the freest opportunity of autonomous development.

"XI. Rumania, Serbia, and Montenegro should be evacuated; occupied territories restored; Serbia accorded free and secure access to the sea; and the relations of the several Balkan states to one another determined by friendly counsel along historically established lines of allegiance and nationality; and international guarantees of the political and economic independence and territorial integrity of the several Balkan states should be entered into.

"XII. The Turkish portions of the present Ottoman Empire should be assured a secure sovereignty, but the other nationalities which are now under Turkish rule should be assured an undoubted security of life and an absolutely unmolested opportunity of autonomous development, and the Dardanelles should be permanently opened as a free passage to the ships and commerce of all nations under international guarantees.

"XIII. An independent Polish state should be erected which should include the territories inhabited by indisputably Polish populations, which should be assured a free and secure access to the sea, and whose political and economic independence and territorial integrity should be guaranteed by international covenant.

"XIV. A general association of nations must be formed under specific covenant for the purpose of affording mutual guarantees of political independence and territorial integrity to great and small states alike.

"In regard to these essential rectifications of wrong and assertions of right we feel ourselves to be intimate partners of all the governments and peoples associated together against the Imperialists. We cannot be separated in interest or divided in purpose. We stand together until the end. . . .

"We have spoken now, surely, in terms too concrete to admit of any further doubt or question. An evident principle runs through the whole programme I have outlined. It is the principle of justice to all peoples and nationalities, and their right to live on equal terms of liberty and safety with one another, whether they be strong or weak. Unless this principle be made its foundation no part of the structure of international justice can stand. The people of the United States could act upon no other principle; and to the vindication of this principle they are ready to devote their lives, their honor, and everything that they possess. The moral climax of this the culminating and final war for human liberty has come, and they are ready to put their own strength, their own highest purpose, their own integrity and devotion to the test."

Further Reading

Useful general accounts of the foreign relations of the period, 1900–21, are found in the appropriate chapters of a number of such widely used textbooks as the following: Thomas A. Bailey, *A Diplomatic History of the American People* (7th ed., New York, 1964); Samuel F. Bemis, *A Diplomatic History of the United States* (5th ed., New York, 1965); Alexander De Conde, *A History of American Foreign Policy* (New York, 1963); Julius W. Pratt, *A History of United States Foreign Policy* (2nd ed., Englewood Cliffs, N.J., 1965). Richard W. Leopold, *The Growth of American Foreign Policy: A History* (New York, 1962), adopts a more analytical approach than the others, gives much attention to the techniques and principles of the diplomatic process, and devotes some seven-eighths of its pages to the period since 1889. Another topically organized narrative, covering the period from 1783 to 1943, is Richard W. Van Alstyne, *American Diplomacy in Action: A Series of Case Studies* (Stanford University, 1944). Briefer textbooks are: Robert H. Ferrell, *American Diplomacy: A History* (New York, 1959); L. Ethan Ellis, *A Short History of American Diplomacy* (New York, 1951); Samuel F. Bemis, *A Short History of American Policy and Diplomacy* (New York, 1959); and, for the period since 1900, the same author's *The United States as a World Power* (revised ed., New York, 1955).

Volumes IX and X of *The American Secretaries of State and Their Diplomacy*, edited by Samuel F. Bemis (10 vols., New York, 1927–29), contain sketches of the Secretaries of the period which are still useful. Briefer sketches are presented in Norman A. Graebner (ed.), *An Uncertain Tradition: American Secretaries of State in the Twentieth Century* (New York, 1961). Noteworthy critiques of American foreign policy, especially its twentieth-century phases, are found in George F. Kennan's small volume *American Diplomacy, 1900–1950* (New York, 1951), and, on a larger scale, in Robert E. Osgood, *Ideals and Self-Interest in America's Foreign Relations: The Great Transformation of the Twentieth Century* (Chicago, 1953), and Hans J. Morgenthau, *In Defense of the National Interest: A Critical Examination of American Foreign Policy* (New York, 1951).

The official compilation of American diplomatic correspondence since 1860 is the Department of State's multivolume series, *Papers Relating to the Foreign Relations of the United States* (since 1931 renamed *Foreign Relations of the United States: Diplomatic Papers*), customarily referred to simply as *Foreign Relations.* The series comprises one or more volumes annually, and for the period of World War I was expanded to include supplementary volumes of correspondence relating to the war, to relations with Soviet Russia, and to the peace conference in Paris. Useful selections drawn from this and other sources are found in Ruhl J. Bartlett (ed.), *The Record of American Diplomacy: Documents and Readings in the History of American Foreign Relations* (4th ed., New York, 1964); Dorothy B. Goebel (ed.), *American Foreign Policy: A Documentary Survey, 1776–1960* (New York, 1961); William A. Williams (ed.), *The Shaping of American Diplomacy: Readings and Documents in American Foreign Relations, 1750–1955* (Chicago, 1956); Robert A. Divine (ed.), *American Foreign Policy* (New York, 1960); Norman A. Graebner (ed.), *Ideas and Diplomacy: Readings in the Intellectual Tradition of American Foreign Policy* (New York, 1964); Daniel M. Smith (ed.), *Major Problems in American Diplomatic History: Documents and Readings* (Boston, 1964).

For the student undertaking to do research in American diplomatic history in any period from independence to 1921 the best handbook is still Samuel F. Bemis and Grace Gardner Griffin, *Guide to the Diplomatic History of the United States, 1775–1921* (Washington, 1935). This should be supplemented by reference to Oscar Handlin *et al.* (eds.), *Harvard Guide to American History* (Cambridge, 1954), which includes items, in diplomatic and other fields, published since Bemis and Griffin compiled their *Guide*.

Different aspects of the period as a whole are treated in a number of specialized works. Thomas A. Bailey, *The Man in the Street: The Impact of American Public Opinion on Foreign Policy* (New York, 1948), explores the subject described in the subtitle. Julius W. Pratt, *America's Colonial Experiment* (New York, 1950), deals with American policy in its newly acquired dependencies and protectorates following the war with Spain. Policy toward Latin America is described at length in Samuel F. Bemis, *The Latin American Policy of the United States* (New York, 1943), and special aspects of it in Dana G. Munro, *Intervention and Dollar Diplomacy in the Caribbean, 1900–1921* (Princeton, 1964); Dexter Perkins, *A History of the Monroe Doctrine* (revised ed., Boston, 1955) and *The United States and the Caribbean* (Cambridge, 1947); J. Fred Rippy, *The Caribbean Danger Zone* (New York, 1940); Wilfrid H. Callcott, *The Caribbean Policy of the United States, 1890–1920* (Baltimore, 1942). The best, though somewhat overly critical, account of Far Eastern policy during the period is A. Whitney Griswold, *The Far Eastern Policy of the United States* (New York, 1938). Popular accounts of relations with the two chief Asiatic powers are two books by Foster Rhea Dulles: *Forty Years of American Japanese Relations* (New York, 1937), and *China and America: The Story of Their Relations Since 1784* (Princeton, 1946). Mr. Dulles has also contributed a volume on United States-Russian relations in *The Road to Teheran: The Story of Russia and America, 1781–1943* (Princeton, 1944). Both this volume and William A. Williams, *American-Russian Relations, 1781–1947* (New York, 1952), are inclined to a somewhat too roseate view of the subject. Better balanced is Thomas A. Bailey, *America Faces Russia: Russian American Relations from Early Times to Our Day* (Ithaca, 1950). A useful general survey of relations with England is Harry C. Allen, *Great Britain and the United States: A History of Anglo-American Relations (1783–1952)* (New York, 1955). For books on special aspects or periods of relations with the above areas or nations, see the sections below.

For United States naval policy during the period covered, see two books by Harold and Margaret Sprout, *The Rise of American Naval Power, 1776–1918* (Princeton, 1939), and *Toward a New Order of Sea Power* (Princeton, 1940); George T. Davis, *A Navy Second to None* (New York, 1940); William R. Braisted, *The United States Navy in the Pacific, 1897–1909* (Austin, Texas, 1958); also two articles by Seward W. Livermore: "Battleship Diplomacy in South America, 1905–1925," *Journal of Modern History,* XVI, 31–48 (March 1944), and "The American Navy as a Factor in World Politics, 1903–1913," *American Historical Review,* LXIII, 863–879 (July 1958).

On the hopeful but generally unfruitful efforts to promote peace, arbitration, and the limitation of armaments, the following are useful: Merle Curti, *Peace or War: The American Struggle, 1636–1936* (New York, 1936); Joseph H. Choate, *The Two Hague Conferences* (Princeton, 1913); Calvin De A. Davis, *The United States and the First Hague Peace Conference* (Ithaca, 1962); and two books by Merze Tate: *The Disarmament Illusion: The Movement for a Limitation of Armaments to 1907* (New York, 1942), and *The United States and Armaments* (Cambridge, 1948). Francis J. Weber, "The Pious Fund of the Californias," *Hispanic American Historical Review,* XLIII, 78–94 (February 1963), tells of the first resort by the United States to the Permanent Court of Arbitration at The Hague.

THE ROOSEVELT-TAFT PERIOD
1901–13

A rich source for the development of Theodore Roosevelt's ideas on public policy is found in the eight volumes of *The Letters of Theodore Roosevelt* edited by Elting E. Morison (Cambridge, 1951–54). Important exchanges between Roosevelt and his friend Senator Lodge are printed in H. C. Lodge (ed.), *Selections from the Correspondence of Theodore Roosevelt and Henry Cabot Lodge* (2 vols., New York, 1925). Roosevelt published his own version of his career in *Theodore Roosevelt: An Autobiography* (New York, 1916). The year after his death

Joseph Bucklin Bishop published the first important biography, *Theodore Roosevelt and His Time Shown in His Own Letters* (2 vols., New York, 1920). Of the many other biographies, mention should be made of the following: William R. Thayer, *Theodore Roosevelt: An Intimate Biography* (Boston, 1919), made much of Roosevelt's handling of the Venezuela crisis with Germany. Lewis Einstein, *Roosevelt, His Mind in Action* (Boston, 1930), compares Roosevelt to the great men of the Italian Renaissance in his combination of intellectual versatility and dedication to action. Henry F. Pringle, in his *Theodore Roosevelt: A Biography* (New York, 1931), treated his subject with a gentle irony that commended the book to thousands of readers. A more complete account is William H. Harbaugh, *Power and Responsibility: The Life and Times of Theodore Roosevelt* (New York, 1961). A brilliant interpretative essay is *The Republican Roosevelt* (Cambridge, 1954), by John M. Blum. Howard K. Beale's scholarly and heavily documented *Theodore Roosevelt and the Rise of America to World Power* (Baltimore, 1956) is an intensive study of Roosevelt's foreign policy which casts important new light on such controversial episodes as the Venezuela crisis of 1902–03 and the Algeciras Conference of 1906. George E. Mowry in *The Era of Theodore Roosevelt, 1900–1912* (New York, 1958), a volume in *The New American Nation Series,* deals at greater length with domestic affairs than with foreign. Foster Rhea Dulles concludes his book, *The Imperial Years* (New York, 1956), with chapters on Roosevelt's policies toward Latin America, the Far East, and Europe.

There are also a number of studies of specific episodes in Roosevelt's foreign policy. Alfred L. P. Dennis, *Adventures in American Diplomacy, 1896–1906* (New York, 1928), covers a number of these as well as some that preceded Roosevelt's accession to the presidency. Improving relations with England and the amicable settlement of controversies over the proposed isthmian canal and the Alaskan boundary form the subject of three books (see also Allen, *op. cit.*): Alexander E. Campbell, *Great Britain and the United States, 1895–1903* (London, 1960); Charles S. Campbell, *Anglo-American Understanding, 1898–1903* (Baltimore, 1957); Lionel M. Gelber, *The Rise of Anglo-Ameri-*

can Friendship: A Study in World Politics, 1898–1906 (New York, 1938). On the acquisition of the Panama Canal Zone, two useful books are Gerstle Mack, *The Land Divided: A History of the Panama Canal and Other Isthmian Canal Projects* (New York, 1944), and Dwight C. Miner, *The Fight for the Panama Route* (New York, 1940). The latter improves upon most other accounts by including a clear analysis of the background of the episode in Colombian politics. See also the lively narrative by one of the chief actors in Philippe Bunau-Varilla, *Panama: The Creation, Destruction, and Resurrection* (New York, 1914). A critical view of Bunau-Varilla's activities is presented by Charles D. Ameringer, "Philippe Bunau-Varilla: New Light on the Panama Canal Treaty," *Hispanic American Historical Review*, XLVI, 28–52 (February 1966). A far from satisfying biography of another participant is *William Nelson Cromwell, 1854–1948*, by Arthur H. Dean (privately printed, New York, 1957). Interesting light on the Alaska boundary question is presented in Thomas A. Bailey, "Theodore Roosevelt and the Alaska Boundary Settlement," *Canadian Historical Review*, XVIII, 123–130 (June 1937).

On Roosevelt's handling of Anglo-German intervention in Venezuela, the conventional view (which discredits Roosevelt's account) is well presented in Dexter Perkins, *The Monroe Doctrine, 1867–1907* (Baltimore, 1937). For support of the essentials of Roosevelt's story, see Beale, *op. cit.*, and Seward W. Livermore, "Theodore Roosevelt, the American Navy, and the Venezuela Crisis of 1902–1903," *American Historical Review*, LI, 452–471 (April 1946).

Useful monographs on specific aspects of Roosevelt's policy in the Far East are Tyler Dennett, *Theodore Roosevelt and the Russo-Japanese War* (Garden City, New York, 1935), and Thomas A. Bailey, *Theodore Roosevelt and the Japanese-American Crises* (Stanford University, 1934). These are now to some extent superseded by Raymond A. Esthus, *Theodore Roosevelt and Japan* (Seattle, 1966), which is based on extensive use of Japanese as well as American sources. A critical view of the round-the-world cruise of the battleship fleet is presented in Robert A. Hart, *The Great White Fleet; Its Voyage around the World, 1907–1909* (Boston, 1965). Louella J. Hall, "The Abortive

German-American-Chinese Entente of 1907–8," *Journal of Modern History*, 219–235 (June 1929), describes the Kaiser's effort on this occasion to align Roosevelt and the American Navy with Germany.

Biographies of Roosevelt's chief lieutenants, John Hay, Elihu Root, and William H. Taft, supplement those of Roosevelt himself. William R. Thayer, *The Life and Letters of John Hay* (2 vols., Boston, 1915)—the origin, in print, of the contention over T. R.'s Venezuela policy—is admiring, while Tyler Dennett, *John Hay: From Poetry to Politics* (New York, 1933), is disillusioned with Hay and more so with Roosevelt. Philip C. Jessup, *Elihu Root* (2 vols., New York, 1938), is a sound biography of an exceptionally able and versatile statesman. Richard W. Leopold, *Elihu Root and the Conservative Tradition* (Boston, 1954), is a perspicacious interpretative essay. Taft has inspired only one important biography, Henry F. Pringle, *The Life and Times of William Howard Taft* (2 vols., New York, 1939). For Philander C. Knox, his Secretary of State, one must rely on the sketches in Volume IX of Bemis (ed.), *The American Secretaries of State and Their Diplomacy*, and in Graebner (ed.), *An Uncertain Tradition*, both previously cited. Herbert Croly, *Willard Straight* (New York, 1924), and Charles Vevier, *The United States and China, 1906–1913* (New Brunswick, N. J., 1955), illuminate the Far Eastern policy of the Taft administration. L. Ethan Ellis, *Reciprocity, 1911: A Study in Canadian-American Relations* (New Haven, 1939), tells the story of one of Taft's failures. C. C. Tansill, *Canadian-American Relations, 1875–1911* (New Haven, 1943), includes the background of the reciprocity fiasco.

THE WILSON PERIOD
1913–21

GENERAL ACCOUNTS. *The Papers of Woodrow Wilson*, a definitive multivolume work under the editorship of Arthur S. Link, is in process of publication by Princeton University Press. Volume I (1856–1880) was published late in 1966. *The Public Papers of Woodrow Wilson*, edited by R. S. Baker and W. E. Dodd,

comprise six volumes (New York, 1925–27), of which the last
four contain material dealing with foreign relations. Until recently
the most authoritative biography of the wartime President
was Ray Stannard Baker, *Woodrow Wilson, Life and Letters* (8 vols., Garden City, N.Y., 1927–39), continued in the same
author's earlier *Woodrow Wilson and World Settlement* (3 vols.,
Garden City, N.Y., 1922). While still useful, this work is in the
course of being supplanted by Arthur S. Link's *Wilson*, of which
five volumes have so far appeared (Princeton, 1947–65). The
fifth volume, subtitled *Campaigns for Progressivism and Peace,
1916–1917*, concludes with the declaration of war against Germany. In addition to his multivolume biography, Link has published a number of other volumes on Wilson or the Wilson
period; notably *Wilson the Diplomatist: A Look at His Major
Foreign Policies* (Baltimore, 1957), a group of lectures; *Woodrow
Wilson and the Progressive Era, 1910–1917* (New York, 1954),
a volume in the *New American Nation Series;* and *Woodrow Wilson: A Brief Biography* (Cleveland, 1963).

A number of other writers have tried their hands at less ambitious biographies than those by Baker and Link. One of the
earliest was *Woodrow Wilson and His Work* (Garden City, N.Y.,
1920), by William E. Dodd, a talented scholar whose sympathetic admiration for Wilson's ideals of democracy and peace was
manifest in his writing. Other biographies are H. F. C. Bell,
Woodrow Wilson and the People (Garden City, N.Y., 1945), and,
most recently, Arthur Walworth, *Woodrow Wilson* (revised ed.,
2 vols. in one, Boston, 1965). A sympathetic interpretative essay
is John M. Blum, *Woodrow Wilson and the Politics of Morality*
(Boston, 1956). Herbert Hoover, in *The Ordeal of Woodrow
Wilson* (New York, 1958), portrayed the struggle for "a just and
lasting peace" by the President whom he had once served as
food commissioner for war-torn Europe.

The peculiarly intimate and later tragically sundered friendship between Wilson and Colonel Edward M. House has attracted
studies which have had to be based largely on the voluminous
Intimate Papers of Colonel House, edited by Charles Seymour (4 vols., Boston, 1926–28), incidentally a prime source for

the Wilson era down to his break with House in 1919. The first
to attempt an analysis of this relationship was George Sylvester
Viereck (a German sympathizer during the war) in *The Strang-
est Friendship in History: Woodrow Wilson and Colonel House*
(New York, 1932). More recently Alexander L. and Juliette L.
George, in *Woodrow Wilson and Colonel House: A Personality
Study* (New York, 1956), have applied modern psychological
techniques, especially to Wilson, reaching the conclusion that his
efforts for a league of nations were virtually foredoomed to failure by deeply ingrained traits of personality.

Of Wilson's three Secretaries of State, William Jennings Bryan,
Robert Lansing, and Bainbridge Colby, there are sketches in
Bemis (ed.), *American Secretaries of State and Their Diplomacy*,
Volume X, and of the first two in Graebner (ed.), *An Uncertain
Tradition*. Of this phase of Bryan's career the most satisfactory
studies are Merle Curti, *Bryan and World Peace* (Smith College
Studies in History, No. 16, 1931), and the relevant chapters in
Paxton Hibben, *The Peerless Leader* (New York, 1929). The
disruption of the State Department and the diplomatic service
by Bryan's application of the spoils system is described in Paolo
E. Coletta, "Secretary of State William Jennings Bryan and 'Deserving Democrats,'" *Mid-America*, XLVIII, 75–98 (April 1966).

Secretary Lansing published, among other things, *The Peace
Negotiations: A Personal Narrative* (Boston, 1921). *The War
Memoirs of Robert Lansing* (New York, 1935) was published
after his death, as were *The Lansing Papers* (2 vols., Washing-
ton, 1940, in the *Papers Relating to the Foreign Relations of the
United States*). Two monographs on Lansing's policies are Daniel
M. Smith, *Robert Lansing and American Neutrality, 1914–1917*
(Berkeley, 1958), and Burton F. Beers, *Vain Endeavor: Robert
Lansing's Attempts to End the American-Japanese Rivalry* (Dur-
ham, 1962).

Something of the work and the attitudes of American diplomats
abroad is revealed in Burton J. Hendrick (ed.), *The Life and
Letters of Walter H. Page* (3 vols., Garden City, N.Y., 1923–25);
James W. Gerard, *My Four Years in Germany* (New York, 1918);
and the first volume of Joseph C. Grew, *Turbulent Era: A*

Diplomatic Record of Forty Years, 1904–1945 (2 vols. Boston, 1952). William Phillips, *Ventures in Diplomacy* (Boston, 1953), writes of the State Department during Wilson's presidency.

Letters and memoirs of members of Wilson's cabinet that throw some light on foreign policy are D. F. Houston, *Eight Years with Wilson's Cabinet* (2 vols., Garden City, N. Y., 1926); W. C. Redfield, *With Congress and Cabinet* (Garden City, N.Y., 1924); A. W. Lane and L. H. Wall (eds.), *The Letters of Franklin K. Lane* (Boston, 1922); Josephus Daniels, *The Wilson Era: Years of Peace, 1910–1917* (Chapel Hill, 1944), and *The Wilson Era: Years of War and After* (Chapel Hill, 1946); also *The Cabinet Diaries of Josephus Daniels, 1913–1921*, edited by David Cronon (Lincoln, Nebraska, 1963). To this list should be added the memoir by Wilson's secretary throughout his eight years in the White House, *Woodrow Wilson as I Know Him*, by Joseph P. Tumulty (Garden City, N.Y., 1921), to be supplemented by John M. Blum, *Joe Tumulty and the Wilson Era* (Boston, 1951); and also the recollections of Wilson's second wife, *My Memoir*, by Edith Bolling Wilson (Indianapolis, 1939).

PROBLEMS OF THE FAR EAST AND LATIN AMERICA. For Wilson's policy in the Far East, apart from the intervention in Siberia (for which see below) the best account is probably R. W. Curry, *Woodrow Wilson and Far Eastern Policy, 1913–1921* (New York, 1957). For his policy toward Latin America other than Mexico see the works by Bemis, Callcott, and Munro cited on page 227, and the biographies by Baker and Link. To these may be added Selig Adler, "Bryan and Wilsonian Caribbean Penetration," *Hispanic American Historical Review*, XX, 198–226 (May 1940), which shows Bryan to have been a would-be practitioner of a novel kind of "dollar diplomacy"; and Daniel M. Smith, "Bainbridge Colby and the Good Neighbor Policy, 1920–1921," *Mississippi Valley Historical Review*, L, 56–78 (June 1963), which brings out a little-known contribution to improved hemisphere relations by Wilson's last Secretary of State.

Wilson's trial-and-error policy toward Mexico and its revolution has inspired a number of books and articles. The best general account is Howard F. Cline, *The United States and Mexico* (revised ed., Cambridge, 1963). Robert E. Quirk, *An Affair of Honor: Woodrow Wilson and the Occupation of Veracruz* (Lexington, Ky. 1962), is justly critical of Wilson's bungling of that episode. The origins of the revolution are set forth in C. C. Cumberland, *The Mexican Revolution: Genesis under Madero* (Austin, Texas, 1952), and Stanley R. Ross, *Francisco I. Madero* (New York, 1955). An American diplomat's irregular role in the overthrow of Madero is made clear in Lowell L. Blaisdell, "Henry Lane Wilson, and the Overthrow of Madero," *Southwestern Social Science Quarterly*, XLIII, 126–135 (September 1962). Later phases are related in Clarence C. Clendenen, *The United States and Pancho Villa* (Ithaca, 1961), and Frank Tompkins, *Chasing Villa* (Harrisburg, Pa., 1934).

An episode not strictly in Latin America but on the border of it is covered, with historical background, in Charles C. Tansill, *The Purchase of the Danish West Indies* (Baltimore, 1932).

THE STRUGGLE FOR NEUTRALITY, 1914–17. The literature on American neutrality and eventual involvement in World War I is endless. The most recent and probably the best analyses are in the third, fourth, and fifth volumes of Link's *Wilson;* in Ernest R. May, *The World War and American Neutrality, 1914–1917* (Cambridge, 1963); and in a briefer work, Daniel M. Smith, *The Great Departure: The United States and World War I, 1914–1920* (New York, 1965). Edward H. Buehrig, *Woodrow Wilson and the Balance of Power* (Bloomington, 1958), examines the part played by that concept in Wilson's thinking, and that of his advisers. Barbara W. Tuchman, *The Zimmermann Telegram* (New York, 1958), and Samuel R. Spencer, *Decision for War, 1917* (Peterborough, N.H., 1953), examine the influence of special episodes on Wilson's decision for war. R. G. Albion and J. B. Pope, *Sea Lanes in Wartime* (New York, 1942), place the issue of neutral rights in its historic setting. The isolationist atmosphere of the 1930s persuaded some historians and popular writers that American entry into the war in 1917 had been a mistake. The most impressive exemplar of this approach is Charles C. Tansill, *America Goes to War* (Boston, 1938). Written from a similar viewpoint but excessively legalistic in method is E. M. Borchard and W. P. Lage, *Neutrality for the United States* (2nd ed., New Haven, 1940). Walter R. Millis, *Road to War, 1914–1917* (Boston, 1935), was a popular handling of essentially the same thesis. C. Hartley Grattan, *Why We Fought* (New York, 1929), foreshadowed the isolationist interpretation. H. C. Peterson, *Propaganda for War* (Norman, Oklahoma, 1939), and H. C. Peterson and G. C. Fite, *Opponents of War, 1917–1918* (Madison, Wisconsin, 1957), present, in effect, opposite sides of the same coin.

Defenses of the American decision for war by men who had shared in making the decision or in negotiating the peace are Newton D. Baker, *Why We Went to War* (New York, 1936), and two books by Charles Seymour: *American Diplomacy during the World War* (Baltimore, 1934), and *American Neutrality, 1914–1917* (New Haven, 1935).

A useful summary of changing interpretations of the reasons for American entry into the war in 1917 is Daniel M. Smith, "National Interest and American Intervention, 1917," *Journal of American History*, LII 5–24 (June 1965).

THE DIPLOMACY OF WARTIME, 1917–1918. The wartime relations of the United States with the Far East and Latin America are described in the books cited in the first paragraph of the section before the last, and in the following: Percy A. Martin, *Latin America and the War* (Baltimore, 1925); James W. Morley, *The Japanese Thrust Into Siberia* (New York, 1957); Frank W. Iklé, "Japanese-German Peace Negotiations during World War I," *American Historical Review*, LXX, 62–76 (October 1965).

America's rather hesitant cooperation with its European "associates" in the war is described in David F. Trask, *The United States in the Supreme War Council: American War Aims and Inter-Allied Strategy, 1917–1918* (Middletown, Conn., 1961); Lord Hankey, *The Supreme Command, 1914–1918* (2 vols., London, 1961); and Arthur Willert, *The Road to Safety: A Study in Anglo-American Relations* (New York, 1953). Informal contacts with a peace-minded opposition group in England are described in Laurence W. Martin, "Woodrow Wilson's Appeal to the People of Europe: British Radical Influence on the President's Strategy," *Political Science Quarterly,* LXXIV, 498–516 (December 1959).

The story of the formulation of American war aims by a group of scholars and publicists under the supervision of Colonel House is told by Lawrence E. Gelfand in *The Inquiry: American Preparation for Peace, 1917–1919* (New Haven, 1963). American interest in the problem of French security during the war and at the peace conference is described in Louis A. R. Yates, *The United States and French Security, 1917–1921: A Study in American Diplomatic History* (New York, 1957). The skillful tactics of Polish leaders in cultivating American support for an independent Poland are well brought out in Louis L. Gerson, *Woodrow Wilson and the Rebirth of Poland, 1914–1920* (New Haven, 1953), which covers part of the same ground as Victor S. Mamatey, *The United States and East Central Europe, 1914–1918* (Princeton, 1957).

The most difficult diplomatic problem that Wilson had to solve during American participation in the war was that of the American attitude toward the Bolshevik (Soviet) government of Russia. This relationship has been made the subject of a detailed study by America's leading "Kremlinologist," George F. Kennan. Of a projected three-volume work entitled *Soviet-American Relations, 1917–1920,* he has published Volumes I and II, subtitled *Russia Leaves the War* and *The Decision to Intervene* (Princeton, 1956 and 1958 respectively). His *Russia and the West under Lenin and Stalin* (Boston, 1961) includes a much less detailed account of the same period. Other works dealing with the American attitude to Bolshevik Russia are Christopher Lasch, *The American Liberals and the Russian Revolution* (New York, 1962), and Leonid I. Strakhovsky, *American Opinion about Russia, 1917–1920* (Toronto, 1961). See also Robert D. Worth, *The Allies and the Russian Revolution* (Durham, 1954).

Strakhovsky has also told the story of the Allied and American intervention in North Russia in two books: *The Origins of American Intervention in North Russia (1918)* (Princeton, 1937), and *Intervention at Archangel: The Story of Allied Intervention and*

Russian Counter-Revolution in North Russia, 1918–1920 (Princeton, 1944). A popular account of the same episode is E. M. Halliday, *The Ignorant Armies* (New York, 1960). The more formidable intervention in Siberia has also been the subject of a number of books. In one of these, *America's Siberian Adventure, 1918–1920* (New York, 1931), General William S. Graves, commander of the American expedition, relates how he skillfully avoided being used by Japanese and Allied agents for their own purposes. Probably the best comprehensive account is Betty M. Unterberger, *America's Siberian Expedition, 1918–1920* (Durham, 1946), but see also John A. White, *The Siberian Intervention* (Princeton, 1950), and Clarence A. Manning, *The Siberian Fiasco* (New York, 1952).

Ronald Radosh, "John Spargo and Wilson's Russian Policy," *Journal of American History*, LII, 548–565 (December, 1965), shows the influence of a former Socialist in setting the United States on a firm course of nonrecognition of the Soviet Union.

THE PARIS PEACE CONFERENCE, 1919. On the peace negotiations of 1919, the studies by Trask, Gelfand, Yates, Gerson, Mamatey, and Kennan (*Russia and the West under Lenin and Stalin*), and Worth, listed in the preceding section, are relevant, as are the biographies of Wilson, especially those by Bell, Walworth, and the Georges. The most comprehensive history of the conference is still H. W. V. Temperley, *A History of the Peace Conference at Paris* (6 vols., London, 1920–24). The nearest approach to an American official history is R. S. Baker's three-volume *Woodrow Wilson and World Settlement*, previously cited, which, however, is marred by excessive devotion to the President. The thirteen documentary volumes, *The Paris Peace Conference* (Washington, 1942–47), in *Papers Relating to the Foreign Relations of the United States*, have not been fully exploited. Numerous participants in the conference have recorded their experiences and impressions. On the British side, David Lloyd George, *Memoirs of the Peace Conference* (2 vols., New Haven, 1939), and Harold Nicolson, *Peacemaking* (Boston, 1933), were highly critical of Wilson, though Nicolson had a high opinion of the American experts and of Colonel House. A young

British economist, later to become world-famous, John Maynard Keynes, in his devastating *The Economic Consequences of the Peace* (New York, 1920), foretold the evil consequences to Europe as a whole of the harsh economic terms imposed upon Germany.

Accounts by American participants (in addition to Baker's cited above) are Robert Lansing, *The Peace Negotiations* (Boston, 1921); Seymour (ed.), *The Intimate Papers of Colonel House*, previously cited; E. M. House and C. Seymour (eds.), *What Really Happened at Paris* (New York, 1921); C. H. Haskins and R. H. Lord, *Some Problems of the Peace Conference* (Cambridge, 1920); Thomas W. Lamont, *Across World Frontiers* (New York, 1951); David Hunter Miller, *The Drafting of the Covenant* (2 vols., New York, 1928); Bernard M. Baruch, *The Making of the Reparation and Economic Sections of the Treaty* (New York, 1920); Bernard M. Baruch, *Baruch: The Public Years* (New York, 1960); Charles Seymour, *Letters from the Paris Peace Conference*, edited by Harold B. Whiteman, Jr. (New Haven, 1965); James T. Shotwell, *At the Paris Peace Conference* (New York, 1937); Stephen Bonsal, *Unfinished Business* (Garden City, N.Y., 1944); Joseph C. Grew, *Turbulent Era*, previously cited; Edith Bolling Wilson, *My Memoir* (Indianapolis, 1939).

Of secondary accounts of the conference, one of the best is Thomas A. Bailey, *Woodrow Wilson and the Lost Peace* (New York, 1944), which actually presents a more favorable view than the title suggests. Paul Birdsall, *Versailles Twenty Years After* (New York, 1941), also emphasizes the positive achievements of the conference. Useful biographies of members of the American delegation are Allan Nevins, *Henry White* (New York, 1930), and Frederick Palmer, *Bliss, Peacemaker: The Life and Letters of General Tasker Howard Bliss* (New York, 1934).

A number of studies deal with special aspects of the negotiations. Seth P. Tillman, *Anglo-American Relations at the Paris Peace Conference* (Princeton, 1961), shows that the American and British delegations for the most part shared the same purposes but never effectually coordinated their efforts. Harold L. Nelson, *Land and Power: British and Allied Policy on Germany's Frontiers, 1916–1919* (Toronto, 1963), analyzes British, French, and American attitudes on the redrawing of Germany's boundaries with Poland, Czechoslovakia, and her western neighbors. Russell H. Fifield, *Woodrow Wilson and the Far East: The Diplomacy of the Shantung Question* (New York, 1952), sets forth Wilson's contention with the Japanese over Shantung. H. Duncan Hall, *Mandates, Dependencies and Trusteeship* (Washington, 1948), includes chapters on the origin of the mandate system at the Peace Conference. On the same subject see William R. Louis, "The United States and the African Peace Settlement of 1919: The Pilgrimage of George Louis Beer," *Journal of African History,* IV, 412–433 (No. 3, 1963). Philip M. Burnett, *Reparations at the Paris Peace Conference From the Standpoint of the American Delegation* (2 vols., New York, 1940), is a detailed study of the handling of that controversial subject. Alfred D. Low, *The Soviet Hungarian Republic and the Paris Peace Conference* (Philadelphia, 1963), shows that the constriction of Hungary's boundaries was determined upon before the short-lived ascendancy of Communism in Budapest.

THE SENATE, THE TREATY, AND THE ELECTION OF 1920, 1919–20. Thomas A. Bailey, *Woodrow Wilson and the Great Betrayal* (New York, 1945), one of the best accounts of the Senate fight over the treaty, is also published in combination with *Woodrow Wilson and the Lost Peace,* previously cited, as *Wilson and the Peacemakers* (New York, 1947). Other scholarly accounts are contained in Denna F. Fleming, *The United States and the League of Nations, 1918–1920* (New York, 1932); the same author's *The United States and World Organization, 1920–1933* (New York, 1933); W. Stull Holt, *Treaties Defeated by the Senate* (Baltimore, 1933); and F. P. Walters, *A History of the League of Nations* (2 vols., London, 1952). Ruhl J. Bartlett, *The League to Enforce Peace* (Chapel Hill, N.C., 1944), describes the part taken in the League contest by this pro-League organization and its head, ex-President Taft. Henry Cabot Lodge, chief organizer of Senate opposition to Wilson's League, maintains in his *The Senate and the League of Nations* (New York, 1925) that his purpose was not to defeat the League, but only to make it safe for the United States. The reader should compare Lodge's account with the conclusions of his chief biographers: Karl Schriftgiesser, *The Gentleman from Massachusetts: Henry Cabot Lodge* (Boston, 1944) and John A. Garraty, *Henry Cabot Lodge, a Biography* (New York, 1953). Stephen Bonsal, *op. cit.*, tells of an apparently liberal offer of compromise from Lodge, which seemingly never reached Wilson and which has disappeared if it ever existed.

Claudius O. Johnson's *Borah of Idaho* (New York, 1936) is a biography of a leading isolationist Senator. The biographies of Wilson, especially those by Bell, Walworth, and the Georges, the sketch by Blum, and Edith Wilson's *My Memoir* (all previously cited), are useful for this topic, as are Blum's *Joe Tumulty*, Pringle's *William H. Taft*, Jessup's *Elihu Root*, Lamont's *Across World Frontiers*, Baruch's *Baruch: The Public Years*, Hoover's *The Ordeal of Woodrow Wilson*, and Claude G. Bowers, *Beveridge and the Progressive Era* (New York, 1932). Selig Adler, *The Isolationist Impulse: Its Twentieth Century Reaction* (New York, 1957), describes in great detail the rise of isolationist opposition to the treaty. See also the first chapter in his *The Uncertain Giant: 1921–1941, American Foreign Policy Between the Wars* (New York, 1965). Dexter Perkins, *A History of the Monroe Doctrine* (cited above), has a chapter on "The Doctrine and the League."

Kurt Wimer has published a number of articles on Wilson's fight for the League; among them, "Woodrow Wilson Tries Conciliation: An Effort That Failed," *The Historian*, XXV, 419–438 (August, 1963); "Woodrow Wilson's Plans to Enter the League of Nations through an Executive Agreement," *Western Political Quarterly*, XI, 800–812 (December 1958); and "Woodrow Wilson's Plan for a Vote of Confidence," *Pennsylvania History*, XXVIII, No. 3, 2–16 (June 1961).

The campaign and election of 1920, including Wilson's obvious but undeclared angling for a third nomination, are covered in most of the biographies and special works listed earlier in this section. See also Charles W. Stein, *The Third-Term Tradition: Its Rise and Collapse in American Politics* (New York, 1943); Wesley M. Bagby, *The Road to Normalcy: The Presidential Campaign and Election of 1920* (Baltimore, 1962); John Chalmers

Vinson, *Referendum for Isolation: Defeat of Article Ten of the League of Nations Covenant* (Athens, Ga., 1961); Andrew Sinclair, *The Available Man: The Life Behind the Masks of Warren Gamaliel Harding* (New York, 1965); and Merlo J. Pusey, *Charles Evans Hughes* (2 vols., 2nd edition, New York, 1963). Edith Bolling Wilson, in *My Memoir,* and Gene Smith, in *When The Cheering Stopped: The Last Years of Woodrow Wilson* (New York, 1964), a sympathetic but sometimes inaccurate narrative, tells the tragic story of Wilson's physical collapse and the pathetic years that followed.

Index

"ABC Powers," 111-12, 116
Alaska boundary, 9-10, 39-43
Albert, Dr. Heinrich, 129
Algeciras Conference, 44-48
Allies, 120, 135, 137, 142, 144-46, 150, 158, 161, 167-69, 170, 172
Alverstone, Lord, 42-43
Amador Guerrero, Dr. Manuel, 18-20
American China Development Company, 55
American Commission to Negotiate Peace, 178ff
American Security League, 133
Angell, Norman, *The Great Illusion*, 82
Arabic, 129-30, 133
Arbitration treaties, 51-52, 70, 81-83
Archangel, 165, 167; U.S. troops at, 169
Article Ten, 86, 196, 200, 202-203, 205, 210, 218
Austria-Hungary, 148, 152, 170-71

Baéz, Ramón, 93
Bailey, Thomas A., 202, 208, 212
Baker, Newton D., 135, 160
Balfour, Arthur, 6, 42, 158
Beer, George L., 181, 186
Bernstorff, Count Johann von, 129-30, 138, 145-46
Bethmann-Hollweg, 123, 127-28, 130n, 139, 143, 146
Beveridge, Albert J., 35
Bliss, General Tasker H., 159-60, 176-77, 186, 189
Bobo, Dr. Ronsalvo, 98-99
Boer War, 6, 10, 23
Borah, William E., 197, 210
Bordas Valdés, José, 92
Boxer crisis, 4, 7
Boxer indemnity, 57n.
Boy-Ed, 129n.
Boyd, Federico, 19-20
Brandegee, Frank B., 197
Brest-Litovsk, treaty of, 164

Brockdorff-Rantzau, Count, 191
Bryan-Chamorro Treaty, 79, 89-90
Bryan, William Jennings, 83, 87-89, 92-93, 97, 105, 109, 118-20, 124, 126, 128, 208-209; and "dollar diplomacy," 84, 88; and Columbia, 85-86; loans to belligerents, 122; and Japan, 156
Bryce, James, 52-53
Bullitt, William C., 179
Bunau-Varilla, Philippe, 13-14, 18-20

Cabrera, Luis, 113
Cáceres, Ramón, 75
Canada, 9-10, 40-43; and reciprocity, 70, 80-81
Caperton, Admiral W. B., 98-100
Caporetto, 152, 159
Carnegie, Andrew, 37, 82
Carranza, Venustiano, 105, 108, 111-18, 149n., 154
Carrizal incident, 115-16
Casement, Roger, 141
Castrillo, 77
Castro, Cipriano, 23-25
Central American Court of Justice, 33, 90
Central American Peace Conference, 33
Central Powers, 120, 136, 166, 170
Chamberlain, Joseph, 6
Chamorro, Diego Manuel, 91
Chamorro, Emiliano, 89-91
China, 54-57, 64, 66, 68, 71-73, 155-57, 188, 193
Churchill, Winston, 157
Clayton-Bulwer Treaty, 3, 8-11, 40
Clemenceau, Georges, 171, 185, 187, 189, 192
Colby, Bainbridge, 213-15
Colombia, 9, 16, 16n., 17-18, 20-21, 34, 36, 85-86, 153
Colt, LeBaron C., 200
Committee on Foreign Relations, 197, 201, 204

Consortium, four-power, 72-73; six-power, 74, 85, 155
Constitutionalists, Mexican, 105-106, 108-11, 114
Costa Rica, 89-90
Council of Four, 185-86, 188
Council of Ten, 178, 180, 185
Cox, James M., 216
Cromwell, William Nelson, 13, 15, 17
Cuba, 7; second intervention in, 34-35
"Czechoslovak legion," 166-67, 169
Czechoslovak National Council, 166, 171
Czolgosz, Leon, 1

Daniels, Josephus, 134
Danish West Indies, 154
Dartiguenave, Sudre, 99-100
Declaration of London, 51, 124, 124n., 141
Delcassé, Théophile, 45
De Lesseps, Ferdinand, 9
Democratic party, 84
Dennett, Tyler, 17
Dewey, Admiral George, 25-27
Díaz, Adolfo, 76-77, 79-80, 88-90
Díaz, Felix, 103
Díaz, Porfirio, 80n., 102-103
"Dollar Diplomacy," 71-74, 78, 84, 88
Dominican Republic, 29-32, 35, 74-75, 87, 92-95
Drago Doctrine, 33, 49-50
Drago, Luis M., 33, 50, 53
Dumba, Dr. Constantin, 129n.
Durand, Sir Mortimer, 59

Ebert, Friedrich, 172
El Salvador, 89-90
Esthus, Raymond A., 67n.
Estrada, Juan J., 76, 79
Estrada Palma, Tomás, 34-35

Falkenhayn, General Eric von, 142
Farnham, Roger L., 97
First Hague Conference, 37, 48
Fiume, 187, 189
Foch, Marshal Ferdinand, 168
Fourteen Points address, 163n., 170, 172, 177, 193, 220ff.

France, 43-48, 96, 120, 170-71, 177-78, 184, 186-88
Francis, David R., 165
Frazier, Arthur Hugh, 185

Garrison, Lindley M., 134-35
Gerard, James W., 140
German-American-Chinese Alliance, proposed, 64, 68
Germany: and Venezuela, 23-27; and Morocco, 43-48; alienates U.S. sympathy, 121; and neutral rights, 123, 125-31; proposes peace conference, 144; unrestricted submarine warfare, 146-48; final offensive by, 170; peace offer of, 170-71; signs armistice, 173; at Versailles, 191-92; signs treaty, 193
Gómez, Miguel, 34
Gore-McLemore Resolution, 138-39
Gore, Thomas P., 138
Graves, General William S., 169
Grayson, Dr. Cary T., 202, 215
Great Britain, 3, 5, 8-11, 23, 25, 28, 39-43, 52-53, 59-60, 81-82, 157-58, 178, 188, 190, 213; and Mexico, 107-108; and Panama Canal tolls, 108; and neutral rights, 123, 125, 130, 141-42; and U.S. protest, 130-32
"Great White Fleet," 65-66
Grew, Joseph C., 178, 185, 194
Grey, Sir Edward, 73, 107, 123, 131, 136-37, 141, 143, 208
Guantanamo Bay, 34
Guillaume Sam, Vilbrun, 98
Gummere, Samuel R., 46

Hague Court, 27, 28n., 36-37, 39, 51, 53, 82, 217
Haiti, 87-88, 94; foreign interests in, 95-97; U.S. treaty with, 99-101; new constitution, 101
Hankey, Sir Maurice, 185
Hanna, Mark, 13
Harding, Warren G., 216-19
Harriman, Edward H., 71-73
Hay-Bunau-Varilla Treaty, 19-20
Hay-Herrán Treaty, 15-16
Hay, John, 23, 51; services under McKinley, 4; death of, 4; Roose-

velt's opinion of, 5; negotiates canal treaties, 9-12, 15; warns Colombia, 17; and Alaska boundary, 40-41
Hay-Pauncefote Treaties, 10-12
Hepburn Bill, 12, 14
Herbert, Sir Michael, 23, 41
Herrán, Dr. Tomás, 15
Herrick, Myron T., 120
Hindenburg, Field Marshal Paul von, 142
Hispaniola, 91
Hitchcock, Gilbert M., 200, 202, 207, 209-11
Hitler, 193, 203
Holleben, Theodor von, 23, 27
Honduras, 77-78
Hoover, Herbert, 209
House, Colonel Edward M., 119, 139, 143, 146, 158-59, 172, 175-79, 208; mission to Europe (1915), 127-29; mission to Europe (1916), 135-37; estrangement from Wilson, 184-85
House-Grey memorandum, 137
Huerta, General Victoriano, 80n., 103-11, 129n.
Hughes, William M., 181
Hukuang loan, 72

Inquiry, the, 163, 177-78, 186
Inter-American Conference, 49
Irías, Julián, 91
Irigoyen, Hipólito, 153
Irish independence, 210
"Irreconcilables," 196-97, 204, 207, 210, 216
Ishii, Kikujiro, 156
Isthmian Canal Act, 17
Isthmian Canal Commission, 9, 12
Isthmian Canal question, 8-15; *see also* Panama

Jagow, Gottlieb von, 130
Japan, 2, 43, 54, 57-69, 62n., 155-57, 157n., 169, 178, 188-89, 204, 206; *see also* Russo-Japanese War
Japanese and San Francisco schools, 62-63
Jiménez, Juan Isidro, 93-94
Johnson, Hiram, 197
Joint High Commissions, Anglo-American, 9, 40; U.S.-Mexican, 116
Jusserand, J. J., 4, 46

Karl, Emperor, 148, 171
Katsura, Count Taro, 58-59
Kemnitz, von, 149n.
Kennan, George F., 161, 164n.
Kerensky, Alexander, 161
Kitchener, General Lord, 143
Knapp, Captain Harry S., 95
Knox-Castrillo Convention, 77, 88-89
Knox, Philander C., 70, 73-74, 76-78, 82-83, 88, 104, 206
Korea, 2, 57-58, 61
Komura, Count Jutaro, 61

Laconia, 149
Lansdowne, Lord, 6, 11, 23, 42, 59
Lansing-Ishii agreement, 156
Lansing, Robert, 87-88, 98, 112, 114, 117, 119-21, 126, 128-29, 131, 137, 139, 143, 156, 176-77, 179, 186, 189; armed merchantmen, proposal by, 138; counters peace move, 144-45; dismissal of, 212
Latin America: and World War I, 152-54; *see also* Roosevelt Corollary; Root; Taft; Wilson
Laurier, Sir Wilfrid, 81
League to Enforce Peace, 141, 182, 208
League of Nations Covenant, 182-83, 186-87, 194, 218
Lenin, Nikolai, 164n., 165
Lind, John, 106
Link, Arthur, 87, 121, 137, 144, 147
Lloyd George, David, 143, 157, 179, 185, 189, 190, 192, 210
Lodge, Henry Cabot, 41, 176, 183, 197-98, 208-10
Lodge reservations, 204-207, 212, 217
Long, Boaz, 90, 97
Lord, Robert H., 186
Lowden, Frank O., 216
Lowell, Abbot L., 209
Ludendorff, General Erich, 142
Lusitania, 127, 130n., 133
Lvov, Prince, 161

McAdoo, William G., 215-16

McCumber, Porter J., 200, 206
McKinley, William, 1
Madero, Francisco I., 80n., 103-104
Madriz, José, 76
Magoon, Charles E., 35
Mahan, A. T., 3, 10
Managua, 76, 80, 91
Manchu dynasty, 54, 73
Manchuria, 67-69, 71
March, General Peyton C., 169
Marroquín, José Manuel, 16, 20
Marshall, Thomas R., 208
May, Ernest R., 141
Mayo, Admiral Henry T., 109-10
Mena, General Luis, 80
Mexico, 102-17, 153-54; Constitution of 1917, 113, 117
Meyer, George von L., 4, 59
"Mild reservationists," 198-201, 204-206
Môle St. Nicholas, 96
Monroe Doctrine, 11, 23-24, 30, 83, 122, 200, 202-203, 212
Moore, John Bassett, 17-18
Morales, Carlos F., 30
Morgan, J. P., 55-72
Morgan, John T., 8, 13-14
Morocco, 44-48
Mukden, Battle of, 60
Murmansk, 167-68

National Bank of Haiti, 95, 97
New Granada, 17-18, 21n.
New Panama Canal Company, 9, 12-13, 15-16
Nicaragua, 75-80, 87, 88-91; canal route, 8-9, 12-14
Nicholas II, Russian czar, 33, 48, 57, 61, 150
Northeastern Fisheries, arbitration, 52-53
Nouel, Adolfo A., 75, 92

Obregón, Alvaro, 105, 111, 113
Open door, in China, 4, 55, 67, 156
Orlando, Vittorio, 185, 189

"Pact of the Embassy," 104
Page, Walter Hines, 119, 131, 157
Panama, canal route, 9-14
Panama Canal tolls, 108
Panama, Republic of, 19, 22, 34

Papen, Franz von, 129n.
Paris Peace Conference: organization of, 178-80; excludes Soviets, 179; plenary sessions of, 180, 191, 193; work of, 180-83, 185-91; German colonies and, 181; mandate system and, 181-82; League of Nations Covenant and, 182-83, 186-87; Germans attend, 191, 193
Payne-Aldrich tariff, 81
Permanent Court of Arbitration, 37; *see also* Hague Court
Pershing, General John J., 114-17, 160
Philippines, 68n., 84, 86
Pious Fund, arbitration, 38-39
Platt, Orville H., 7
Platt Amendment, 7, 22, 34-35, 89, 98
Port Arthur, 57, 60
Port au Prince, 96-97
Portsmouth Peace Conference, 60-61
Protectorates, U.S., in Caribbean, 22-36, 74-80, 87-101; results of, 101
Puerto Rico, 86

Reid, Whitelaw, 25, 47n.
Reparations Commission, 191
Reparations controversy, 189-91
Republican Senators, division on treaty, 198
Robins, Colonel Raymond, 164n., 165
Roman Catholic Church, in Mexico, 108
Roman Catholic clergy in the U.S., 114
Roosevelt Corollary, 28, 78; reception abroad of, 32-33, 35
Roosevelt, Franklin D., 4, 157, 214, 216
Roosevelt, Theodore, 35, 83, 86, 120-21, 133, 219; accession to Presidency, 1; basic beliefs, 2-3, 5; naval policy, 3; distrust of treaties, 3; personal diplomacy, 3-4. 59; criticizes canal treaty, 10-11; acquires Panama Canal Zone, 17-20; allied blockade of Venezuela and, 23-28, 26-27n.; announces Corollary to Monroe Doctrine, 28; establishes protectorate over Do-

minican Republic, 29-32; and arbitration, 37, 82; and Alaska boundary, 39-43; and Morocco, 44-48; and Second Hague Conference, 48; and Japan, 54, 58-69; and China, 54-57, 68; and Chinese immigration, 56-57; and Korea, 56; and Russo-Japanese War, 58-60; and Portsmouth Conference, 60-61; and Nobel Peace Prize, 61; and San Francisco schools, 62-63; and Gentlemen's Agreement, 63; and Japanese war scare, 64-65; sends fleet around the world, 65-66; and the Philippines, 68n.; warns Taft, 69; on Wilson, 175; death of, 194

Root, Elihu, 3, 7, 28-29, 34-35, 41, 49-50, 63, 63n., 90, 102, 121, 161, 176, 196, 217; Secretary of War, 4; Secretary of State, 4-6; and Latin America, 33, 74; and arbitration treaties, 51-52; and Fisheries arbitration, 52-53; and Takahira, 66

Root-Takahira agreement, 66-68

Rosen, Baron Roman, 60

Rouvier, Maurice, 45

Rowe, Leo S., 214

Russia, 43-45; and open door, 55; war with Japan, 57-61; March revolution, 150; Bolshevik Revolution, 159-61; provisional government, 160-61; Soviet peace drive, 162-64; treaty of Brest-Litovsk, 164; Allied aims in (1917–18), 165-67

Russo-Japanese War, 54, 57-60

Saar Basin, 187-88

San Francisco school crisis, 62-63, 157n.

Santo Domingo (city), 30, 36, 74, 94

Sarajevo assassinations, 120

Second Hague Peace Conference, 33, 48-51

Seibold, Louis, 215

Senate, U.S., and Hay-Pauncefote treaties, 10-12; and canal bills, 12-14; and Dominican treaties, 31; and Algeciras treaty, 48; and

arbitration treaties, 51-52, 82-83; and Bryan-Chamorro Treaty, 89; and Treaty of Versailles, 195-202, 204, 207, 210-11

Seymour, Charles, 186, 194

Smuts, Jan Christiaan, 181

Sonnino, Sidney, 189

South Manchurian Railway, 71, 73

Spargo, John, 214, 215n.

Spooner Amendment, 12-13

Spring Rice, Sir Cecil, 4, 58-59, 157

Sternburg, Speck von, 3, 3n., 23, 45-47, 64

Stevens, John F., 161

Stone, William J., 138, 146

Straight, Willard, 71, 73

Suárez, Pino, 104

Sullivan, James M., 92

Supreme War Council, 159-60, 165, 167-68, 172, 176

Sussex, 131; crisis, 139-41, 143, 151

Taft, William H., 102, 176, 184, 186, 208-209; as Secretary of War, 34-35, 75, 83; Katsura interview, 58-59; warned by Roosevelt, 69; as President, 70-83; and China, 71-74; and Hukuang loan, 72; and Latin America, 74; and the Roosevelt Corollary, 78; and Canada, 80-81; and Mexico, 80n., 104, 108; and arbitration treaties, 81-83

Takahira, Baron Kogoro, 61; and Root, 66

Tampico incident, 109

Teller Resolution, 35n.

Thayer, W. R., 26n.

Théodore, Davilmar, 97

Thirty-one Republicans for Harding and League, 217-18

Tirpitz, Admiral Alfred von, 126

Treaty of Versailles, 193, 193n.; Republican criticism of, 196-97; liberal criticism, 197-98; Senate action, 204-207; first defeat in Senate, 207; pressure for compromise, 208-209; last attempt at compromise, 210; second defeat in Senate, 211

Trotsky, Leon, 164n., 167

Tsushima Straits, naval battle, 60

Tumulty, Joseph, 175 , 215
Turner, George, 41
Tyrrell, Sir William, 107

Ugarte, Manuel, 36

Venezuela, European intervention in,
    22-28, 41
Villa, Pancho, 105, 110n., 111-12,
    114-15, 117
Virgin Islands of the United States,
    154
Vladivostok, 165; U.S. troops at,
    169

"War guilt" clause, 191
Welles, Sumner, 214
Westermann, William L., 186
White, Henry, 4, 26n., 42, 46, 176-
    77, 186
Wilhelm II, German Kaiser, 3, 60,
    126, 140, 143, 146, 172; and Roose-
    velt on Venezuela, 25-27, 27n.; on
    Morocco, 44-45, 47; proposes a
    German - American - Chinese alli-
    ance, 64, 68
Wilson, Edith Bolling (Mrs. Wood-
    row), 175, 207-208, 215
Wilson, Henry Lane, 103-106
"Wilson Plan," 93, 98
Wilson, Woodrow, 74, 83, 138, 219;
    and China, 84-85; and Latin
    America, 85-87, 152-54; speech at
    Mobile, 85, 107; and Nicaragua,
    88-91; and Dominican Republic,
    92-95; and Haiti, 95-101; and
    Mexico, 104-17, 154; and Panama
    Canal tolls, 108; "watchful wait-
    ing," 108; and Tampico incident,
    109; Veracruz occupation, 110;
    and Carranza, 112-17; and Mex-
    ico, appraisal of, 117; conducts
    foreign policy, 118-19; and neu-
    trality, 120ff.; appeal for "imparti-
    ality in thought," 120; warns Ger-
    many, 126; and Lusitania, 128-30,
    130n.; and preparedness, 133-35;
    and House mission, 136-37; and
    Sussex crisis, 139-41; and League
    to Enforce Peace, 141; resents
    British attitude, 141-42; plans
    peace move, 143; asks peace terms,

144; for "peace without victory,"
    145-46; break with Germany, 147;
    arms merchant ships, 148; decides
    on war, 149-51; war address to
    Congress, 151; relations with Al-
    lies, 157-60, 172; and Soviet Rus-
    sia, 161-69; Fourteen Points ad-
    dress, 163, 163n., 220-24; mes-
    sage to Russian people, 164; and
    U.S. troops in Russia, 165-69; de-
    fines purpose of landings, 168-69;
    and Austria-Hungary, 170-71; and
    German peace offer, 171; appeal
    for Democratic Congress, 174-75;
    choice of peace delegation, 175-
    77; vague peace program, 177-78;
    and mandate system, 181; League
    of Nations Covenant, 182-83, 186-
    87; return to Washington, 182-
    84; defends Covenant, 183-84;
    estrangement from House, 184-
    85; in Council of Four, 185-91;
    concessions to Allies, 187-89;
    and reparations, 189-91; defends
    treaty, 192; work at Paris ap-
    praised, 193-94; submits treaty to
    Senate, 195; and "mild reservation-
    ists," 199-201; decides on speak-
    ing tour, 201; offers concessions,
    202; public appeal for treaty, 202-
    204; collapse and illness, 204, 207;
    denounces Lodge reservations, 207;
    contemplates challenging Sena-
    tors, 208; Jackson Day letter, 209;
    vetoes compromise, 211; responsi-
    ble for defeat of treaty, 211-12;
    dismisses Lansing, 212; denounces
    Allies, 213; vetoes peace resolu-
    tion, 213; and third term, 215-16
Wiseman, Sir William, 158
Witte, Count Serge, 60, 61
Wood, General Leonard, 216
World War I, 119ff.

"Yankeephobia," 36, 74, 153
Yüan Shih-k'ai, 73, 155

Zamor, Oreste, 97
Zapata, Emiliano, 105, 111-12
Zelaya, José Santos, 75, 80, 91
Zimmermann   telegram,   148-49,
    149n., 154